T0305191

Exchange Rates, Interest Rates and Commodity Prices

Exchange Rates, Interest Rates and Commodity Prices

Edited by

Meher Manzur

School of Economics and Finance
Curtin University of Technology
Perth, Australia

Edward Elgar
Cheltenham, UK • Northampton, MA, USA

Published by
Edward Elgar Publishing Limited
Glensanda House
Montpellier Parade
Cheltenham
Glos GL50 1UA
UK

Edward Elgar Publishing, Inc.
136 West Street
Suite 202
Northampton
Massachusetts 01060
USA

A catalogue record for this book
is available from the British Library

Library of Congress Cataloguing in Publication Data
Exchange rates, interest rates, and commodity prices / edited by Meher Manzur.
    p. cm.
  Includes bibliographical references and index.
  1. Foreign exchange rates. 2. Interest rates. 3. Primary commodities—Prices.
  4. International finance. I. Manzur, Meher, 1953–

HG3851 .E938 2003
332'.042—dc21   2002034711

ISBN 1 84064 843 0

Printed and bound in Great Britain by MPG Books Ltd, Bodmin, Cornwall

Contents

Figures

Tables

Preface

The volatility of nominal and real exchange rates has been the major highlight of events since the switch to floating by major currencies in the early 1970s. Interestingly, large fluctuations in exchange rates are observed to have been in concert with those of interest rates, and prices for agricultural, energy and mineral commodities. Whilst exchange rates are fundamentally linked with interest rates (through interest parity conditions), the system is still quite noisy with substantial independent variations in nominal and real interest rates across countries. More intriguing is the alleged link between exchange rates and commodity prices. It is true that exchange rates and commodity prices are both asset prices that respond to news instantaneously, but can something stronger be said about causation? Is exchange rate volatility responsible for the wide swings in commodity prices, or vice versa? These questions themselves concern the broader problems of exchange rate determination and price formation in open economies, which are among the fundamental issues occupying the frontiers of international finance.

The purpose of this volume is to provide a set of selected self-contained studies analysing a number of interrelated questions about interactions of exchange rates, interest rates and commodity prices. While there remains much that is little understood, the conclusions concerning the validity of the theory of purchasing power parity are becoming more and more reliable; the expectations hypothesis of the term structure continues to perform poorly; interest rates are yet to equalise in real terms across countries; and there is evidence of important linkages between commodity prices and exchange rates, and vice versa. Consistent with the main findings, efforts have been made, as and when appropriate, to draw attention to what action and decisions businesses and governments can take to modify adverse effects and to capitalise on opportunities in the future.

M.M.

Acknowledgements

I wish to express my gratitude to the authors for their contributions to this volume. I extend my gratitude to Elsevier Science Ltd for granting permission to reprint material from *Journal of International Money and Finance*, Vol. 18, 1999, pp. 225–249, L.L. Ong et al 'The world interest rate....'; Vol. 19, 1998, pp. 407–439, L.A. Sjaastad: 'On exchange rates....' ; Vol. 15, 1996, pp. 879–897, L.A. Sjaastad et al: 'The price of gold....', and to Taylor and Francis Ltd (www.tandf.co.uk) for permission to reproduce material from *Applied Economics* Vol. 31, 1999, pp. 1383–1391, M. Manzur et al 'Measuring international competitiveness....'.

I am indebted to Kennneth Clements, not only for his useful contribution to this volume, but also for his constructive help and continuous encouragement through out the course of this work. Paula Haslehurst has done a professional job in preparing the manuscript, with Melvin Poa providing excellent research assistance. Thanks are also due to Subramaniam Anathram for his useful help during the final stage of this work. I am also thankful to Edward Elgar and his colleagues, Francine O'Sullivan, Alex Minton and Caroline McLin, all from Edward Elgar Publishing for their exhaustive efforts in the development of the manuscript. The text has also benefited from the comments of an anonymous reviewer. Financial assistance from the Curtin Business School is gratefully acknowledged.

M.M.

Contributors

Kenneth W. Clements is Professor of Economics and Director of the Economic Research Centre at The University of Western Australia.

John Freebairn is Professor and Head of the Department of Economics at the University of Melbourne.

H.Y. Izan is Professorial Fellow at the Graduate School of Management, The University of Western Australia.

Yihui Lan is working on her PhD thesis, 'The Big Mac Approach to Economics', at the University of Western Australia.

Meher Manzur is Senior Lecturer in Finance and Banking at the Curtin University of Technology.

Li Lian Ong is Asian Regional Economist (based in Hong Kong) at Macquarie Bank in Sydney.

Fabio Scacciavillani is Economist at the European Central Bank.

Larry A. Sjaastad is Professor of Economics at The University of Chicago and Adjunct Professor at The University of Western Australia.

1. Exchange Rates, Interest Rates and Commodity Prices: An Introduction

Meher Manzur

Why is purchasing power parity (PPP) always and everywhere controversial? Despite overwhelming evidence that sterilised central bank interventions are impotent, why do major industrialised countries (such as the G8) continue to look for accords to stem exchange rate volatility? In a world of increasing globalisation, why are interest rate movements so poorly correlated across countries? Why are the currencies of the resource-based economies depreciating when the commodity prices are holding up? Has the link between exchange rates and commodity prices collapsed? These are among the fundamental questions confronting contemporary research and policy-making in international finance. These questions themselves concern the more fundamental problems of exchange rate determination and price formation in open economies, and the degree of monetary independence and its implications for macroeconomic policy.

This book contributes to an understanding of the key issues relating to the intriguing questions of the link between the exchange rate instability and domestic inflation; the real exchange rate and interest rate manifestations; and the covariability of exchange rates and commodity prices. The book is made up of nine self-contained chapters with a common theme – the behaviour of asset prices and interest rates in international markets. The approach is broadly empirical and applies econometric and modelling techniques to a wide range of recent data for a cross-section of countries.

The purpose of this chapter is to set the stage for the subsequent chapters to follow. We start in the next section with a skeletal review of how the three key variables under focus – exchange rates, interest rates and commodity prices – hold together historically. This descriptive analysis will be followed by an overview of the other chapters of this book.

1.0 HISTORICAL PERSPECTIVES

Exchange rates and interest rates are fundamentally linked by the interest parity condition. The *uncovered version* of this condition stipulates that the interest differential (that is, domestic interest rate minus foreign interest rate) coincides with the expected depreciation of the domestic currency. Since the expected future spot exchange rate is not observable, the uncovered version is modified by replacing the expected future spot rate by the forward exchange rate to obtain the *covered version*, implying that the interest differential is equal to the forward discount or premium.[1] The link between exchange rates and commodity prices derives from PPP. Under PPP, commodity prices are arbitraged internationally so that they are the same in all locations when expressed in terms of a common currency.[2]

In what follows, we provide a brief description of the broad features of major exchange rates in the 1990s, and compare these features with those of the 1960s. Also included is a brief analysis of whether these features are manifested in real interest rates and commodity prices. The purpose here is to describe the features rather than analyse them.

We use quarterly exchange rates for the Group of Seven (G7) countries for 1991(1)–1998(4) to capture the most recent experience with the current floating rate system, and 1961(1)–1968(4), the 'matured' part of the Bretton Woods period of adjustable par values. All data are from *International Financial Statistics* published by the International Monetary Fund. Since the two periods have substantially different implications with respect to the behaviour of nominal exchange rates and monetary policy, we focus on real rather than nominal exchange rates.

Real exchange rates are defined as nominal rates adjusted for inflation. Since prices for individual countries, when expressed in a common currency, are subject to the variability of exchange rates, bilateral real exchange rates based on individual country price levels may be infected with measurement errors. The use of one reference country, such as the USA, gives rise to asymmetries. Following Sjaastad (1990), we resolve these problems by using 'multilateral' real exchange rates which involve defining all prices and exchange rates on an appropriately weighted 'basket' of currencies rather than a single currency. In our context, the basket comprises the G7 currencies; and the average export shares of these countries are used as weights. Alternative weighting schemes were tested and gave the same results.[3]

Table 1.1 gives the mean and standard deviation of the real exchange rate changes for the 1990s and 1960s. As can be seen, the means are more or less comparable for the two periods, but the standard deviations in the 1990s are considerably larger – on average more than five times larger. This indicates that real exchange rates have been much more volatile in the 1990s compared with the 1960s, that is, the variability of real exchange rates is increased when the nominal exchange rate is floating. This is consistent with Mussa (1987).

Note that greater variability of real exchange rates in a floating rate regime is 'inherent' in the adjustment mechanism. By definition, the exchange rate is the relative price of two national monies (assets), and like other asset prices, is determined in a forward-looking manner in which expectations concerning the future course of events play a key role. Consequently, exchange rates are very sensitive to the receipt of new information. On the other hand, aggregate price levels, which reflect the prices of goods and services, adjust only slowly, and do not jump as new information becomes available. The 'stickiness' of aggregate price levels does not necessarily represent market imperfections, rather it reflects the costs of price adjustment as a result of nominal contracts of finite length (see Frenkel, 1981). This characterisation of exchange rates *vis-à-vis* national price levels is embodied in the 'asset market' theory of exchange rates (see Mussa, 1982).

We now turn to the properties of other prices such as commodity prices and real interest rates. For commodity prices, we use the monthly series of world commodity prices contained in *International Financial Statistics* published by the International Monetary Fund.

Table 1.1 Real exchange rates: G7 (log changes x 100)

Statistic	UK	France	Germany	Japan	Canada	Italy	USA
1960s							
Mean	0.35	−0.21	0.08	−0.70	0.30	−0.29	0.13
Std deviation	2.48	0.66	0.74	1.05	1.00	0.78	0.46
1990s							
Mean	0.25	0.07	0.20	−0.08	0.37	0.16	0.24
Std deviation	6.81	6.93	7.21	7.84	3.12	6.45	3.41

To eliminate seasonal effects, we use twelve-month rates of change rather than monthly changes. For real interest rates, we use the ninety-day US treasury bill rates corrected for US inflation over the following twelve months. As a check, we also defined the real interest rate as the ninety-day

US treasury bill rate adjusted for quarterly inflation in the USA; moreover, we repeated the exercise using the yield on US long-term government bonds and the results (not included here) were very similar. The data on the US treasury bill rates, the yield on long-term bonds and the CPI are all from OECD MEI Database, VAR Econometrics.

The statistics for the twelve-month rates of change of commodity price index and the level of real interest rates are given in Table 1.2. As can be seen, the mean changes for the two series are more or less comparable, but standard deviations of both of them are about five times more variable in the 1990s than in the 1960s. This result is quite similar to the increased volatility of exchange rates, discussed previously. Note that as changes in exchange rates and commodity prices are dimensionally consistent, they are comparable with *levels* of real interest rates.

Table 1.2 Changes in commodity prices and real interest rates

	Commodity prices		Real interest rates	
	1960s	1990s	1960s	1990s
Mean	−1.30	−1.02	−0.02	−0.04
Standard deviation	5.88	19.89	0.32	1.61

To summarise, we observe that exchange rates have been markedly volatile since the switch to floating by the major currencies. Interestingly, we also observe that the additional variability of exchange rates tends to echo those of commodity prices and interest rates. This raises a number of important questions such as why these prices are so volatile, whether there is any systematic link among their variances, business and policy implications of this increased volatility, and so on. Proper resolution of these questions involves a thorough re-examination of the fundamental issues in exchange rate economics. In the eight chapters to follow, we provide new insights to these issues.

2.0 A PREVIEW OF OTHER CHAPTERS

PPP has, historically, occupied the centre stage of research in international finance. In Chapter 2, Yihui Lan provides an up-to-date survey of the contemporary literature on PPP. It covers the literature that has appeared up until July 2000, with the major focus on the research from the last decade.

This chapter has several attractive features. First, it employs an analytical approach to quantify the research into and interest in PPP, as compared to other major topics in international finance. Second, it provides a stylised geometric analysis of the PPP theory. Third, the study uses scientific measures (for example, the half-life measure) to deal with issues related to deviations from the parity and the speed of adjustment. Finally, it provides a succinct analysis of the recent empirical evidence on PPP.

Chapter 3 focuses on the crucial area of exchange rate dynamics. In this chapter, Larry Sjaastad provides an empirical test of the proposition that floating exchange rates can insulate small, open economies from external inflation. For this purpose, an Australian 'commodity currency' model is developed first, which is then extended to deal with real exchange rates as well. An attractive feature of this study is that the nominal version of the model is rich enough to admit tests of various hypotheses, including PPP, monetary independence, interest rate parity, terms-of-trade neutrality and foreign exchange market efficiency. The author uses Swiss data for the post-Bretton Woods period to test the nominal and real versions of the exchange rate model. The results indicate, among others, that the model tracks the Swiss franc nominal exchange rate *vis-à-vis* the dollar and the major European currencies very well, but Swiss PPP real exchange rates are found to be heavily contaminated with measurement error. According to the author, as that error explains the large co-movements in nominal and PPP real exchange rates, those co-movements are largely irrelevant to the PPP debate.

Chapter 4 deals with an important application of PPP. In this chapter, Meher Manzur investigates the relative usefulness of PPP in the measurement of international competitiveness. For this purpose, a new, alternative measure of real exchange rates is first constructed as an indicator of international competitiveness. This new measure, called the 'basket approach', involves defining all prices and exchange rates on an appropriately weighted basket of currencies rather than a single currency. Using data for Japan, Korea, Thailand, Malaysia and Singapore, real exchange rates are calculated based on both PPP and the basket approach. To check for the relative performance of the two measures, cointegration tests are employed. The results indicate that the new measure tends to outperform PPP in tracking the export growth for the sample countries. Moreover, the PPP-based real exchange rates tend to understate the measures of competitiveness for these countries. This result has important implications in terms of the levels of these countries' exchange rates as well as the well-known Balassa hypothesis.

Chapter 5 deals with a particular version of interest rate parity, namely, the equalisation of the real interest rates across countries. A key feature of this study is that it uses the emerging stochastic index numbers approach. In this chapter, Li Lian Ong et al. show that the standard regression model of real exchange rates for the world can be interpreted as an application of the stochastic approach to index numbers. The results indicate a rejection of the strict real interest rate equalisation. However, when wholesale prices, which give more prominence to traded goods, are used as the deflator, the results are supportive of the hypothesis. Note that such equalisation has profound effects. If interest rates in real terms are the same internationally, then the cost of borrowing is independent of where that borrowing occurs and in what currency the loan is denominated. Moreover, the equalisation of real rates means that the role of monetary policy within any one country is very much circumscribed; in the limit, monetary policy can only affect domestic interest rates via its influences on the world interest rate. A world with highly mobile capital and integrated financial markets would seem to be not inconsistent with these implications of the equalisation of real interest rates.

Meher Manzur re-examines the various forms of the expectations hypothesis of the term structure of interest rates in Chapter 6. A special attraction of this chapter is that the analysis is carried out on recent data from the major industrialised countries (G7) jointly, rather than focusing on one country in isolation from the rest of the world. This multi-country approach is capable of capturing the shocks which might hit a number of countries simultaneously. The results indicate the presence of a time-varying risk premium. However, the evidence suggests that the yield spread, at least partially, is able to predict the change of future short rates, which is encouraging for the expectations hypothesis. To explain the results, a variety of tests involving interest rate volatility, stock market developments, nominal and real exchange rate volatility, are employed. Unfortunately these variables do not appear to adequately explain the time-varying term premium. These results are consistent with the existing literature on this topic.

Chapter 7 provides analytical notes on the interactions between exchange rates and commodity prices. Using PPP as the building block, Kenneth Clements and Meher Manzur introduce a stylised model in which PPP holds for traded goods only. This model determines the impact of real exchange rate changes on the relative prices of commodities. The model illustrates the general principle that producers of a commodity dominated by a country whose currency appreciates will be better off, and producers of a commodity dominated by a country whose currency depreciates will be worse off. This chapter sets the stage for further rigorous analysis on this topic to follow in the subsequent chapters.

Chapter 8 follows on from the previous chapter and Larry Sjaastad and

Fabio Scacciavillani develop an international pricing model, which predicts that changes in major currency exchange rates do impact on the prices of many commodities in all currencies – major and minor alike. In the empirical section, the case of gold is analysed using forecast error data. Among other things, it is found that, since the dissolution of the Bretton–Woods international monetary system, floating exchange rates among the major currencies have been a major source of price instability in the world gold market and, as the gold market is dominated by the European currency bloc, appreciations or depreciations of European currencies have strong effects on the price of gold in other currencies.

It seems to be conventional wisdom that if world commodity prices were to rise by, say, 10 per cent, then the Australian dollar will appreciate by about 5 per cent. Thus, in terms of domestic currency, Australian exporters benefit by only about a half of the world price increase. As this could be expected to work in reverse for a fall in commodity prices, it can be seen that the co–movement of the Australian dollar and commodity prices serves to buffer exporters. According to this model of the exchange rate, the Australian dollar can be described as a 'commodity currency'. Chapter 9 investigates the extent to which the commodity currency model applies to the Australian dollar and its economy-wide implications. In this chapter, John Freebairn first articulates the workings of the commodity currency model. Evidence is then presented to support the view that the Australian dollar is a commodity currency. The chapter finally analyses the implications of the model for profitability of the different sectors of the economy. As all sectors are shown to be linked to commodity prices by one means or another, this analysis clearly illustrates the fundamental importance of these prices to the Australian economy.

REFERENCES

Frenkel, J.A. (1981), 'Flexible exchange rates, prices, and the role of "news": lessons from the 1970s', *Journal of Political Economy*, **89**, pp. 665–705.

Mussa, M.L. (1982), 'A model of exchange rate dynamics', *Journal of Political Economy*, **90**, pp. 74–104.

Mussa, M.L. (1987), 'Nominal exchange rate regimes and the behaviour of real exchange rates: evidence and implications', in K. Brunner and A. Meltzer (eds), *Real Business Cycles, Real Exchange Rates and Actual Policies*, Carnegie–Rochester Conference Series on Public Policy, Amsterdam: North-Holland.

Sjaastad, L.A. (1990), 'Exchange rates and commodity prices: the Australian case', in K. Clements and J. Freebairn (eds), *Exchange Rates and Australian Commodity*

Exports, Melbourne and Perth: Centre for Policy Studies, Monash University, and Economic Research Centre, The University of Western Australia.

NOTES

1   See Chapter 5 of this volume for formal representation of these conditions.
2   See Chapter 7 of this volume for a systematic treatment of this relationship. Also see Chapters 8 and 9 of this volume for empirical investigations.
3   See Chapter 5 of this volume for more details on the calculation of the basket approach to real exchange rates.

2. The Explosion of Purchasing Power Parity

Yihui Lan

The theory of purchasing power parity (PPP) is one of the fundamental principles in international finance. It states that prices across countries should be equal when converted to a common currency (absolute PPP), or less strictly, the change in the exchange rate should be equal to the difference between the changes in the domestic and foreign prices (relative PPP). It is widely agreed that Gustav Cassel (20 October 1866–15 January 1945) is the father of the PPP doctrine, although this line of intellectual thought actually originated with Spanish scholars in the sixteenth century. Rigorous empirical examination of the theory did not appear until the 1960s, when evidence was found supporting PPP over long periods of time (see, for example, Friedman and Schwartz, 1963, and Gaillot 1970). The productivity bias hypothesis proposed by Balassa (1964) and Samuelson (1964) obtained considerable empirical support, and continues to be highly influential. During the past three decades, there have been heated debates about the validity of PPP and professional confidence in the theory has experienced considerable ups and downs.

With the move to flexible exchange rates in the early 1970s, it was generally assumed that the nominal exchange rate would quickly adjust to changes in relative price levels. However, the high volatility of exchange rates, in both nominal and real terms, rendered PPP theory almost untenable. Dornbusch (1976) proposed an overshooting model, temporarily mitigating some unease in the literature. He argued that the stickiness of goods prices, together with continuously clearing asset markets, are the main reasons for deviations from PPP. Before the mid-1980s empirical tests were concerned with simple specifications of PPP which centred on coefficient restrictions, using the methods of ordinary and generalised least squares, which tended to strongly reject PPP except for hyperinflation countries. This line of research reached its high-water mark in the early 1980s with a paper published by Frenkel (1981) entitled 'The Collapse of Purchasing Power Parities during the 1970s'. It is now widely agreed that such straightforward tests for PPP, which Froot and Rogoff (1995) term the 'Stage-One tests', took no account of the possible non-stationarity in relative prices and exchange rates, and thus produced possibly spurious results.

In the second half of the 1980s, with the advancement of time-series techniques, many PPP studies concentrated on testing the efficient markets version of PPP (that is, the hypothesis of random walk behaviour in real exchange rates), but could not reject the null of a random walk (see, for example, Adler and Lehmann, 1983; Meese and Rogoff, 1988; and Mark, 1990). There was also a sizeable amount of work which failed to find cointegration between nominal exchange rates and relative prices (see, for example, Corbae and Ouliaris, 1988; Enders, 1988; and Patel, 1990). The failure of PPP to pass empirical scrutiny further sapped confidence in its practical usefulness.

The late-1980s saw a rebirth of interest in PPP, mainly due to the advent of unit-root econometrics. As conventional unit root tests have low power, researchers have circumvented the problem by using (i) longer periods of data; and (ii) cross-country time-series analysis, known as 'panel data' techniques. Research from long-horizon data generally finds increasing evidence of convergence to PPP. Well-known examples of long-horizon studies include Frankel (1986), Edison (1987), Diebold et al. (1991), and Lothian and Taylor (1996). However, there still remains scepticism about inferences of real exchange rate behaviour based on data across exchange rate regimes (Frankel and Rose, 1996, and Lothian, 1998), or over long historical periods of peace and war (Johnson, 1993, and Grilli and Kaminsky, 1991). As data are available over long time spans only for industrial countries, the favourable results may be exaggerated by the survivorship bias problem raised by Froot and Rogoff (1995). The large size bias of tests for PPP based on long-horizon data has been confirmed in several studies (see, for example, Engel and Kim 1999, and Engel 2000). By the late 1990s, there has been only a few additional investigations of PPP using long time-series data (for example, Guimarães-Filho, 1999; Kuo and Mikkola, 1999; and Parkes and Savvides, 1999). It seems that this remedy for the problem of low test power has now lost favour.

The use of panel data has become increasingly popular among researchers to examine the behaviour of real exchange rates over relatively short time periods, such as during the post-Bretton–Woods era. Hakkio (1984) and Abuaf and Jorion (1990) were early papers that applied panel data methods to PPP tests. Evidence in favour of long-run PPP using cross-sectional datasets from industrial countries is reported in Wei and Parsley (1995), Frankel and Rose (1996), Oh (1996), Wu (1996), Papell (1997), Papell and Theodoridis

(1998), and Higgins and Zakrajšek (1999). On the other hand, mixed results have been found for parity reversion for a limited number of panel analyses from developing countries. Phylaktis and Kassimatis (1994) support the validity of long-run PPP for eight Pacific Basin countries over the period 1974 to 1987, while Wu and Chen (1999) find no evidence of PPP using the data from the same eight countries for the period of 1980 to 1996. Through unit root tests from heterogeneous panels and variance ratio tests, Luintel (2000) finds support for PPP using data for eight Asian developing countries. A number of other methodologies have been used to test for PPP during the last decade, including the still-popular cointegration techniques, variance ratio tests, structural-break tests, non-linear approaches to mean reversion and so on.

The revival of interest in PPP has been documented in a number of comprehensive and influential surveys – see Breuer (1994), Froot and Rogoff (1995), MacDonald (1995) and Rogoff (1996). This chapter aims to provide an up-to-date survey of the contemporary literature on PPP. It covers the literature that has appeared up until July 2000, with the major focus on the research from the last decade. The next section examines the research into and interest in PPP, while Section 2.0 gives a geometric analysis of PPP theory. Section 3.0 is devoted to issues related to deviations from parity, including two measures of PPP deviations. In Section 4.0 we summarise recent empirical evidence on PPP and the last section offers some concluding remarks.

1.0 HOW MUCH IS BEING WRITTEN ON PPP?

The amount of research into PPP has exploded during the past three decades. The Big Mac Index (BMI), invented by *The Economist* magazine in 1986, has played a major role in popularising PPP and bringing its practical implications to the attention of financial markets. As a way of measuring the extent of professional interest in PPP, this section reports results of searching for (i) PPP in Econlit, a widely-used economic indexing database produced by the American Economic Association;[1] and (ii) the Big Mac Index in Google, a popular search engine on the world wide web.

To quantify the growth in the literature on PPP, we conducted a keyword search for the term 'purchasing power parity' or 'PPP' in EconLit. As we need to compare the amount published on PPP with something, we also searched for four broad additional economic terms – inflation, unemployment, interest rate and exchange rate – and another relatively narrow term, foreign direct investment (FDI).[2] We recorded the number of research articles on each topic in the 1970s, 1980s, 1990s and from January to July 2000. Figure 2.1 plots, on the left-hand axis, the number of articles in each decade for the six topics. As the vertical axis uses a logarithmic scale, the change in the height of the bars from one decade to the next indicates the exponential rate of growth for each topic. The right-hand vertical axis gives the average growth rate, on an annual basis, for each topic. It can be seen that PPP has grown at an average annual rate of 18 per cent p.a., second only to FDI. This growth rate clearly reflects that the research interest in PPP has been expanded very substantially over the last thirty years. Thus, rather than 'collapsing', PPP research can be described as 'exploding'.

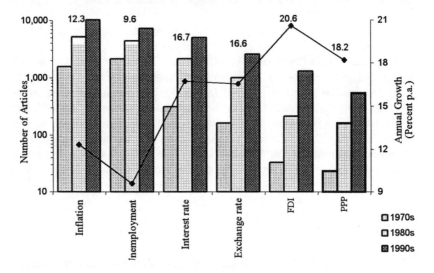

Figure 2.1 The growth of economic research

Since the introduction of the Big Mac Index (BMI) by *The Economist* in 1986, financial markets have become interested in PPP as a practical approach to valuing currencies and in making international price comparisons. Economic research on this index has evolved into an important strand of literature called 'Burgernomics'.[3] As a way to measure the extent of such interest, we searched for the exact phase 'Big Mac Index' in a web search engine Google.[4] This resulted in 697 entires.[5] We categorised these BMI web sites according to the language they use and their institutional domains and the results are presented in Table 2.1. The left panel shows that around 70 per cent of the search results are written in the 17 frequently-used languages and the remaining 30 per cent are in the language not specifically identified by Google. English web sites are the most frequent, followed by European languages. Developing countries are also aware of this widely-quoted invention from *The Economist*. From the right panel of Table 2.1, it can be seen that BMI is used in all sectors. About 40 per cent of the BMI web pages are created by commercial institutions, suggesting the widespread practical usefulness of the BMI. Another 20 per cent of the BMI pages are related to educational activities. The popularity of the Index in different sectors points to its practical versatility – presumably due to the simple and timely nature of this metric.

Table 2.1 Big Mac Index search results

Language of web page	Number	Institutional Domain	Number
English	405	.com	271
Danish, French, German, Japanese, Swedish	66	.edu	131
Chinese, Dutch, Italian, Korea, Norwegian, Russian, Spanish	27	.org	45
Czech, Finnish, Hungarian, Portuguese	7	.net	38
Other	192	Other	260
Total	697	Total	697

Source: http://www.google.com.

2.0 THE GEOMETRY OF PPP

This section presents a geometric analysis of PPP theory by examining the two perspectives on traditional PPP: (1) The exchange rate–relative price relationship; and (2) the relationship among exchange rates, money and prices.

A natural starting point of the traditional view of PPP is its central building block – the law of one price, which states that the price of an identical good in two countries should be equal when converted to a common currency. The basic mechanism is arbitrage – buying in those countries where the price is low and selling where it is high – will eliminate the price differentials, at least over the medium term. Applying this idea to the price of a market basket, we have $P_t = S_t P_t^*$, where P is the domestic price level,

P^* the foreign price level, and S the exchange rate. This implies the absolute version of PPP, that is, $S_t = P_t / P_t^*$, whereby the absolute PPP of a currency is determined by the ratio of the domestic price level to the foreign price level. In terms of natural logarithms, we have

$$s_t = p_t - p_t^*. \tag{2.1}$$

Given the difficulties with the construction of an appropriate common basket of goods for implementing absolute PPP, a weaker version of PPP is often considered. This relative version of PPP is based on price movements, which are measured by changes in prices relative to a base period. Relative PPP allows for a constant gap in absolute PPP described in equation (2.1),

$$s_t = p_t - p_t^* - k. \tag{2.2}$$

Let expression (2.2) hold for the base period, 0, so that $s_0 = p_0 - p_0^* - k$. We can then subtract this equation from (2.2) to yield

$$s_t - s_0 = \tilde{p}_t - \tilde{p}_t^*, \tag{2.3}$$

where $\tilde{p} = p_t - p_0$ and $\tilde{p}^* = p_t^* - p_0^*$ are (log) changes in price levels of the domestic and foreign country respectively, with the same base starting–point, i.e., inflation at home and aboard. Expression (2.3) is the usual presentation of relative PPP in textbooks. It states that the change in the exchange rate should offset the inflation differential.[6] To allow for stochastic deviations from relative PPP, we add a stationary error term to equation (2.2),

$$s_t = p_t - p_t^* - k + e_t.^7 \tag{2.4}$$

We draw on the conceptual framework of MacDonald and Stein (1999) to illustrate the above three versions of traditional view of PPP. Figure 2.2 plots the nominal exchange rate s against the relative price, $r = p - p^*$. Panel A presents the case when $k = e = 0$, so that the $45°$ line passing through the origin corresponds to absolute PPP. Any combination of s and r that lies above the line implies an undervaluation of the home country currency, while points below represent overvaluation. Panel B allows $k \neq 0$ and $e = 0$, which is relative PPP. Here the $45°$ line does not pass through the origin, but an increase in the relative price still leads to an equi-proportional depreciation of the currency, as is illustrated by the movement from the point A to B, whereby $s_2 - s_1 = r_2 - r_1$. The central line in Panel C corresponds to relative PPP and is the centre-of-gravity relationship when there are stochastic shocks in the short run. Suppose for simplicity that e is a discrete random variable and that $e_1 < 0$ and $e_2 > 0$ are its only possible values. When the shock is $e_1 < 0$, we obtain a new, lower $45°$ line, which has an intercept of $-k + e_1$; similarly, $e_2 > 0$ results in the upper line in Panel C.

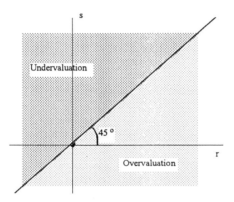

Figure 2.2A Exchange rates and relative prices: absolute PPP

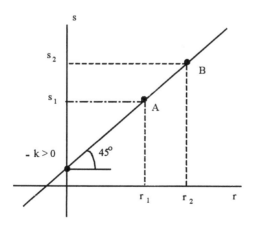

ure 2.2B Exchange rates and relative prices: relative PPP

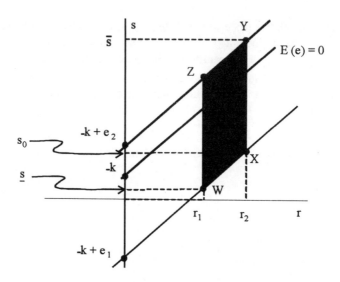

Figure 2.2C Exchange rates and relative prices: stochastic deviations from relative PPP

Consider the situation in which s is the exchange rate and r_1 is the relative price, so we are located at the point W in Panel C. If there is now the same increase in the relative price as before, so that r rises from r_1 to r_2, then, in the presence of the shock e_1, we move to the point X with the rate depreciating to s_0. With the shock e_2, the same relative price r_2 leads to an exchange rate of $\bar{s}$, as indicated by point Y. More generally, if relative prices change within the range $[r_1, r_2]$ and if the shocks can now vary continuously within the range $[e_1, e_2]$, then the exchange rate/relative price point lies somewhere in the shaded parallelogram WXYZ. It is to be noted that as the height of this parallelogram exceeds its base, the possible range of the exchange rate, $\bar{s} - \underline{s}$, exceeds that of prices, $r_2 - r_1$. This 'overshooting' accords with the idea that in the short run exchange rates are considerably more variable than relative prices. This contrasts with the situation in Panels A and B where the exchange rate is proportional to prices and illustrates the importance of stochastic shocks to the PPP relationship.

Next, we examine the PPP theory from the perspective of the quantity theory of money and present a geometric analysis of the relationships among exchange rates, money and prices.[8] The quantity theory of money (QTM) is built on the equation of exchange which shows the relationship between the money supply, velocity, prices and volume of transactions.

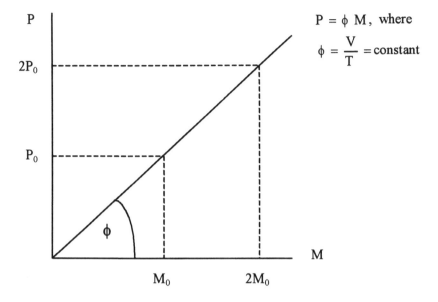

Figure 2.3 The quantity theory of money

The transactions version of QTM is $MV=PT$, where M is the supply of money balances, V is the velocity or rate of circulation of these money balances, P is the general level of prices of all transactions, and T is the number of transactions. As V and T are fixed, an increase in the supply of money will lead to a proportionate increase in the price level, that is, $\hat{P} = \hat{M}$, where a circumflex ('^') denotes percentage change. Figure 2.3 shows this relationship. To relate QTM to PPP, we decompose the goods that make up the general price level P into traded and non–traded goods. Then we have the price level function $P = P(P_T, P_N)$, which is homogeneous of degree one. This function is plotted as the downward sloping convex curve AA in Figure 2.4 and is called the 'absolute price schedule' along which the price level is a constant. The distance of the absolute price schedule from the origin measures the price level. Suppose that the relative price $r = P_T/P_N$ is constant, so that the two prices must lie somewhere along the ray OP. For the economy to simultaneously satisfy monetary equilibrium and for the relative price to be r, overall equilibrium must be located at the point E where the two curves intersect. A doubling of the money supply moves the absolute price schedule from AA to A'A', the price level doubles and with the relative price unchanged, the new equilibrium is at the point E'. The homogeneity of the price level function $P = P(P_T, P_N)$ means that the effect of the doubling the quantity of money is to double both sectoral prices P_T and P_N.

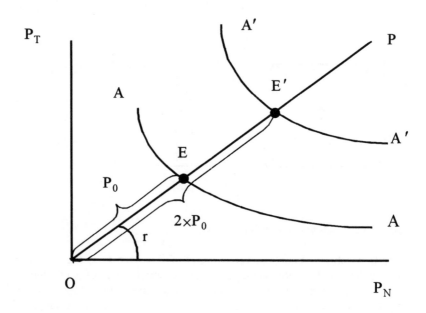

Figure 2.4 Traded and non-traded goods prices

Figure 2.5 combines the above two figures with the money stock added to the lower quadrant of Figure 2.4. PPP theory comes into play with the additional assumption that it holds for traded goods, that is, $P_T = S P_T^*$, where P_T^* is the foreign price level of traded goods. The left quadrant of Figure 2.5 shows this relationship. As before, a doubling of the money stock doubles the general price level and the domestic price of traded goods also doubles. With the foreign traded goods price unchanged at P_{T0}^*, the exchange rate depreciates by 100 per cent, that is, $S_1 = 2S_0$, as can be seen from the left-hand panel of Figure 2.5.

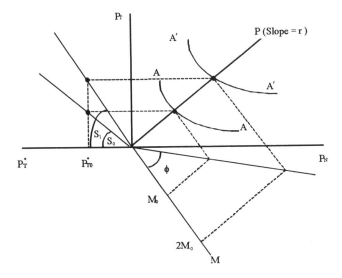

Figure 2.5 Exchange rates, money and prices

An important case of an interaction between real and monetary phenomena in this area is the 'productivity bias' hypothesis of Balassa (1964) and Samuelson (1964). The above framework can be used to illustrate the key idea. Suppose there are two countries, one rich and one poor. The productivity bias hypothesis states that the rich country has higher productivities in producing both traded and non-traded goods, but is proportionately more productive in traded goods, relative to the poor country. This could be because non-traded goods tend to be services, which are labour intensive, and are not so amenable to productivity improvement. The higher productivity of the traded goods sector in both countries raises wages not only in its own sector, but also economy-wide wages. As non-traded goods are usually labour intensive, this has the effect of making the relative price of these goods higher in the rich country, where wages are higher. In other words, traded goods (in terms of non-traded goods) are cheaper in the rich country as compared to the poor country, so that $r^R < r^P$. To isolate the impact of the differing structure of relative prices, let the two countries share the same absolute price schedule, so that the overall price level is the same in the two countries. Application of PPP to these price levels would then imply that the cost of unit of foreign exchange would be identical in the two countries, $S^R = S^P$. But, the situation is different if we apply PPP to the traded goods only. As Figure 2.6 shows, $r^R < r^P$ implies that $S^R < S^P$, so that the rich country's currency is now more highly valued than that of the poor country.

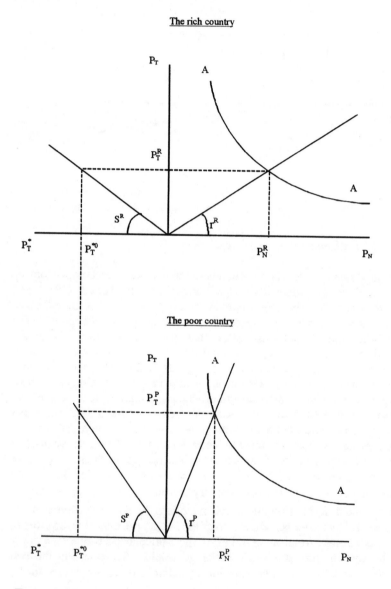

Figure 2.6 Productivity and exchange rates

The implications of the above analysis are as follows:

- Application of PPP to price levels indicates that the currencies of the two counties should have the same value.
- PPP for traded goods only indicates that the currency of the rich country is worth more.
- If currencies are in fact priced according to traded goods PPP, whereas one values them according to price level PPP, (i) and (ii) above jointly imply that the currency of the rich (poor) country is over (under) valued. This is the productivity bias hypothesis.

3.0 DEVIATIONS FROM PARITY AND THE SPEED OF ADJUSTMENT

As Rogoff (1996) points out, every reasonable theoretical model suggests that there should be at least some temporary component to PPP deviations. This section first explores the notion of deviations from PPP from both the traditional and efficient-markets perspectives of PPP. Then we discuss the concept of the half-life as a measure of the speed of convergence to long-run PPP. Finally, a summary of estimates of the half-life of PPP deviations from a variety of studies is presented.

Recall from Section 2.0 that stochastic deviations from traditional PPP are described in equation (2.4) as $s_t = p_t - p_t^* - k + e_t$, whereby the real exchange rate is $k - e_t$. The nature of the error term e_t determines the validity of PPP. Following Maeso-Fernández (1998), we write e_t as a moving average of a white-noise process, $\{\varepsilon_t\}$: $e_t = a(L)\varepsilon_t$, where $a(L)$ is a polynomial in the lag operator L and $a(L) = \sum_{i=0}^{N} a_i L^i$. There are three possibilities for the PPP deviations e_t:

- If the polynomial $a(L)$ is of zero degree (that is, $N = 0$, so that $a(L) = a_0$), PPP deviations e_t are serially-uncorrelated white noise. In such a case, the shocks to PPP only have a transitory effect.
- If $a(L)$ is of greater-than-zero degree $(N > 0)$ and its roots are *outside* the unit circle, a real shock has permanent effects on the current level of the real exchange rate, but the effects gradually die out. In this case, PPP deviations are persistent, but relative PPP holds in the long run. The real exchange rate thus displays mean reversion.

- If $a(L)$ has greater-than-zero degree and its roots are *inside* the unit circle, all previous real shocks have permanent effects on the current exchange rate level. In this case, e_t is a non-stationary process, implying that the relative PPP does not hold in the long run.

The above analysis examines the traditional view of PPP, that is, PPP as a relationship between the exchange rate and relative prices. Next, we examine deviations from PPP from the perspective of the efficient-markets view of PPP and review two alternative measures of the speed of convergence. The traditional and efficient-markets views are closely related to each other and test for PPP from different angles, although they seem to be contradictory with opposite economic implications.[9]

The efficient-markets view, initiated by Magee (1978), Roll (1979) and Darby (1980), examines the stochastic behaviour of real exchange rates. It states that if expectations are rational, changes in the real exchange rates should be serially uncorrelated. Thus the real exchange rate should follow a random walk process. One of the implications of this random walk hypothesis is that changes in the real exchange rate cannot be predicted using past information. The baseline test for the efficient-markets view of PPP is equivalent to testing for a unit root in the real exchange rate against the stationarity alternative. Consider the following simple data-generating process:

$$H_o : q_t = \alpha + \beta q_{t-1} + u_t, \quad \beta = 1 ,$$
$$H_1 : q_t = \alpha + \beta q_{t-1} + u_t, \quad 0 < \beta < 1 ,$$

where q_t is the real exchange rate defined as $q_t = p_t - s_t - p_t^*$; α and β are the intercept and the speed-of-adjustment parameters and u_t is a disturbance term.[10] From equation (2.4), we can see that $q_t = k - e_t$, so that the real exchange rate represents the deviation from PPP. Stationarity of the real exchange rate implies that deviations from PPP are transitory and eventually die out.

Consider again the above data-generating process,

$$q_t = \alpha + \beta q_{t-1} + u_t , \tag{2.5}$$

averaging over $t = 2, ... , T$, we have

$$\bar{q}_t = \alpha + \beta \bar{q}_{t-1} + \bar{u}_t \tag{2.6}$$

where the bars denote means. For a process with sufficiently long time intervals, $\bar{q}_t = \bar{q}_{t-1} = \bar{q}$. Subtracting equation (2.6) from equation (2.5) and ignoring the disturbance terms (which represent the deviations from the deterministic relationship), we obtain through successive substitution

$$d_t = d_0 \, \beta^t, \tag{2.7}$$

where $d_t = q_t - \bar{q}$ is the value of the current deviation and d_0 is the value of the initial deviation. Under stationarity, the speed-of-adjustment parameter β in equation (2.5) is less than one, thus $\beta^t \to 0$ and the deviation $d_t \to 0$ when $t \to \infty$. A value of β of 0.97, for example, means that 3 per cent of the PPP deviation vanishes per period.

More generally, let the real exchange rate be generated by a more complex process:

$$q_t = \alpha + \sum_{j=1}^{m} \beta_j \, q_{t-j} + u_t. \tag{2.8}$$

As in equilibrium $E(q_t) = E(q_{t-j})$ for $j = 1, \dots, m$, the speed of convergence is the sum of the coefficients of all the lags, that is, $\sum_{j=1}^{m} \beta_j$. Accordingly, stationarity of $\{q_t\}$ requires $0 < \sum_{j=1}^{m} \beta_j < 1$.

An alternative measure of the speed of adjustment is the 'half-life' of a process, a concept originally from physics. It measures the decay of a substance comprising of a large number of identical particles. The half-life is the time taken by a given amount of substance to decay to half its mass. Figure 2.7 shows the remaining amount of particles as a function of time.

Here, H is the half-life of the process. After a second half-life, one half of the remaining particles will have decayed, leaving 1/4 of the original amount. After three half-life intervals, 1/8 of the original amount remains and so on. Thus the decay process can be expressed as:

$$d_t = d_0 \, e^{-\frac{t}{T}}, \tag{2.9}$$

where T is the time required for the total amount to decay, usually called the 'life-time'. According to the definition of the half-life, $e^{-H/T} = d_H / d_0 = 1/2$, so that

$$H = T \ln 2. \tag{2.10}$$

This relationship shows that the half-life is an alternative measure of the total time required for mean reversion, T. It indicates how long it takes for the impact of a unit shock to dissipate by half. Comparing expressions (2.7) and (2.9), we obtain the relationship between the lifetime T and the mean reversion speed $\beta : T = -1 / (\ln \beta)$. Substituting this into (2.10), we obtain

$$H = - \ln 2 / (\ln \beta). \tag{2.11}$$

If the data-generating process is in the form of equation (2.8), expression (2.11) then becomes $H = - \ln 2 / [\ln (\sum_{j=1}^{m} \beta_j)]$.

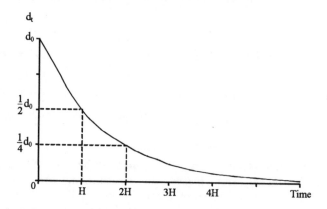

Figure 2.7 The time path of a mean reversion process

Empirically, the half-life of PPP can be estimated not only from an autoregressive data-generating process of the real exchange rate, but also from variance ratios. The simplest variance ratio for a time series $\{y_t\}$, proposed by Cochrane (1988), is $R(k) = \text{var}(y_{t+k} - y_t) / \text{var}(y_{t+1} - y_t)$, where $k = 2, \cdots$. This expression is the variance of the kth difference divided by that of the first difference. When the value of k is sufficiently large, it can be shown that $R(k)$ is approximately the variance of the unit-root component of the real exchange rate. Thus the time required for $R(k)$ to diminish to half of its size is an alternative estimator of the half-life of real exchange rate innovations.

Table 2.2 Estimates of PPP half-lives

Author(s)		Half-life (Years)	Data
Frankel (1990)		4.6	Dollar–pound
Abuaf and Jorion (1990)		3.3	Ten industrial countries
Manzur (1990,1993)		5	Seven industrial countries
Fung and Lo (1992)		6.5	Six industrial countries
Wei and Parsley (1995)	(i)	4.25	European Monetary System
	(ii)	4.75	Non-European Monetary System
Frankel and Rose (1996)		4	150 countries
Cumby (1996)		1	Big Mac currencies
Lothian and Taylor (1996)	(i)	2.8	Franc–pound
	(ii)	5.9	Dollar–pound
Papell (1997)	(i)	1.9	EC (The European Community)
	(ii)	2.8	EMS
Higgins and Zakrajšek (1999)	(i)	5	Europe, CPI
	(ii)	3	Europe, WPI
	(iii)	2.5	OECD, WPI
	(iv)	11.5	Open economies, CPI
Cheung and Lai (2000)	(i)	(2–5)	Industrial countries
	(ii)	(under 3)	Developing countries
Median		4	
Mean		4.1	
Standard error of mean		2.3	

Notes:

a Where a study contains more than one estimate of half-life, we use (i),(ii), (iii) and so on to distinguish different estimates, with additional information provided in the final column of the corresponding row.

b Where a study does not report the half-life directly, we compute it from the speed-of-adjustment estimate (on an annual basis) using $H = -\ln 2 / (\ln \beta)$ or $H = -\ln 2 / [\ln(\sum_{j=1}^{t} \beta_j)]$.

c In those cases where the underlying data are not annual and the parameter estimated is β, we compute the speed of adjustment per annum as β^n, where n is the number of periods per year.

d Cheung and Lai (2000) report the range of half-life estimates for two groups of countries. To compute the mean and its standard error in the last two rows of this table, we use 3.5 and 2 years as the respective point estimates.

Table 2.2 summarises estimates of half-lives from various studies in the PPP literature; these estimates are presented in descending order in Figure 2.8. It can be seen that most of the estimates lie between 3 and 5 years. The median and mean of half-lives are 4 and 4.1 years, respectively. These figures are in broad agreement with the length of the long run insofar as PPP is concerned reported in the survey paper of Froot and Rogoff (1995) – four to five years. This increasing consensus boosts professional confidence in long-run PPP despite the fact that PPP deviations are quite persistent.

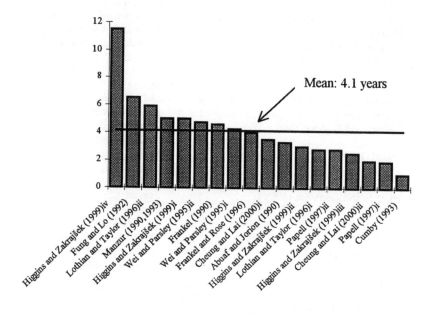

Figure 2.8 Estimates of PPP half-lives

4.0 RECENT EMPIRICAL FINDINGS

This section gives an overview of the most recent empirical evidence regarding PPP which has emerged during the course of the theory's resurrection over the 1990s. Table 2.3 gives a list of the most recent work on PPP.[11]

To review the empirical evidence using a variety of techniques, we classify these papers into three kinds of samples: (1) Industrial countries; (2) mixed samples of both developed and developing countries; and (3) purely developing countries.

Panel A of Table 2.3 shows that recent evidence from industrial countries is generally supportive of long-run PPP, and interestingly, such favourable results are obtained through a diverse variety of econometric techniques. Bayoumi and MacDonald (1999), Flôres et al. (1999), Koedijk et al. (1998), Papell (1997), and Papell and Theodoridis (1998) are some examples in favour of PPP using panel frameworks. Maeso-Fernández (1998) find evidence of mean reversion of real exchange rates using variance ratio tests. Edison et al. (1997) employ cointegration techniques. Michael et al. (1997) apply a non-linear approach to mean reversion. Parkes and Savvides (1999) use a sequential model to search for endogenous breaks and find that the real sterling rate reverts to a shifting mean. Sjaastad (1998) uses a commodity–currency approach to model exchange rates and commodity prices.

Negative results for PPP from industrial countries are reported in Baum et al. (1999), Engel (2000), Li (1999) and O'Connell (1998). It is to be noted that most studies examine real exchange rates against the US dollar, and there are only a limited number of studies using the German mark as the base currency (for example, Anker, 1999; Engel et al., 1997; Flôres et al., 1999; Koedijk et al., 1998, and Papell, 1997).[12] The common finding is that PPP holds more strongly for the German mark than the US dollar exchange rates. Lothian (1998) argues that this is caused by the large depreciation of the dollar during the early and mid 1980s and the strong appreciation afterwards.

Mixed evidence is found in studies whose samples include both industrial and developing countries; see Panel B of Table 2.3. Wu and Chen (1999) fail to find evidence for PPP using two panel unit root tests. Lee (1999) tests PPP for 13 Asia Pacific countries using a generalised error correction model and finds support for PPP for countries. Favourable empirical results from mixed samples are reported in Higgins and Zakrajšek (1999) who include eight developing countries in their open-economy panel, and Cheung and Lai (2000) who find evidence of PPP mean reversion through a country-by-country unit-root testing approach.

Due to limited data availability and quality, there are only a handful of studies which examine the validity of long-run PPP for developing economies. Panel C of Table 2.3 lists such papers. Empirical results from the developing world are in disagreement. Using cointegration techniques, Doğanlar (1999) finds evidence in favour of PPP for only one among five Asian developing countries. Salehizadeh and Taylor (1999) examine 27 emerging economies in Europe, the Americas, Asia and Africa. Their results obtained from cointegration support PPP for more than half of the countries and strongly reject the symmetry and proportionality conditions.[13]

Table 2.3 Recent empirical evidence on PPP

Author(s)	Nature of data[a]	Countries in sample	Sample period	Price index used	Approach	Does PPP hold?
A. Industrial Countries						
Anker (1999)	Panel	18 (14) industrial countries	1974–97 (Q)	CPI (WPI)	Panel unit root test (GLS)	Yes
Baum et al. (1999)	Time–series	17 countries, 12 countries	1973–95 (M)	CPI & WPI	Fractional cointegration and structural break tests	No
Bayoumi and MacDonald (1999)	Panel	20 countries, 48 states (US), 9 provinces (Canada)	1973–93, 1972–94, 1963–92 (A)	CPI & WPI	Panel unit root test	Yes
Edison et al. (1997)	Time–series	13 countries	1974–92 (Q)	CPI	Cointegration	Yes
Engel (2000)	Time–series	US/UK	1970–95 (Q)	GDP def.	Unit root and cointegration tests	No
Engel et al. (1997)	Panel	4 pairs of cities in the US and Europe	1978–94 (M)	CPI	GLS applied to a system of error-correction models	No
Flôres et al. (1999)	Panel	10 industrial countries	1973–94 (M)	CPI	Panel unit root test (SUR–GLS)	Yes
Koedijk et al. (1998)	Panel	17 industrial countries	1972–96 (Q)	CPI	A numeraire-invariant panel methodology	Yes

28

Study	Method	Countries	Period	Price index	Test	Stationarity test
Kuo and Mikkola (1999)	Time-series	US/UK	1859–1992 (A)	WPI & GNP def.	Stationarity test	Yes
Li (1999)	Time-series	29, 26 and 25 OECD countries	1974–96 (A)	CPI	Hierarchical model	No
Maeso-Fernández (1998)	Time-series	19 developed countries	1974–92 (M, A)	CPI & WPI	Variance ratio	Yes
Michael et al. (1997)	Time-series	US, UK, France, Germany	1921–25 (M), 1800–1992 (A)	WPI	Nonlinear adjustment (STAR model)	Yes
O'Connell (1998)	Panel	64 countries	1973–95 (Q)	CPI	Panel unit root test (GLS)	No
Papell (1997)	Panel	17 and 20 countries	1973–94 (M, Q)	CPI	Panel unit root test (FGLS incorporating serial correlation)	Yes
Papell and Theodoridis (1998)	Panel	20 industrial countries	1973–96 (Q)	CPI	Panel unit root test (GLS)	Yes
Parkes and Savvides (1999)	Panel	G7 countries	1917–94 (A)	CPI & WPI	SUR and sequential test for structural breaks	Yes
Sjaastad (1998)	Time-series	Switzerland	1974–91 (Q)	GDP deflator, CPI & PPI	Commodity currency	Yes

Table 2.3 (contd)

Author(s)	Nature of data	Countries in sample	Sample period	Price index used	Approach	Does PPP hold?
Taylor and Sarno (1998)	Panel	US, UK, France, Germany, Japan	1973–96 (Q)	CPI & GDP def.	Panel unit root test (SUR–GLS)	Yes
B. Industrial and Developing Countries						
Cheung and Lai (2000)	Time-series	94 countries	1973–94 (M)	CPI	Fractional integration	Yes
Higgins and Zakrajšek (1999)	Panel	11 European countries, 12 OECD countries and 17 open economies	1973 (or 76 or 79)–97 (Q)	CPI & WPI	Four panel unit root tests	Yes
Lee (1999)	Time-series	13 Asia Pacific countries	1957–94 (Q)	CPI & WPI	Generalised error correction	Yes
Wu and Chen (1999)	Panel	8 Pacific Basin countries	1980–96 (M)	CPI & WPI	Two panel unit root tests	No
C. Developing Countries						
Bahmani-Oskooee (1998)	Time-series	11 Middle Eastern countries	1971–94 (Q)	CPI	Stationarity and ADF tests	Yes

Boyd and Smith (1999)	Panel	31 developing countries	1966–90 (Q)	CPI	Panel unit root and cointegration tests	Yes
Doğanlar (1999)	Time-series	India, Indonesia, Pakistan, Turkey and Philippines	1980–95 (Q)	CPI	Cointegration	No
Guimarães-Filho (1999)	Time-series	Brazil	1855–1990 (Q)	Unknown	Robust rank test	No
Luintel (2000)	Panel	8 Asian developing countries	1958–89 (M)	CPI	Panel unit root and variance ratio tests	Yes
Nagayasu (1998)	Panel	16 African countries	1981–94 (A)	CPI and WPI	Cointegration	Yes
Salehizadeh and Taylor (1999)	Time-series	27 American, European, African and Asian emerging economies	1975–97 (M)	CPI	Cointegration	Yes
Sarno (2000)	Time-series	11 Middle Eastern countries	1973–94 (Q)	CPI	Multivariate nonlinear models	Yes

Notes: In the column headed 'Sample period', M denotes monthly data, Q quarterly and A annual.

31

In Boyd and Smith (1999), who focus on 31 developing countries, PPP is strongly supported using panel unit root tests, but only weakly supported using cointegration tests. The panel cointegration analysis of Nagayasu (1998) reveals that the behaviour of parallel market exchange rates of 16 African countries is consistent with long-run PPP.

There are a number of studies for developing countries using tests other than cointegration. Luintel (2000) confirms the stationarity of black-market real exchange rates for eight Asian developing countries using both panel unit root and variance ratio tests. Using the robust rank test, Guimarães-Filho (1999) cannot reject the existence of a unit root in Brazilian real exchange rates for more than a century. Evidence of PPP from Middle-Eastern countries are provided in Bahmani-Oskooee (1998) and Sarno (2000); the former uses conventional univariate tests and find mixed results, and the latter strongly supports PPP using multivariate nonlinear models.

5.0 CONCLUSIONS

In a nutshell, research on PPP has been exploding in the past three decades, especially during the last ten years. With the use of increasingly powerful test techniques, the conclusions concerning the validity of PPP are becoming more and more reliable. The increasing evidence favouring PPP has strengthened confidence in PPP. As Taylor and Sarno (1998) put it, '...it seems that the profession's confidence in long-run PPP, having been low for a number of years, may itself be mean reverting' (p. 308).

The implications of PPP holding in the long run are no less than profound. For example, PPP means that nominal devaluations are just inflationary in the long run and have no impact on the country's competitiveness. A further implication of PPP holding in the long run is that it can be used as a convenient way to define equilibrium exchange rates. For example, Lan (2001) estimates the equilibrium rates for 16 countries using the Big Mac Index published by *The Economist* magazine.

It is found that real exchange rates are stationary using this single-good index, and the estimated equilibrium exchange rates are quite similar to those derived from more complex methodologies. The attractions of this approach are its modest data requirement (Big Mac prices), the minimal economic structure on the problem and, above all, its simplicity.

Concerning the future direction of the research on PPP, there are at least two important issues to be resolved. First, the purchasing power parity puzzle summarised by Rogoff (1996): how can one reconcile the excessively high volatility of real exchange rates in the short term with seemingly 'long' half-life of deviations from PPP, that is, four to five years? Second, the economic underpinnings of deviations from PPP, as pointed out by Higgins and Zakrajšek (1999): economists should move beyond the purely statistical issue of whether the real exchange rate contains a unit root, to focus on the economic sources of deviations from PPP, which may comprise persistent and/or transitory components.

ACKNOWLEDGEMENTS

This chapter is based on my PhD thesis at The University of Western Australia. I would like to thank Ken Clements for his excellent supervision and constant encouragement. The help from the editor, Meher Manzur, and useful comments from Paula Madson are also gratefully acknowledged. All errors are my own.

REFERENCES

Abuaf, N. and P. Jorion (1990), 'Purchasing power parity in the long run', *Journal of Finance*, **45**, pp. 157–174.

Adler, M. and B. Lehmann (1983), 'Deviations from purchasing power parity in the long run', *Journal of Finance*, **39**, pp. 1471–1487.

Anker, P. (1999), 'Pitfalls in panel tests of purchasing power parity', *Weltwischaftliches Archiv*, **135**, pp. 437–453.

Annaert, J. and M.J.K. Ceuster (1997), 'The Big Mac: More than a junk asset allocator?', *International Review of Financial Analysis*, **6**, pp. 179–192.

Bahmani-Oskooee, M. (1998), 'Do exchange rates follow a random walk process in Middle Eastern countries?', *Economics Letters*, **58**, pp. 339–344.

Balassa, B. (1964), 'The purchasing-power parity doctrine: A reappraisal', *Journal of Political Economy*, **72**, pp. 584–596.

Baum, C.F., Barkoulas, J.T. and M. Caglayan (1999), 'Long memory or structural breaks: Can either explain nonstationary real exchange rates under the current float?', *Journal of International Financial Markets, Institutions and Money*, **9**, pp. 359–376.

Bayoumi, T. and R. MacDonald (1999), 'Deviations of exchange rates from purchasing power parity: A story featuring two monetary unions', *International Monetary Fund Staff Papers*, **46**, pp. 89–102.

Boyd, D. and R. Smith (1999), 'Testing for purchasing power parity: econometric issues and an application to developing countries', *The Manchester School of Economic & Social Studies*, **67**, pp. 287–303.

Breuer, J.B. (1994), 'An assessment of the evidence on purchasing power parity', in J. Williamson (ed.), *Estimating Equilibrium Exchange Rates*, Washington, DC: Institute for International Economics, pp. 245–277.

Cheung, Y.–W. and K.S. Lai (2000), 'On cross-country differences in the persistence of real exchange rates', *Journal of International Economics*, **50**, pp. 375–97.

Clements, K.W. (1981), 'The monetary approach to exchange rate determination: A geometric analysis', *Weltwirtschaftliches Archiv*, **117**, pp. 20–29.

Click, R.W. (1996), 'Contrarian MacParity', *Economics Letters*, **53**, pp. 209–212.

Cochrane, J.H. (1988), 'How big is the random walk in GNP?', *Journal of Political Economy*, **96**, pp. 893–920.

Corbae, D. and S. Ouliaris (1988), 'Cointegration and tests of purchasing power parity', *Review of Economics and Statistics*, **70**, pp. 508–521.

Cumby, R.E. (1996), 'Forecasting exchange rates and relative prices with the hamburger standard: Is what you want what you get with McParity?', *NBER Research Paper 5675*, Massachusetts: National Bureau of Economic Research,

Darby, M.R. (1980), 'Does purchasing power parity work?', *NBER Working Paper 607*, Massachusetts: National Bureau of Economic Research.

Diebold, F., Husted, S. and M. Rush (1991), 'Real exchange rate under the gold standard', *Journal of Political Economy*, **99**, pp. 1151–1158.

Doğanlar, M. (1999), 'Testing long-run validity of purchasing power parity for Asian countries', *Applied Economics Letters*, **6**, pp. 147–151.

Dornbusch, R. (1976), 'Expectations and exchange rate dynamics', *Journal of Political Economy*, **84**, pp. 1161–1176.

Edison, H.J. (1987), 'Purchasing power parity in the long run: A test of the dollar/pound exchange rate (1890–1978)', *Journal of Money, Credit and Banking*, **19**, pp. 376–387.

Edison, H.J. and E. Fisher (1991), 'A long-run view of the European Monetary System', *Journal of International Money and Finance*, **10**, pp. 53–70.

Edison, H.J., Gagnon, G.E. and W.R. Melick (1997), 'Understanding the empirical literature on purchasing power parity: The post-Bretton Woods era', *Journal of International Money and Finance*, **16**, pp. 1–17.

Enders, W. (1988), 'ARIMA and cointegration tests of PPP under fixed and flexible exchange rate regimes', *Review of Economics and Statistics*, **70**, 504–508.

Engel, C. (2000), 'Long-run PPP may not hold after all', *Journal of International Economics*, **51**, pp. 243–273.

Engel, C., Hendrickson, M.K. and J.H. Rogers (1997), 'Intra-national, intra-continental and intra-planetary PPP', *International Finance Discussion Papers*, No. 589, Washington DC: Board of Governors of the Federal Reserve System.

Engel, C. and C.J. Kim (1999), 'The long-run U.S./U.K. real exchange rate', *Journal of Money, Credit and Banking*, **31**, pp. 335–356.

Fisher, E. and J. Park (1991), 'Testing purchasing power parity under the null hypothesis of co-integration', *The Economic Journal*, **52**, pp. 1476–1484.

Flôres, R., Jorion, P., Preumont, P. and A. Szafarz (1999), 'Multivariate unit root tests of the PPP hypothesis', *Journal of Empirical Finance*, **6**, pp. 335–353.

Frankel, J. (1986), 'International capital mobility and crowding out in the U.S. economy: Imperfect integration of financial markets or goods markets?', in R. Hafer (ed.), *How Open is the US Economy?*, Lexington, MA: Lexington Books, pp. 33–67.

Frankel, J. (1990), 'Zen and the art of modern macroeconomics: a commentary', in W. Haraf and T. Willett (eds), *Monetary Policy for a Volatile Global Economy*, Washington DC: American Enterprise Institute for Public Policy Research, pp. 117–123.

Frankel, J. and A. Rose (1996), 'A panel project on purchasing power parity: mean reversion within and between countries', *Journal of International Economics*, **40**, pp. 209–224.

Frenkel, J.A. (1981), 'The collapse of purchasing power parities during the 1970s', *European Economic Review*, **16**, pp. 145–165.

Friedman, M. and A.J. Schwartz (1963), *A Monetary History of the United States: 1867–1960*, Princeton, NJ: Princeton University Press, for National Bureau of Economic Research.

Froot, K. and K. Rogoff (1995), 'Perspectives on PPP and long-run real exchange rates', in G. Grossman and K. Rogoff (eds), *Handbook of International Economics*, Amsterdam: North-Holland Press, pp. 1647–1688.

Fung, H.G. and W.C. Lo (1992), 'Deviations from purchasing power parity', *The Financial Review*, **27**, pp. 553–570.

Gaillot, H.J. (1970), 'Purchasing power parity as an explanation of long term changes in exchange rates', *Journal of Money, Credit and Banking*, **2**, pp. 348–357.

Grilli, V. and G. Kaminsky (1991), 'Nominal exchange rate regimes and the real exchange rate: Evidence for the United States and Great Britain, 1885–1986', *Journal of Monetary Economics*, **27**, pp. 191–212.

Guimarães-Filho, R.F. (1999), 'Does purchasing power parity hold after all? Evidence from a robust test', *Applied Financial Economics*, **9**, pp. 167–172.

Hakkio, C. (1984), 'A reexamination of purchasing power parity', *Journal of International Economics*, **17**, pp. 265–277.

Higgins, M. and E. Zakrajšek (1999), 'Purchasing power parity: Three stakes through the heart of the unit root null', Staff Reports No. 80, Federal Reserve Bank of New York.

Johnson, D.R. (1993), 'Unit roots, cointegration and purchasing power parity: Canada and the United States, 1870–1991', in the Bank of Canada, *The Exchange Rate and the Economy: Proceedings of a Conference Held at the Bank of Canada*, 22–23 June 1992, Ottawa: Bank of Canada, pp. 133–198.

Koedijk, K.G., Schotman, P.C. and M.A. Van Dijk (1998), 'The re-emergence of PPP in the 1990s', *Journal of International Money and Finance*, **17**, pp. 51–61.

Kuo, B. and A. Mikkola (1999), 'Re-examining long-run purchasing power parity', *Journal of International Money and Finance*, **18**, pp. 251–266.

Lan, Y. (2001), 'The long-run value of currencies: A Big Mac perspective', Paper presented to the PhD Conference in Economics and Business, 7–9 November, Perth, Australia.

Lee, D.Y. (1999), 'Purchasing power parity and dynamic error correction: Evidence from Asia Pacific economies', *International Review of Economics and Finance*, **8**, pp. 199–212.

Li, K. (1999), 'Testing symmetry and proportionality in PPP: A panel-data approach', *Journal of Business and Economic Statistics*, **17**, pp. 409–418.

Lothian, J.R. (1998), 'Some new stylized facts of floating exchange rates', *Journal of International Money and Finance*, **17**, pp. 29–39.

Lothian, J.R. and M.P. Taylor (1996), 'Real exchange rate behaviour: The recent float from the perspective of the past two centuries', *Journal of Political Economy*, **104**, pp. 488–510.

Luintel, K.B. (2000), 'Real exchange rate behaviour: Evidence from black markets', *Journal of Applied Econometrics*, **15**, pp. 161–185.

MacDonald, R. (1995), 'Long-run exchange rate modeling', *International Monetary Fund Staff Papers*, **42**, pp. 437–489.

MacDonald, R. and I. Marsh (1999), 'Purchasing power parity: Long and short run testing', Chapter 3 in R. MacDonald and I. Marsh (eds), *Exchange Rate Modelling*, Boston/Dordrecht/London: Kluwer Academic Publishers.

MacDonald, R. and J.L. Stein (1999), 'Introduction: Equilibrium exchange rates', Chapter 1 in R. MacDonald and J.L. Stein (eds), *Equilibrium Exchange Rates*, Boston/Dordrecht/London: Kluwer Academic Publishers.

Maeso-Fernández, F. (1998), 'Econometric methods and purchasing power parity: short and long-run PPP', *Applied Economics*, **30**, pp. 1443–1457.

Magee, S.P. (1978), 'Contracting and spurious deviations from purchasing power parity', in J.A. Frenkel and H.G. Johnson (eds), *Studies in the Economics of Exchange Rates*, Addison-Wesley, pp. 67–74.

Manzur, M. (1990), 'An international comparison of prices and exchange rates: A new test of purchasing power parity', *Journal of International Money and Finance*, **9**, pp. 75–91.

Manzur, M. (1993), *Exchange Rates, Prices and World Trade: New Methods, Evidence and Implications*, London: Routledge.

Mark, N. (1990), 'Real exchange rates in the long run: An empirical investigation', *Journal of International Economics*, **28**, pp. 115–136.

Meese, R. and K. Rogoff (1988), 'Was it real? The exchange rate interest differential relation over the modern floating exchange rate period', *Journal of Finance*, **43**, pp. 933–948.

Michael, P., Nobay A. and D. Peel (1997), 'Transaction costs and non-linear adjustments in real exchange rates: An empirical investigation', *Journal of Political Economy*, **105**, pp. 862–879.

Nagayasu, J. (1998), 'Does the long-run PPP hypothesis hold for Africa? Evidence from panel co–integration study', International Monetary Fund Working Paper, WP/98/123.

O'Connell, P.G.J. (1998), 'The overvaluation of purchasing power parity', *Journal of International Economics*, **44**, pp. 1–19.

Oh, K.Y. (1996), 'Purchasing power parity and unit root tests using panel data', *Journal of International Money and Finance*, **15**, pp. 405–418.

Ong, L.L. (1997), 'Burgernomics: the economics of the Big Mac standard', *Journal of International Money and Finance*, **16**, pp. 865–878.

Ong, L.L. (1998a), 'Burgernomics and the ASEAN currency crisis', *Journal of the Australian Society of Security Analysts*, **1**, pp. 15–16.

Ong, L.L. (1998b), 'Big Mac and wages to go, please: Comparing the purchasing power of earnings around the world', *Australian Journal of Labor Economics*, **2**, pp. 53–68.

Ong, L.L. and J.D. Mitchell (2000), 'Professors and hamburgers: An international comparison of real academic salaries', *Applied Economics*, **32**, pp. 869–876.

Pakko, M.R. and P.S. Pollard (1996), 'For here to go? Purchasing power parity and the Big Mac', *Federal Reserve Bank of St. Louis Review*, **78**, pp. 3–21.

Papell, D.H. (1997), 'Searching for stationarity: Purchasing power parity under the current float', *Journal of International Economics*, **43**, pp. 313–332.

Papell, D.H. and H. Theodoridis (1998), 'Increasing evidence of purchasing power parity over the current float', *Journal of International Money and Finance*, **17**, pp. 41–50.

Parkes, A.L.H. and A. Savvides (1999), 'Purchasing power parity in the long run and structural breaks: Evidence from real sterling exchange rates', *Applied Financial Economics*, **9**, pp. 117–127.

Patel, J. (1990), 'Purchasing power parity as a long-run relation', *Journal of Applied Econometrics*, **5**, 367–379.

Phylaktis, K. and Y. Kassimatis (1994), 'Does the real exchange rate follow a random walk? The pacific basin perspective', *Journal of International Money and Finance*, **13**, pp. 476–495.

Rogoff, K. (1996), 'The purchasing power parity puzzle', *Journal of Economic Literature*, **34**, pp. 647–668.

Roll, R. (1979), 'Violations of purchasing power parity and their implications for efficient international commodity markets', in M. Sarnat and G.P. Szego (eds), *International Finance and Trade*, Cambridge: Ballinger Publishing Company, pp. 3–76.

Salehizadeh, M. and R. Taylor (1999), 'A test of purchasing power parity for emerging economies', *Journal of International Financial Markets, Institutions and Money*, **9**, 183–193.

Samuelson, P.A. (1964), 'Theoretical notes on trade problems', *Review of Economics and Statistics*, **46**, pp. 145–154.

Sarno, L. (2000), 'Real exchange rate behaviour in Middle East: A re-examination', *Economics Letters*, **66**, pp. 127–136.

Sjaastad, L. (1998), 'On exchange rates, nominal and real', *Journal of International Money and Finance*, **17**, pp. 407–439.

Taylor, M.P. and L. Sarno (1998), 'The behavior of real exchange rates during the post-Bretton Woods period', *Journal of International Economics*, **46**, pp. 281–312.

Wei, S. and D. Parsley (1995), 'Purchasing power disparity during the floating rate period: Exchange rate volatility and trade barriers', NBER Working Paper No. 5032. Massachusetts: National Bureau of Economic Research.

Wu, J.-L. and S.-L. Chen (1999), 'Are real exchange rates stationary based on panel unit–root tests? Evidence from Pacific Basin countries', *International Journal of Finance and Economics*, **4**, pp. 243–252.

Wu, Y. (1996), 'Are real exchange rates non stationary? Evidence from a panel data test', *Journal of Money, Credit and Banking*, **28**, pp. 54–63.

NOTES

1   The source material of Econlit includes international economic journals, essays, research papers, books, dissertations, book reviews, and working papers. Years of coverage are from 1969 to the present with approximately 26,000 records added annually. Our search is done through the licensed Econlit website at The University of Western Australia: http://ovid.library.uwa.edu.au/ovidweb/ovidweb.cgi.

2   Foreign direct investment is chosen as a keyword due to its extraordinary growth over the past few decades.

3   In the Burgernomics literature, Cumby (1996) is the first paper which uses the BMI to tests for PPP. Pakko and Pollard (1996) and Click (1996) examine the nature of deviations from PPP, while Annaert and Ceuster investigate the value of BMI from an investment perspective. Ong (1997) improves upon BMI and proposes the 'No-Frills Index' to value currencies. Applications of Burgernomics include Ong (1998a) who analyses the Asian currency crisis, Ong (1998b) and Ong and Mitchell (2000) which examine the purchasing power of earnings around the world and real academic salaries.

4   The address of the Google search engine is http://www.google.com.

5   Note that (1) to narrow down the search, we use an additional constraint 'not computer'; (2) all the search results in Google refer to the returned entries excluding pages similar to those displayed; and (3) another 18 entries from Google contain only the word 'Burgernomics', but not the phrase 'Big Mac Index'.

6   Equations (2.2) and (2.3) are two presentations of relative PPP. Note that relative PPP expressed in (2.2) includes absolute PPP as a special case with $k = 0$. It can only be tested with price levels, whereas (2.3) can be tested directly with price indexes, or price indexes computed from price levels.

7   Maeso-Fernández (1998) points out a frequent mistake that most researchers make when formulating stochastic deviations from relative PPP – adding the stationary error term to (2.3). In such a case, the real exchange rate follows a random walk and relative PPP does not hold.

8   This material mainly draws on the lecture notes of International Finance 415 by Ken Clements at The University of Western Australia. See also Clements (1981).

9   See, for example, MacDonald and Marsh (1999) and Maeso-Fernández (1998), for discussions of the two views of PPP.

10   In testing for the efficient-markets view of PPP, in practice a more extended time-series model is typically used. The most common data-generating process used is the augmented Dickey-Fuller framework: $\Delta q_t = \alpha + \rho q_{t-1} + \sum_{j=1}^{m} \lambda_j \Delta q_{t-j} + \eta_t$, where the lagged real exchange rate changes are added to control for serial correlation. Under the null, $\alpha = \rho = 0$. Under the alternative, $\rho < 0$.

11   Note that this review of the recent empirical evidence was completed in July 2000.

12   Some earlier examples using the German mark as the base currency are Mark (1990), Edison and Fisher (1991) and Fisher and Park (1991).

13   Recall from Section 2.0 that the absolute PPP is expressed in equation (2.1) as $s_t = p_t - p_t^*$. Expressing this in regression form, we have $s_t = \alpha_1 p_t - \alpha_2 p_t^* + u_t$. Symmetry requires that $\alpha_1 = \alpha_2$ and proportionality requires that $\alpha_1 = \alpha_2 = 1$.

3. On Exchange Rates, Nominal and Real

Larry A. Sjaastad

This study addresses two closely related questions concerning exchange rate behavior: (i) can a freely-floating exchange rate insulate an open economy from external price shocks?; and (ii) do real exchange rates – hereafter referred to as purchasing power parity (PPP) real exchange rates – that normally are used to judge the empirical performance of PPP faithfully reflect movements in 'true' real exchange rates (that is, the relative price of internationally-traded goods)? If the answer to the first question is yes, then the answer to the second must be no; the floating of exchange rates will both increase the variance of PPP real exchange rates and reduce their correlation with 'true' real rates.

It is undisputed that the variance of both nominal and PPP real exchange rates increased markedly after the collapse of the Bretton Woods international monetary system in the early 1970s.[1] Indeed, Jones and Purvis (1983) described the 'prevailing conventional wisdom' concerning PPP as follows. (1) 'PPP does *not* hold in the short run. (2) There are strong tendencies towards PPP so that it does hold in the long run' (p. 34).

Moreover, stocks to both nominal and PPP real exchange rates have become more persistent and the prolonged deviations in PPP real exchange rates have been identified with a failure of purchasing power parity under floating exchange rates.[2] Nonetheless, PPP real rates appear to be mean reverting.[3]

The short run failure of PPP may be due in part to the fact that PPP real exchange rates are inherently more variable under a floating regime simply because 'news' is reflected immediately in both nominal and PPP real exchange rates (which explicitly involve nominal rates), whereas under fixed rates the price level is the adjustment mechanism and, since price levels are heavily weighted with perishables, 'news' is incorporated into prices – and hence PPP real exchange rates – only over time.[4] PPP real rates also embody the distortions in nominal rates due to exchange control, commercial policy, and so on. Finally, the persistence of shocks to PPP real exchange rates may arise from measurement error (which is not to be confused with data transcription error) due to shocks to third-country price levels and nominal exchange rates that generate persistent deviations between the price level of the reference country and external prices of the home country's traded goods.[5] This source of measurement error is shown to be particularly serious.

Identification of PPP with stable real exchange rates can be – and often has been – read into the following passage from Cassel (1922):

> When two currencies have undergone inflation, the normal rate of exchange will be equal to the old rate multiplied by the quotient of the degree of inflation in the one country and in the other ... But the rate that has been calculated by the above method must be regarded as the new parity between the two currencies, the point of balance towards which, in spite of all temporary fluctuations, the exchanges rates will always tend. This parity I call *purchasing power parity*. (p. 140, emphasis in original)

If PPP held perfectly, PPP real exchange rates would be constant. But it will be argued that, for a small, open economy, PPP is more appropriately tested by the true real exchange rate than by its empirical proxy, the PPP real exchange rate. Support for this view also is found in Cassel's original tract Cassel (1922):

> Our calculation of the purchasing power parity rests strictly on the proviso that the rise in prices in the countries concerned has affected *all commodities in a like degree. If that proviso is not fulfilled, then the actual exchange rate may deviate from the calculated purchasing power parity.* (p. 154, emphasis added)

A faithful interpretation of Cassel clearly must allow for movements in relative prices; the concept of PPP should not necessarily be rejected simply because of fluctuations in PPP real exchange rates between two open economies. Indeed, Cassel's proviso suggests that one should reject the theory underlying PPP only when persistent deviations in the PPP real exchange rate are shared by the true real exchange rate.

The remainder of this chapter is divided into four parts. Section 1 develops a simple floating exchange rate model that admits tests of PPP, independence of monetary policy, interest rate parity, foreign exchange market efficiency and the impact of the terms of trade on a floating exchange rate. More fundamentally, the model addresses the proposition that a freely floating exchange rate can impart monetary neutrality on an open economy; tests of that model are based on Swiss time series data. Since these propositions and hence the theory underlying PPP are supported in the tests, in Section 2 we then turn to the question of why the empirical performance of PPP real exchange rates, as conventionally measured, has so often appeared at variance with the theory. It is shown that, even when the true real exchange is in fact 'real', its PPP counterpart is too contaminated with measurement error to behave as a real variable; that proposition also is tested on Swiss data. Section 3 presents estimates of that measurement error and Section 4 contains a summary of main results.

1.0 THE NOMINAL EXCHANGE RATE MODEL

The following basic notation will be used through the article:

EX	=	the domestic-currency price of foreign exchange;
$EXP(IMP)$	=	a domestic-currency price index of exports (imports);
$PT(PNT)$	=	a domestic-currency price index of traded (non-traded) goods;
P	=	$w \cdot PNT + (1 - w) \cdot PT$, an overall price-level index for the country in question;
TT	=	$EXPF - IMPF$, the external terms of trade;
ytt	=	first-order income effect of the external terms of trade; and
INT	=	the domestic minus the foreign rate of interest.

Upper case letters indicate natural logarithms, Δ indicates first differences and an *'F'* is appended to a variable when it is measured in foreign currency. Final-form multipliers, the final effect on a variable W of a permanent shock to another variable Z, are denoted by $\delta(W) / \delta(Z)$.[6]

1.1 Basic Relationships

The extremely frugal model that is developed below is intended to test the proposition that floating exchange rates can insulate small, open economies from external inflation. Traded and non-traded goods are both consumed and produced in the country in question and tastes and technology satisfy the homogeneity postulate such that, at a given moment, the relative price that clears the non-traded goods market is unique. Changes in the foreign currency prices of traded goods are unanticipated (apart, perhaps, from a trend due to inflation). While monetary variables remain in the background, some aspects of monetary policy can be inferred from the parameters of the model.

The model reflects the Australian 'commodity-currency' approach to exchange rate determination, the central idea of which is that the more successful (and hence dominant) agents in the foreign exchange market will have correctly perceived the objective of domestic monetary policy and hence their actions will cause the exchange rate to behave in a manner consistent with that objective; in effect, those agents act on behalf of the neutral bank.[7] If that objective is price stability, then the exchange rate will neutralize fluctuations in the external prices of traded goods without direct central bank intervention.

The first relationship of the model expresses the deterministic component of EX_x^y, the price of currency Y in terms of currency X, as a function of the price of non-traded goods in Country X, PNT_x, the price of Country X's traded goods in currency Y, PTF_x^y, and the interest rate differential, INT_x^y:

$$EX_{xt}^y = A(L) \cdot PNT_{x,t} + B(L) \cdot PTF_{x,t}^y + \rho(L) \cdot INT_{x,t}^y \qquad (3.1)$$

where $A(L) = \sum_{i=0}^{N} a_i \cdot L^i$ is a polynomial in positive powers of the lag operator L and similarly for $B(L)$ and $\rho(L)$. The role of the interest rate differential in equation (3.1) is unspecified; $\rho(L) \cdot INT_{x,t}^y$ might capture interest rate parity, but it may reflect other effects as well. Certain parametric restrictions on $A(L)$ and $B(L)$ are developed in the following subsection.

The second relationship, which is similar to those used to analyze international transmission of inflation (such as Genberg, 1978) embodies the homogeneity postulate as it concerns the relative price of non-traded goods. As shocks to the external prices of traded goods impact on the non-traded goods market via both substitution and income effects, two variables are needed.[8] The substitution effect is captured by the domestic-currency price index for traded goods, PT_x, and the terms-of-trade income effect by ytt_x, which is measured in units of GDP.[9] The deterministic component of the second relationship is simply:

$$PNT_{x,t} = C(L) \cdot PT_{x,t} + D(L) \cdot ytt_{x,t} \qquad (3.2)$$

By the homogeneity postulate, equation (3.2) is homogenous of degree one in PT_x so $(\delta PNT_x / \delta PNT_x)_s = C(1) = 1$, the subscript s indicating 'substitution effect' only (that is, constant terms of trade). The ytt_x variable is defined in first differences as $\Delta ytt_{x,t} \equiv (x_{x,t} \cdot \Delta rexpf_{x,t}) - (m_{x,t} \cdot \Delta rimpf_{x,t})$ where x_x and m_x are ratios of exports and imports to GDP_x, and $rexpf_x$, and $rimpf_x$ are indices of the real external prices of exports and imports, respectively. The relative price of non-traded goods presumably is an increasing function of ytt_x.

The endogenous variables are EX_x^y, PNT_x, and PT_x; PNT_x is eliminated by substituting equation (3.2) into equation (3.1) and PT_x is eliminated using the identity $PT_x \equiv PTF_x^y + EX_x^y$, which should not to be confused with the law of one price as that identity merely converts domestic-currency prices into foreign-currency prices. The deterministic component of the resulting reduced form is:

$$\alpha(L) \cdot EX_{x,t}^y = \beta(L) \cdot PTF_{x,t}^y + \gamma(L) \cdot ytt_{x,t} + \rho(L) \cdot INT_{x,t}^y ,$$

in which the new parameters are $\alpha(L) = 1 - A(L) \cdot C(L)$, $\gamma(L) = A(L) \cdot D(L)$ and $\beta(L) = A(L) \cdot C(L) + B(L)$; α_0 is normalized to unity by dividing the entire equation by $(1 - a_0 \cdot c_0)$. It is assumed throughout that the reduced form is stable.

Since a traded goods price index is not available, we assume that imports and domestically produced import-competing goods are perfect substitutes and define that index as a weighted average of EXP_x and IMP_x:

$$PT_x^y = \Omega \cdot EXP_x^y + (1 - \Omega) \cdot IMP_x^y$$
$$= IMP_x^y + \Omega \cdot TT_x ,$$

which implies:

$$PTF_x^y = IMPF_x^y + \Omega \cdot TT_x ,$$

and hence the reduced form can be written as:

$$\alpha(L) \cdot EX_{x,t}^{y} = \beta(L) \cdot (IMPF_{x,t}^{y} + \Omega \cdot TT_{x,t})_t$$
$$+ \gamma(L) \cdot ytt_{x,t} + \rho(L) \cdot INT_{x,t}^{y} \quad . \tag{3.3}$$

As PT_x is intended to capture only substitution effects, the weight Ω must be correct if equation (3.2) and the reduced form are to satisfy the homogeneity postulate.[10] But if equation (3.3) is estimated by non-linear methods, Ω is a free parameter in that estimation process, so there should be no specification error and hence the homogeneity postulate will be assumed to hold.

1.2 Properties of the Nominal Exchange Rate Model

While deceptively simple, the exchange rate model is rich enough to admit tests of various hypotheses, including PPP, monetary independence, interest rate parity, terms-of-trade neutrality and foreign exchange market efficiency; each of these properties will be taken up in turn in the following subsections.

1.2.1 Purchasing power parity
If PPP holds continuously, then $EX_{x,t}^{y} = P_{x,t} - P_{y,t}$; if it holds only in the long run, then $\delta EX_x^y / \delta P_y = \delta P_x / \delta P_y - 1$. As PPP can be satisfied by adjustments in either exchange rates or price levels, the long-run version imposes only weak restrictions on the model, which can be illustrated by appeal to the law of one price for traded goods. In a world of M open economies, prices of those goods are governed by national price and exchange rates, equation (3.17) of Appendix 1 indicates the relationship between the prices of Country X's traded goods and the M price levels, all expressed in the currency of Country Y:

$$PTF_x^y = \sum_j^M \Theta_j^i \cdot (P_j + EX_y^j) + G(Z_x) , \tag{3.4}$$

where the Θ_x^j are non-negative weights that measure the relative price-making power of Country j over Country X's traded goods. As $\sum_j^M \Theta_j^i = 1$, PTF_x^y is a weighted average of the price levels (expressed in a single currency) of all countries, including Country X. The term $G(Z_x)$ captures all other relevant variables (the 'fundamentals'), which are neglected in much of what follows.[11]

Neglecting the term $G(Z_x)$, equation (3.3) can be written as:

$$\alpha(L) \cdot EX^y_{x,t} = \beta(L) \cdot \left[\sum_j^M \Theta^j_x \cdot (P_{j,t} + EX^j_{y,t}) \right]$$
$$+ \gamma(L) \cdot ytt_{x,t} + \rho(L) \cdot INT^y_{x,t} \ .$$

If purchasing power parity holds universally in the long-run, a permanent shock to the price level of Country Y implies $\delta(P_j + EX^j_y)/\delta P_y = 1$ for all j, and so $\delta EX^y_x / \delta P_y = \beta(1)/\alpha(1)$, whose magnitude depends upon monetary policy (and the exchange rate regime) but is logically confined to the $[0, -1]$ interval, so long-run PPP imposes only a weak restriction, $\beta(1) \in [0, -\alpha(1)]$, on equation (3.3).

1.2.2 Monetary independence

Monetary policy is *independent* when the monetary authorities neither accommodate external price shocks nor intervene in the foreign exchange market, so the exchange rate is endogenous and the domestic price level exogenous with respect to external prices, which imposes strong restrictions on equation (3.3). As Stockman (1988) pointed out, under a policy of monetary independence the role of the exchange rate is to neutralize external price shocks; that is $\delta EX^y_x / \delta PTF^y_x = \beta(1)/\alpha(1) = -1$. But $\beta(1)/\alpha(1)$ is indeterminate since monetary independence also implies the restriction $\alpha(1) = \beta(1) = 0$. To so demonstrate, we combine equation (3.1), the price level equation, and the identity $EX^y_x \equiv PT_x - PTF^y_x$ to obtain:

$$P_{x,t} = [w + (1-w) \cdot A(L)] \cdot PNT_{x,t} + (1-w) \cdot [1 + B(L)] \cdot PTF^y_{x,t}$$
$$+ (1-w) \cdot \rho(L) \cdot INT^y_{x,t} \ .$$

When monetary policy is independent, external price shocks, holding the terms of trade constant, will have no long-run effect on relative prices or the price level, so $\delta P_x / \delta PTF^y_x = (1-w) \cdot [1 + B(1)] = 0 \Rightarrow B(1) = -1$. Moreover, although domestic stocks may impact on PNT_x, shocks involving only nominal variables, such as the money supply will have no long-run effect on the relative price structure, so $\delta P_x / \delta PNT_x = w + (1-w) \cdot A(1) = 1 \Rightarrow A(1) = 1$.

Together with the homogeneity postulate, $C(1) = 1$, these two restrictions imply $\alpha(1) = \beta(1) = 0$.

However, if $\alpha(L)$ is of degree N, then there exists a second polynomial $\tilde{\alpha}(L)$ of degree $N-1$ which is defined by $\alpha(L) \equiv (1-L) \cdot \tilde{\alpha}(L) + L^N \cdot \alpha(1)$, where $\tilde{\alpha}_k = \sum_{i=0}^{k} \alpha_i$ and $\tilde{\alpha}(1) = N \cdot \alpha(1) - \sum_{i=1}^{N} i \cdot \alpha_i$. So if $\alpha(1) = \beta(1) = 0$, it follows that $\delta EX_x^y / \delta PTF_x^y = \tilde{\beta}(1)/\tilde{\alpha}(1) \equiv \pi$ which is determinate. An independent monetary policy, then, implies three restrictions: $\alpha(1) = 0$, $\beta(1) = 0$ and $\pi = -1$. Note that with a fixed exchange rate, which precludes monetary independence, equation (3.3) becomes $\Delta EX = 0$ so $\alpha(L) = 1 - L$, $\beta(L) = 0$ and $\alpha(1) = \beta(1) = 0$, but as $\tilde{\alpha}(1) = \alpha_0 = 1$ and $\tilde{\beta}(1) = 0$, the third restriction is violated as $\pi = 0$.

1.2.3 Foreign exchange market efficiency
If the foreign exchange market is both efficient and rational, there can be no systematic lags in the response of EX_x^y to external price shocks; if lags do exist, relevant information is unexploited. By rewriting equation (3.3) as:

$$EX_{x,t}^y = [\beta(L)/\alpha(L)] \cdot PTF_{x,t}^y + [\gamma(L)/\alpha(L)] \cdot ytt_{x,t}$$
$$+ [\rho(L)/\alpha(L)] \cdot INT_{x,t}^y , \qquad (3.3A)$$

it is clear that foreign exchange market efficiency implies the following restriction $\beta(L) \equiv -\alpha(L)$ or ($\beta(L) \equiv -\tilde{\alpha}(L)$ if monetary independence holds).

1.2.4 The terms-of-trade effect
The terms-of-trade effect on relative price of non-tradeables is induced by the exchange rate. The impact of a permanent change in the terms of trade is $\delta\ EX_x^y/\delta\ ytt_x = [\gamma(1)/\alpha(1)] \equiv \lambda_N$; if $\lambda_N = 0$, the terms of trade are neutral, and if $\alpha(1) = \gamma(1) = 0$, the restriction becomes $\tilde{\gamma}(1) = 0$.

1.2.5 Interest rate parity
The effect a permanent shock to INT_x^y, defined as the domestic minus foreign interest rate, is $\delta\ EX_x/\delta\ INT_x = \rho(1)/\alpha(1) \equiv \mu$; if $\alpha(1) = \rho(1) = 0$, then $\mu = \tilde{\rho}(1)/\tilde{\alpha}(1)$. If interest rate parity held strictly under floating rates, equation (3.1) would become $\Delta EX_{x,t}^y = INT_{x,t-1}^y$ so $\alpha(L) = 1$

$-L$, $\rho(L) = L$, μ is unbounded and EX_x^y is the sum of all past values of INT_x^y. But Fama (1984) and others have found that high interest rates (more precisely, positive forward premia) are associated with currency appreciations, suggesting that $\mu < 0$.

1.3 Tests of the Nominal Exchange Rate Model: the Swiss Franc Case

Tests of the nominal exchange rate model were based on quarterly data for Swiss franc exchange rates *vis à vis* the US dollar and a 'mini' ECU for the post-Bretton Woods period. As the franc has floated throughout that period, and Switzerland has not participated in joint floats, has eschewed exchange control and exchange market intervention, and has had a highly stable commercial policy, the Swiss case is ideal for examining exchange rate behavior.[12] Given its status as *primus inter pares*, the Swiss franc provides an acid test of the PPP approach to exchange rate determination.

1.3.1 The data
All exchange rate series are quarterly averages of monthly averages, and the mini-ECU/dollar exchange rate, designated *EUROX*, was defined on a basket of four major European currencies (France, Germany, Italy and the UK) using their relative GDPs as weights; *EUROX* is (the natural logarithm of) the mini-ECU price of the US dollar.[13] The Swiss franc price indices for imports and exports are seasonally adjusted and, in constructing the *ytt* variable, the US GDP deflator was used to convert the nominal dollar prices of Swiss imports and exports into real prices.[14]

All real exchange rates were based on three price level measure: the GDP deflator (*DEF*), consumer prices (*CPI*) and producer prices (*PPI*). The 'European' price levels, based on the four major countries, were constructed by converting GDP and price level data for each country into Deutsche marks and aggregating, quarter by quarter, across the four countries using their relative GDPs as weights. Interest rate differentials were based on averages of monthly data for 3-month US dollar CDs, Swiss franc Eurodeposits (available only from 1974) and DM 3-month interbank transactions, and are labeled USACDRAT, CHEEUROD and DEUFIBOR, respectively, in the RATS–OECD database.

Dickey–Fuller unit-root tests appear in Table 3.1.[15] Except for the US PPI, the Swiss GDP deflator, and the Swiss/US *INT* variables, unit roots are rejected at the 3 per cent level for all variables and unit roots are rejected for all variables at the 2 per cent level when first differenced.

1.3.2 The Swiss franc/US dollar exchange rate

Using the identity $\alpha(L)=(1-L)\cdot\tilde{\alpha}(L)+L^N\cdot\alpha(1)$, and similarly for $\beta(L)$ and $\gamma(L)$, equation (3.3) was reparameterized as follows:

$$
\begin{aligned}
\tilde{\alpha}(L)\cdot\Delta EX^{us}_{ch,t} =\ & \beta(L)\cdot(\Delta IMPF^{us}_{ch,t} + \Omega\cdot\Delta TT_{ch,t}) \\
& + \tilde{\gamma}(L)\cdot\Delta ytt_{ch,t} + \rho_0\cdot\Delta INT^{us}_{ch,t} \\
& + \alpha(1)\cdot EX^{us}_{ch,t-N} \\
& + \beta(1)\cdot(IMPF^{us}_{ch,t-N} + \Omega\cdot TT_{ch,t-N}) \\
& + \gamma(1)\cdot ytt_{ch,t-N} + \rho(1)\cdot INT^{us}_{ch,t-1}
\end{aligned}
\tag{3.3'}
$$

which simplifies tests (and imposition) of the α, β, γ and ρ restrictions.

Table 3.1 Augmented Dickey–Fuller unit-root tests on basic data:
1974:01–1991:04

Variable	Levels			First differences		
	β	t-stat	P-value	β	t-stat	P-value
IMP	0.9387	−2.3923	0.0099	0.7274	−3.0475	0.0017
EXP	0.9246	−2.4226	0.0092	0.6227	−2.9392	0.0023
ytt	0.9106	−2.5082	0.0074	0.4802	−4.0612	0.0001
TT	0.9318	−2.1134	0.0194	0.5610	3.7561	0.0002
$EX_{(US)}$	0.9045	−2.0728	0.0212	0.2993	−3.5141	0.0004
$EX_{(EU)}$	0.9282	−2.1765	0.0167	0.3285	−3.5765	0.0003
$EUROX$	0.9325	−1.9987	0.0251	0.4856	−2.9107	0.0025
$DEF_{(US)}$	0.9578	−2.5384	0.0069	0.7473	−2.3685	0.0105
$CPI_{(US)}$	0.9560	−2.3396	0.0113	0.7560	−2.1122	0.0194
$PPI_{(US)}$	0.9695	−1.5627	0.0617	0.6809	−2.2098	0.0154
$DEF_{(CH)}$	0.9718	−1.4694	0.0735	0.7853	−2.3596	0.0108
$CPI_{(CH)}$	0.8900	−3.3082	0.0008	0.6849	−2.1118	0.0194
$PPI_{(CH)}$	0.9233	−2.5419	0.0068	0.5377	−3.6444	0.0003
$DEF_{(EU)}$	0.8992	−2.5395	0.0069	0.4073	−3.2036	0.0011
$CPI_{(EU)}$	0.9188	−2.3205	0.0119	0.4818	−2.9135	0.0025
$PPI_{(EU)}$	0.9155	−2.2135	0.0153	0.4391	−3.0071	0.0019
$INT_{(CH-US)}$	0.8694	−1.5220	0.0666	−0.5244	−3.9546	0.0001
$INT_{(CH-GERM)}$	0.6750	−2.7898	0.0035	−0.5709	−4.2318	0.0000

Equation (3.3') was estimated for the franc/dollar exchange rate during the post-Bretton Woods period by non-linear least squares (NLLS) and with standard errors obtained by White's robust method (designated NLLS–ROB) (White, 1980); since both TT_{ch} and ytt_{ch} were found to be endogenous (see Appendix 2), the equation also was estimated by Hansen's generalized method of moments (NLLS–GMM) (Hansen, 1982).[16] The key results, summarized in Panels A and B of Table 3.2, are the following:

1. both standard errors of estimate are very small (0.62 per cent) but the NLLS–GMM standard errors are considerably smaller;
2. neither long-run PPP nor monetary independence are rejected, but terms-of-trade neutrality is decisively rejected; and
3. the estimate of β_0 is not significantly different from -1.0, so the exchange rate neutralizes external price shocks as they occur.[17]

The joint restriction $\{\alpha\,(1)=\beta\,(1)=\gamma\,(1)=\rho\,(1)=0\}$ was not rejected, so all level variables in equation (3.3′) were deleted to impose that restriction, and the identities $\tilde{\beta}\,(1) \equiv \Pi \cdot \tilde{\alpha}\,(1)$, $\tilde{\gamma}\,(1) \equiv \lambda_N \cdot \tilde{\alpha}\,(1)$, and $\rho_0 \equiv \mu \cdot \tilde{\alpha}\,(1)$ were embedded to estimate Π, λ_N and μ. The results, using the same instruments, are reported in Panel C of Table 3.2; the main points are the following:

1. the estimates of Ω, 0.69 (0.58), are very tight, and the precision of the fit is extraordinary for first-differenced data as the standard error of estimate is a mere 0.61 (0.63) per cent;
2. the estimates of π are not significantly different from -1.0, so monetary independence is not rejected;
3. the highly significant estimates of λ_N indicate that a 1 per cent increase in national income (0.4 standard deviations of ytt_{ch}) due to improved terms-of-trade results in nearly a 2 per cent rise in the relative price of non-traded goods effected via an appreciation of the franc;
4. since the estimates of ρ_0 and μ are significantly negative, interest rate parity is rejected, which is consistent with Fama's results (Fama, 1984); the estimates indicate that a permanent rise in Swiss (quarterly) interest rate of 100 basis points appreciates the franc *vis à vis* the dollar by 0.80 (0.72) per cent; and
5. since the restricted estimates are very similar to those reported in Panels A and B of Table 3.2, total first differencing is quite benign.

Table 3.2 Swiss franc/US dollar exchange rate: 1974:02–1991:04

A. Summary of NLLS–ROB and NLLS–GMM estimates of equation (3.3′)

Parameter	Estimate		t-statistic[a]		P-value	
	ROB	GMM	ROB	GMM	ROB	GMM
Ω	0.6477	0.6131	4.6934	5.9823	−0.0000	0.0000
β_0	−1.0136	−1.0099	−0.9146[b]	−0.8934[b]	0.3648	0.3759
ρ_0	−0.5330	−0.4459	−3.0185	3.1623	0.0025	0.0016
$\alpha(1)$	0.0009	0.0058	0.0756	0.5668	0.9397	0.5708
$\beta(1)$	0.0031	0.0104	0.2502	0.9784	0.8025	0.3279
$\gamma(1)$	0.0121	−0.0364	0.1819	−0.5890	0.8556	0.5559
$\rho(1)$	−0.1492	−0.1402	−1.5907	−1.6039	0.1117	0.1087

$\bar{R}^2$ = 0.9893 (0.9890); SEE = 0.0062 (0.0062); D–W = 1.9462 (1.8979)
$Q(4)$ = 5.7192 (5.7154), P-value = 0.2211 (0.2214)

B. Chi-square tests on joint restrictions on equation (3.3′)

Restrictions:	NDF	χ^2		P-value	
α and β:	2	0.3704	1.8206	0.8309	0.4024
α and γ:	2	0.1084	0.4147	0.9472	0.8127
α, β and γ:	3	3.3643	4.2105	0.3388	0.2396
α, β, γ and ρ:	4	4.3656	5.7023	0.3588	0.2225
Monetary independence:	3	0.5092	1.9630	0.9169	0.5801
Terms-of-trade neutrality:	3	14.2663	29.7651	0.0026	0.0000

C. Restricted NLLS–ROB and NLLS–GMM estimates of equation (3.3′)

Parameter	LAG	Estimate		t-statistic[c]		P-value	
		ROB	GMM	ROB	GMM	ROB	GMM
Ω	–	0.6944	0.5786	4.8212	6.0222	0.0000	0.0000
β_0	0	−1.0203	−1.0108	−1.5010[b]	−1.1274[b]	0.1392	0.2645
ρ_0	0	−0.4352	−0.4271	−2.5300	−3.2200	0.0114	0.0013
π_0	–	−1.0303	−1.0036	−0.8359[b]	−0.1256[b]	0.4069	0.9005
λ_0	–	−1.6551	−1.8666	−3.2467	−6.0108	0.0012	0.0000
μ_0	–	−0.7959	−0.7202	−2.3419	−2.7568	0.0192	0.0058

$\bar{R}^2$ = 0.9897 (0.9887); SEE = 0.0061 (0.0063); D–W = 1.8939 (1.9018)
$Q(4)$ = 3.0396 (3.7931), P-value = 0.5512 (0.4347)

D. Market efficiency tests: OLS–ROB and OLS–GMM estimates of equation (3.3A)

Restriction	$\chi^2(6)$		P-value	
$\tilde{\beta}(L) = -\tilde{\alpha}(L)$	6.2482	7.1992	0.3960	0.3028

$\bar{R}^2$ = 0.9748 (0.9746); SEE = 0.0095 (0.0095); D–W = 0.9855 (0.9754)
$Q(4)$ = 19.4164 (19.6235), P-value = 0.0007 (0.0006)

Notes:
a Standard errors computed with three lags and damp factor of 0.75 (1.0) for NLLS–ROB
   (NLLS–GMM).
b t–Statistics are against minus unity.
c Standard errors computed with three lags and damp factor of 0.65 (1.0) for NLLS–ROB
   (NLLS–GMM).

Finally, OLS–ROB and OLS–GMM estimates of equation (3.3A) with PTF^{us}_{ch} defined on the NLLS–ROB estimate of Ω were tested for foreign exchange market efficiency; as the χ^2 statistic on the restriction $\{\tilde{\beta}(L) \equiv -\tilde{\alpha}(L)\}$, reported in Panel D of Table 3.2, is not significant, the necessary condition for foreign exchange market efficiency (as herein defined) is not rejected.[18]

1.3.3 The Swiss franc/mini-ECU case

The exercise was repeated using the franc/mini-ECU exchange rate and the estimates of equation (3.3′) are summarized in Panels A and B of Table 3.3; the main difference with the franc/dollar case is that the interest rate differential was significant.[19] Again the standard errors of estimate are very small, the estimates of β_0 do not differ significantly from minus unity, neither long-run PPP nor monetary independence are rejected, but terms-of-trade neutrality is strongly rejected. The joint restriction $\{\alpha(1)=\beta(1)=\gamma(1)=\rho(1)=0\}$ also is not rejected, so it was imposed and equation (3.3′) was re-estimated using the same instruments. The main results, which appear in Panels C and D of Table 3.3, can be summarized as follows:

1. the standard error of estimate is only 0.64 (0.66) per cent;
2. the estimates of Ω and the final-form multipliers π and λ_N are very similar to those of the franc/dollar case; and
3. weak foreign exchange market efficiency, tested on equation (3.3A) with five lags and the same instruments, cannot be rejected.

A most striking aspect of the foregoing results is the degree to which the Swiss franc has responded systematically to external price shocks to insulate the Swiss economy from those shocks during the post-Bretton Woods period but, in so doing, it presumably increases the variance in the conventional PPP real exchange rate; nonetheless, PPP is not rejected as a long-run proposition. We now move on to analyze the relationship between the internal relative price structure (the 'true' real exchange rate) and the PPP real exchange rate.

Table 3.3 Swiss franc/mini-ECU exchange rate: 1974:02–1991:04

A. Summary of NLLS–ROB and NLLS–GMM estimates of Eq. (3.3′)

Parameter	Estimate		t-statistic[a]		P-value	
	ROB	GMM	ROB	GMM	ROB	GMM
Ω	0.5605	0.6141	4.1965	4.8018	0.0000	0.0000
β_0	−0.9879	−0.9835	0.3382[b]	−0.5718[b]	0.7366	0.5699
$\alpha(1)$	−0.0218	−0.0055	−1.4199	−0.2795	0.1556	0.7798
$\beta(1)$	−0.0122	0.0096	−0.9886	0.6169	0.3338	0.5373
$\gamma(1)$	0.0149	−0.0380	0.3220	−0.7113	0.7475	0.4769

$\bar{R}^2$ = 0.9571 (0.9541); SEE = 0.0064 (0.0066); D–W = 1.8374 (1.9411)
$Q(4)$ = 5.1791 (6.3744), P-value = 0.2694 (0.1729)

B. Chi–square tests on joint restrictions on equation (3.3′)

Restrictions:	NDF	χ^2		P-value	
α and β:	2	4.1843	3.2145	0.1234	0.2004
α and γ:	2	2.0420	0.5226	0.3602	0.7701
α, β and γ:	3	4.3171	3.5186	0.2292	0.3184
Monetary independence:	3	4.4261	4.2858	0.2190	0.2322
Terms-of-trade neutrality:	3	21.8740	15.8705	0.7475	0.0012

C. Restricted NLLS–ROB and NLLS–GMM estimates of equation (3.3′)

Parameter	LAG	Estimate		t-statistic[c]		P-value	
		ROB	GMM	ROB	GMM	ROB	GMM
Ω	–	0.5883	0.6090	4.4429	4.7824	0.0000	0.0000
β_0	0	−1.0104	−0.9978	−0.3358[b]	0.0913[b]	0.7383	0.9276
π	–	−0.9418	−0.9036	0.5768[b]	1.3799[b]	0.5664	0.1732
λ_N	–	−2.2622	−2.2162	−5.4444	−5.1239	0.0000	0.0000

$\bar{R}^2$ = 0.9581 (0.9564); SEE = 0.0063 (0.0064); D–W = 1.7928 (1.9335)
$Q(4)$ = 4.7107 (6.4357), P-value = 0.3183 (0.1689)

D. Market efficiency tests: OLS–ROB and OLS–GMM estimates of equation (3.3A)

Restriction	$\chi^2(6)$		P-value	
$\tilde{\beta}(L) = -\tilde{\alpha}(L)$	8.5311	4.9437	0.2017	0.5535

$\bar{R}^2$ = 0.9020 (0.8975); SEE = 0.0096 (0.0099); D–W = 0.9248 (0.9263)
$Q(4)$ = 25.6813 (21.0913), P-value = 0.0000 (0.0003)

Notes:
a Standard errors computed with three lags and damp factor of 0.75 (1.0) for NLLS–ROB (NLLS–GMM).
b t-Statistics are against minus unity.
c Standard errors computed with three lags and damp factor of 0.65 (1.0) for NLLS–ROB (NLLS–GMM).

The key question is whether fluctuations in PPP real exchange rates violate the theory underlying purchasing power parity, or whether those movements are largely benign characteristics of any floating exchange rate regime.

2.0 PROPERTIES OF SWISS REAL EXCHANGE RATES

The true real exchange rate for Country X is the relative price of traded goods, defined as $(PT_x - NT_x)$. As PNT_x is difficult to measure, a more convenient working definition of the true real exchange rate is obtained by using the overall price level $P_x = w_x \cdot PNT_x + (1 - w_x) \cdot PT_x$, to eliminate it:

$$
\begin{aligned}
TRER_x &\equiv PT_x - P_x \\
&= w_x \cdot (PT_x - PNT_x)
\end{aligned}
\qquad (3.5)
$$

which differs from the real thing only by a factor of proportionality, w_x, the weight of non-traded goods in the price level. For empirical convenience, the common version of the PPP real exchange rate for Country X vis à vis Country Y is obtained by replacing PT_x with the price level of Country Y (in the currency of Country X) and PNT_x with the domestic price level:

$$
PRER_x^y \equiv (EX_x^y + P_y) - P_x
\qquad (3.6)
$$

and hence the PPP real exchange rate explicitly involves the nominal rate.[20]

Occasionally, the PPP real exchange rate is given a multilateral flavor by defining it as a *weighted average* of several PPP real exchange rates:

$$
PRER_x = \sum_j v_x^j \cdot PRER_x^j
\qquad (3.6')
$$

the v_x^j being arbitrary (such as, SDR or trade) weights. Using equations (3.4) and (3.5), $TRER_x$ can also be expressed as a *linear combination* of PPP real rates:

$$
TRER_x = \sum_{j \ne x}^{M} \Theta_x^j \cdot PRER_x^j + G(Z_x)
\qquad (3.5')
$$

the sum of the weights being $(1 - \Theta_x^x)$. While equation (3.5′) is similar to the *multilateral* PPP real rate as defined by equation (3.6′), they differ in that (i) $PRER_x$ omits $G(Z_x)$; (ii) a *weighted average* is correct only if $\Theta_x^x = 0$; and (iii) the v_x^j weights bear no logical relationship to the Θ_x^k; indeed, the Θ_x^k ensure that any measurement errors in the $PRER_x^k$ in equation (3.5′) *exactly* cancel out, which will occur only by change with the v_x^j weights.

2.1   The Behavior of Swiss Exchange Rates: an Overview

The Swiss nominal and real exchange rates have fluctuated widely since 1973. Departures of the Swiss franc/US dollar nominal and real exchange rates from their period averages appear in Figure 3.1; both real exchange rates were defined on GDP deflators and all exchange rates were filtered by a three-quarter centered moving average to improve visual clarity. The sample variance of the PPP real exchange rate is nearly five times that of $TRER_{ch}$, and it is evident that real and nominal exchange rates are positively correlated, the PPP rate particularly so. Correlations between the various exchange rates are reported in the left half of Panel A of Table 3.4, and those correlations lead to two key observations.[21] First, the correlations between nominal and all real exchange rates are high and increase upon first differencing for the PPP real rates, but diminish for the true real rate.[22] Changes in the nominal exchange rate clearly dominate the PPP real exchange rates, but not the true real rate. Second, the correlations between the PPP and true real exchange rates are surprisingly low.

Correlations between the real exchange rates and the residuals (RES) from regressions of P_{us} on PTF_{ch}^{us} appear in the right half of Panel A of Table 3.4. As RES is orthogonal with P_{us}, it captures the influence of all other factors (for example third-country price levels and exchange rates) on PTF_{ch}^{us}. While *RES* is not significantly correlated with any version of $TRER_{ch}$, it is highly correlated with all versions of $PRER_{ch}^{us}$ in both levels and first differences, suggesting that the other factors do influence the PPP real rate. It also is clear from Figure 3.2 that both $TRER_{ch,def}$ and $TRER_{ch,ppi}$ have negative time trends while that of $TRER_{ch,ppi}$ is positive. Evidently producer goods are mainly tradeables, so a real exchange rate defined on them is the relative price of two sets of tradeables and henceforth the emphasis will be on real exchange rates defined on DEF_{ch} and CPI_{ch}.

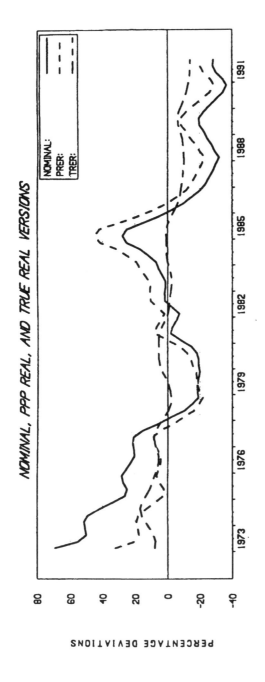

Figure 3.1 Swiss franc exchange rates 1973–1991 (nominal, PPP real and true real versions)

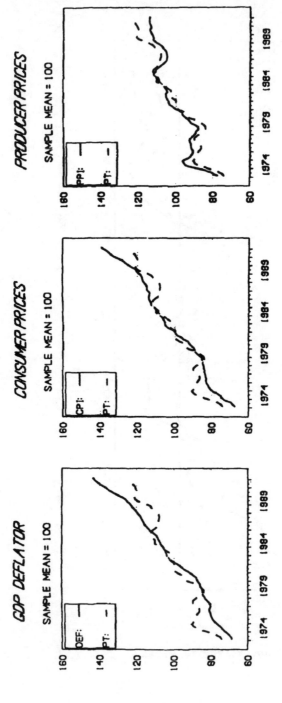

Figure. 3.2 Prices of Swiss traded goods vs. price levels

Table 3.4 Correlations and unit-root tests, franc/dollar exchange rates: 1973:01–1991:04

A. Correlations among real and nominal exchange rates

Exchange rates	Levels	First differences	Variables	Levels	First differences
EX and *PRER:*			*PRER* and *RES:*		
DEF	0.8202	0.9785	DEF	−0.8911	−0.9741
CPI	0.7103	0.9730	CPI	−0.9663	−0.9784
PPI	0.5289	0.9398	PPI	−0.9888	−0.9853
EX and *TRER:*			*RER* and *RES:*		
DEF	0.8152	0.4414	DEF	−0.1763*	−0.2893*
CPI	0.8317	0.2947	CPI	−0.1583*	−0.2017*
PPI	−0.6746	0.2072*	PPI	−0.2552*	−0.0760*
PRER and *TRER:*			*PT:*		
DEF	0.5563	0.4893	DEF	0.9684	0.1593*
CPI	0.3628	0.3579	CPI	0.9792	0.4767
PPI	−0.1366*	0.2369	PPI	0.9800	0.8058

B. Unit root tests of real exchange rates

Variable	Levels			First differences		
	β	*t*-stat	*P*-value	β	*t*-stat	*P*-value
TRER(DEF)	0.8734	−3.1378	0.0013	0.6246	−3.5723	0.0003
TRER(CPI)	0.7700	−4.3577	0.0000	0.4145	−4.1573	0.0001
TRER (PPI)	0.8025	−2.5772	0.0062	−0.0768	−4.7774	0.0000
PRER(DEF)	0.9032	−2.1056	0.0197	0.3096	−3.4424	0.0005
PRER(CPI)	0.9048	−2.0969	0.0201	0.3192	−3.3689	0.0007
PRER (PPI)	0.9071	−2.0150	0.0242	0.2794	−3.3110	0.0008

*Notes: * Not significant at the 1 per cent level.*

2.2 Sources of Measurement Error in PPP Real Exchange Rates

Measurement error is a likely cause of the weak association between the true and PPP real exchange rates. To determine how measurement error might infect real exchange rates, equations (3.2)–(3.6) were combined into reduced forms for PTF_x^ζ and the two real exchange rates, in which $G(Z_x)$ has been ignored:

$$\alpha_R(L) \cdot PTF^y_{x,t} = \alpha(L) \cdot \sum_{j \neq x} \Theta^j_x \cdot (P_j - EX^y_j) - [\Theta^x_x \cdot \gamma_R(L)] \cdot ytt_{x,t}$$

$$- [\Theta^x_x \cdot \rho_R(L)] \cdot INT^y_{x,t}, \tag{3.7}$$

$$\alpha(L) \cdot TRER_{x,t} = \beta_R(L) \cdot PTF^y_{x,t} + \gamma_R(L) \cdot ytt_{x,t} + \rho_R(L) \cdot INT^y_{x,t} \tag{3.8}$$

$$\alpha(L) \cdot PRER^y_{x,t} = [\beta_R(L) - \alpha(L)] \cdot PTF^y_{x,t} + \alpha(L) \cdot P_{y,t}$$

$$+ \gamma_R(L) \cdot ytt_{x,t} + \rho_R(L) \cdot INT^y_{x,t}. \tag{3.9}$$

The new coefficients, $\Theta^k_x \equiv \Theta^k_x / (1 - \Theta^x_x)$, are variants of Θ^k_x that measure the relative market power of Country k *excluding* the market power possessed by Country X.[23] The new polynomials are defined as $\beta_R(L) = w_x \cdot [1 + B(L)] \cdot [1 - C(L)]$, $\alpha_R(L) = \alpha(L) + \Theta^x_x \cdot \beta_R(L)$, $\gamma_R(L) = w_x \cdot [A(L) - 1] \cdot D(L)$ and $\rho_R(L) = w_x \cdot \rho(L) \cdot [1 - C(L)]$.

From equation (3.8), the final-form multiplier of the true real exchange rate with respect to PTF^y_x is $\beta_R(1) / \alpha(1) \equiv \Phi_T$. But it follows from the homogeneity postulate, $C(1) = 1$, that $\beta_R(1) = 0$, so shocks to nominal variables appearing in PTF^y_x have only transitory effects on $TRER_x$. If that property holds, then, the true real rate is *orthogonal*; moreover, if $\beta_R(L) \equiv 0$, then $TRER_x$ is *strongly orthogonal* as it depends only real variables even in the short run.

It follows from equation (3.9) that the final-form multiplier of the PPP real exchange rate with respect to PTF^y_x is $[\beta_R(1) - \alpha(1)] / \alpha(1) = \Phi_T - 1 \equiv \Phi_P$ and, by the homogeneity postulate, $\Phi_P = -1$. It follows, then, that shocks to any nominal variable appearing in PTF^y_x will, by equation (3.9), be fully reflected in PPP real exchange rates *for the entire duration of those shocks*.[24] Accordingly, those shocks introduce measurement error into PPP real rates in the sense that, even if PPP holds globally in the long run, PPP real rates will exhibit short-run behavior that has no counterpart in the true real rates.[25]

There is one exception to the above. $PRER^y_x$ will be orthogonal if $\Theta^j_x = 0$ for all $j \neq X$, Y in equation (3.4); that is, when Countries X and Y together are *price makers* in world markets for goods traded by Country X. But if some $\Theta^j_x \neq 0$, $j \neq X$, Y, then third countries have power over the prices of Country

X's traded goods and hence any shocks to their price levels (or exchange rates *vis à vis* Country *Y*) will introduce measurement error into $PRER_x^y$.[26] As the issue is an empirical one, we turn next to estimates of equations (3.8) and (3.9).

2.2.1 Tests of the Swiss true real exchange rate

Equation (3.8), parameterized with five lags, was estimated simultaneously for two price levels by the generalized method of moments with ESTIMA RATS non-linear system routine – NLSYSTEM–GMM.[27] The key results appear in the upper part of Table 3.5:

1. the joint restriction $\rho_R(L) \equiv 0$ was not rejected even when imposed simultaneously, so the interest rate differential was dropped;
2. the joint zero restrictions on, α, β_R and γ_R were not rejected when imposed simultaneously on both equations; and
3. as the restriction $\beta_R(L) \equiv 0 \Rightarrow \tilde{\beta}_R(L) = 0$ could not be rejected, the Swiss true real exchange rate is *strongly* orthogonal since it depends only upon ytt_{ch} even in the short-run.

The zero restrictions on α, β_R and γ_R were imposed and, by embedding $\beta_R(1) = \Phi_T \cdot \tilde{\alpha}(1)$ and $\tilde{\gamma}_R(1) = \lambda_R \cdot \tilde{\alpha}(1)$ into equation (8), direct estimates of Φ_T and $\lambda_R = \delta\, TRER_{ch} / \delta\, ytt_{ch}$ were obtained. The restricted NLSYSTEM–GMM estimates, reported in the lower part of Table 3.5, can be summarized as follows:

1. despite very small standard errors, all estimates of Φ_T are grossly insignificant, both singly and collectively; and
2. the estimate of λ_R, the final-form multiplier with respect to the terms of trade, −2.38, is large and highly significant; the terms of trade have a strong effect on the true real exchange rate.

The estimates of λ_R and λ_N (see Tables 3.2 and 3.3) provide an insight into the target of Swiss monetary policy. Since $\lambda_N \equiv \delta\, EX_{ch}^{us} / \delta\, ytt_{ch} = \delta\, PT_{ch} / \delta\, ytt_{ch}$, it follows that $\lambda_R \equiv \delta\,(PT_{ch} - P_{ch})/\delta\, ytt_{ch} = \lambda_N - \delta\, P_{ch}/\delta\, ytt_{ch}$. If the authorities target the price level, $E(\delta\, P_{ch}/\delta\, ytt_{ch}) = 0$ so $E(\lambda_R - \lambda_N) = 0$, where E is the expected value operator. But if the price of non-traded goods (that is wages) is the target, the $E(\delta P_{ch}/\delta ytt_{ch}) < 0$ so $E|\lambda_R| < E|\lambda_N|$. As the estimates of λ_R exceed those of λ_N the Swiss authorities appear to target the price level.

Table 3.5 Orthogonality tests of Swiss true real exchange rate: 1974:01–1991:04; NLSYSTEM–GMM estimates of equation (3.8)

Restriction:	Test:	Price level measures		
		DEF	CPI	Both
1: $\rho_R(L) \equiv 0$	χ^2 (2):	1.3956	3.7399	5.9568
	P-value	*0.4977*	*0.1541*	*0.2024*
2: α, β_R and γ_R	χ^2 (3):	3.5738	2.1131	5.7523
	P-value	*0.3113*	*0.5493*	*0.4515*
3: $\Phi_T = 0$	χ^2 (3):	3.1374	2.9287	7.1636
	P-value	*0.3709*	*0.4028*	*0.3060*
4: $\beta_R(L) \equiv 0$	χ^2 (6):	6.4056	11.5341	17.4142
	P-value	*0.3793*	*0.0732*	*0.1347*

NLSYSTEM–GMM regression results (α, β_R and γ_R restrictions imposed):

	DEF	CPI	Both
Restricted estimates of Φ_T :	−0.0350	−0.0160	−0.0365
Standard error:	0.0348	0.0557	0.0352
t-Statistic (against zero):	−1.0062	−0.2875	−1.0356
P-value:	0.3143	0.7737	0.3004
χ^2 (2) stat. on Φ_T =0 restriction:	–	–	1.0795
P-value:	–	–	0.5829
χ^2 (1) Stat. on equality restriction:	–	–	0.1540
P-value:	–	–	0.6948
Restricted estimates of λ_R :	−2.4572	−2.2878	−2.3821
Standard error:	0.2788	0.4653	0.2856
t-Statistic (against zero):	−8.8148	−4.9173	−8.3403
P-value:	0.0000	0.0000	0.0000
χ^2 (1) stat. on equality restriction:	–	–	0.1944
P-value:	–	–	0.6593

2.2.2 Tests of the franc/dollar and franc/mini-ECU PPP real exchange rates

Since the Swiss true real exchange rate is orthogonal, the franc/dollar PPP real exchange rate will be orthogonal only if no third countries can influence

PTF_{ch}^{us}; that is, only if $\theta_{ch}^{us} = 1$. As a first step, equation (3.7) was estimated to test the hypothesis that the dollar and mini-ECU blocs, together with the Swiss, dominate world markets for Swiss traded goods (that is, $\theta_{ch}^{eu} + \theta_{ch}^{us} = 1$). With the unit-sum and $\beta_R(L) \equiv 0$ restrictions imposed, equation (3.7) becomes:

Table 3.6 Tests of 'unit-sum' restriction: Switzerland, 1974:02–1991:04; NLSYSTEM–GMM estimates of equation (3.7) on import and export prices

	Price level measures			
	DEF	CPI	PPI	All
Unit-sum test results, export prices:				
Sum of estimated θ_{ch}^{eu} and θ_{ch}^{eu}:	1.0555	0.8305	1.0235	–
χ^2 statistic on unit-sum restriction	0.3824	2.1510	0.0562	–
P-value:	0.5363	0.1425	0.8126	–
Restricted estimates of θ_{ch}^{eu}	0.6629	0.7348	0.7625	0.7028
t-Statistic (against zero):	22.2015	19.7850	14.4220	24.1385
P-value:	0.0000	0.0000	0.0000	0.0000
t-Statistic (against unity):	−11.2904	−7.1405	−4.4916	−10.2071
P-value	0.0000	0.0000	0.0000	0.0000
χ^2 (2) stat. on equality restriction	–	–	–	6.0117
P-value:	–	–	–	0.0495
Unit-sum test results, import prices:				
Sum of estimated θ_{ch}^{eu} and θ_{ch}^{eu}	1.0010	0.9010	1.0399	–
χ^2 statistic on unit-sum restriction	0.0001	0.6790	0.1064	–
P-value:	0.9924	0.4099	0.7433	–
Restricted estimates of θ_{ch}^{eu}	0.5658	0.6103	0.5998	0.6774
t-Statistic (against zero):	14.5136	11.7160	10.9038	12.9984
P-value:	0.0000	0.0000	0.0000	0.0000
t-Statistic (against unity):	−11.1362	−7.4824	−7.2751	−6.1905
P-value:	0.0000	0.0000	0.0000	0.0000
χ^2 (2) stat. on equality restriction:	–	–	–	1.2279
P-value:	–	–	–	0.5412

$$\alpha(L) \cdot PTF^{us}_{ch,t} = \alpha(L) \cdot (\theta^{eu}_{ch} \cdot PF^{us}_{eu,t} + \theta^{us}_{ch} \cdot P_{us,t})$$
$$- [\theta^{ch}_{ch} \cdot \gamma_R(L)] \cdot ytt_{ch,t} \qquad (3.7')$$

As equation (3.7') holds equally well for export and import prices, it was estimated simultaneously by NLSYSTEM–GMM for both with PF^{us}_{eu} and P_{us} defined on all price levels; the results appear in Table 3.6.[28] All estimates of θ^{eu}_{ch} and θ^{eu}_{Ch} differed significantly from zero and, although two estimates of the sum of θ^{eu}_{ch} and θ^{us}_{ch} fell short of unity, the unit-sum restriction was not rejected in any of the six cases for either export or import price indices. The restricted estimates of θ^{eu}_{ch} were 0.70 and 0.68 for export and import prices, respectively, and both were significantly different from both zero and unity at the 0.00 per cent level.

The unit-sum restriction simplifies equations (3.4) and (3.9); the former reduces to $PTF^{us}_{ch} = P_{us} - \theta^{eu}_{ch} \cdot PRER^{us}_{eu}$ and $PTF^{eu}_{ch} = P_{eu} - \theta^{us}_{ch} \cdot PRER^{eu}_{us}$, denominated in US dollars and the mini-ECU, respectively. Using those relations and imposing the $\beta_R(L) \equiv 0$ restriction, the reduced form for $PRER^{y}_{ch}$ becomes:

$$\begin{cases} \alpha(L) \cdot PRER^{us}_{ch,t} = [\Theta^{eu}_{ch} \cdot \alpha(L)] \cdot PRER^{us}_{eu,t} + \gamma_R(L) \cdot ytt_{ch,t} + \rho_R(L) \cdot INT^{us}_{ch,t} \\ and, \qquad\qquad\qquad\qquad\qquad\qquad\qquad\qquad\qquad\qquad\qquad\qquad (3.9') \\ \alpha(L) \cdot PRER^{eu}_{ch,t} = [\Theta^{us}_{ch} \cdot \alpha(L)] \cdot PRER^{us}_{eu,t} + \gamma_R(L) \cdot ytt_{ch,t} + \rho_R(L) \cdot INT^{eu}_{ch,t} \end{cases}$$

As the responses of $PRER^{y}_{ch}$ to a shock, to say, P_{us} are $\delta PRER^{us}_{ch} / \delta P_{us} = \theta^{eu}_{ch}$ and $\delta PRER^{eu}_{ch} / \delta P_{us} = \theta^{us}_{ch}$, equations (3.9') lend themselves to orthogonality tests. The joint restriction $\{\alpha(1) = \theta^{eu}_{ch} \cdot \alpha(1) = \gamma_R(1) = \rho_R a(1) = 0\}$ on a simultaneous NL–SYSTEM–GMM estimate of the first of equations (3.9'), reported in the upper part of Table 3.7, was not rejected. The key results, with that restriction imposed are reported in the lower panel of Table 3.7:[29]

1. as the restricted estimates of θ^{eu}_{ch} 0.70 and 0.76, are consistent with those reported in Table 3.6 and differ from both zero and unity at the 0.00 per

cent level, orthogonality of both the franc/dollar and the franc/mini-ECU PPP real exchange rates is definitively rejected; and

2. the restricted estimates of λ_R are –4.69 and –4.18 and highly significant.

Table 3.7 Orthogonality tests of Swiss PPP real exchange rate: 1974:02–1991:04; NLSYSTEM–GMM estimates of equation (3.9')

Restriction:	Test:	Price level measures		
		DEF	CPI	Both
α, $\theta_{ch}^{eu} \cdot \alpha, \gamma_R$ and ρ_R;	$\chi^2(4)$:	6.2174	6.9942	7.1724
	P-value:	0.3993	0.3214	0.6192

NLSYSTEM–GMM Regression Results (α, $\theta_{ch}^{eu} \cdot \alpha, \gamma_R$ and ρ_R Restrictions Imposed):

	DEF	CPI	Both
Restricted estimates of θ_{ch}^{eu}	0.7023	0.7557	–
Standard error:	0.0346	0.0365	–
t-Statistic (against zero):	20.2985	20.7016	–
P-value:	0.0000	0.0000	–
t-Statistic (against unity):	–8.6064	–6.6923	–
P-value:	0.0000	0.0000	–
$\chi^2(1)$ Stat. on equality restriction:	–	–	18.8835
P-value:	–	–	0.0000
Restricted estimates of λ_R:	–4.6932	–4.1788	–
Standard error:	0.9011	0.8857	–
Standard error:	0.9011	0.8857	–
t-Statistic (against zero):	–5.2085	–4.7182	–
P-value:	0.0000	0.0000	–
$\chi^2(1)$ stat. on equality restriction:	–	–	5.0188
P-value:	–	–	0.0251

As the standard error of ytt_{ch} is 2.4 per cent of the Swiss GDP, the external terms of trade have been a major source of fluctuations in the Swiss PPP real exchange rate.[30]

2.3   Cointegration Tests of Swiss Nominal and Real Exchange Rates

As Dickey et al. (1991) suggest that the elements of cointegrating vectors can be interpreted as final–form multipliers, a final test of the real and nominal exchange rate models involved estimating those vectors with the Hansen and Juselius (1995) ESTIMA 'CATS in RATS' routine. The cointegrating vector for nominal exchange rates involved all variables in equation (3.3), and for the true real rate all variables in equation (3.8). The vector for PPP real rates used all variables in equation (3.9) but with $\alpha(L) \cdot P_{y,t}$ shifted to the left-hand side:

$$\alpha(L) \cdot PF^y_{ch,t} = [\alpha(L) - \beta_R(L)] \cdot PTF^y_{ch,t}$$
$$- \gamma_R(L) \cdot ytt_{ch,t} - \rho_R(L) \cdot INT^y_{ch,t} \qquad (3.9'')$$

These three equations involve the variables EX^y_{ch}, $TRER_{ch}$, PF^y_{ch}, PTF^y_{ch}, ytt_{ch} and INT^y_{ch}, of which PTF^y_{ch}, ytt_{ch} and INT^y_{ch} were specified as exogenous.

With all variables first differenced, cointegration was not rejected by the eigenvalue or trace tests, nor did trace tests reject a cointegration rank of three at the 5 per cent level (these results are not reported but available upon request). The estimated vectors are reported in Table 3.8.[31]

Apart from the variable INT^{us}_{ch}, the estimate of the cointegrating vector for the nominal franc/dollar rate is consistent with the regression results, the same being true for the franc/mini-ECU nominal rate. Since the restrictions $\delta\, TRER_{ch}/\delta\, PTF^j_{ch} = 0$, $\delta\, PRER^j_{ch}/\delta\, PTF^j_{ch} = 1$, $j =$ US, EU, on the real exchange rates cannot be rejected at the 40 per cent level, the cointegration results provide further evidence that the Swiss true real exchange rate is orthogonal, but that property is not enjoyed by the PPP real exchange rates.[32]

3.0 ESTIMATES OF THE MEASUREMENT ERROR IN SWISS PPP REAL EXCHANGE RATES

The magnitude of the measurement error in Swiss PPP real exchange rates was examined using an identity obtained by subtracting equation (3.5) from equation (3.6):

$$PRER^y_{ch} \equiv TRER_{ch} + E^y_{ch} \qquad (3.10)$$

where $E^y_{ch} = P_y - PTF^y_{ch}$ is error. To ascertain how E^y_{ch} is distributed between $PRER^y_{ch}$ and $TRER_{ch}$, identity (3.10) was decomposed into two linear relationships:

Table 3.8 Estimated cointegrating vectors for Swiss exchange rates: 1974:02–1991:04

Franc/dollar case[a] — Test statistics

EX^{us}_{ch}	$TRER_{ch,gdp}$	$PF^{us}_{ch,cpi}$	PTF^{us}_{ch}	INT^{us}_{ch}	ytt_{ch}	χ^2	d.f.	P-value
1.000	–	–	1.052	0.264	1.292			
			(0.036)	(0.673)	(0.298)			
–	1.000	–	0.036	–0.073	1.382	N.A.	–	–
			(0.033)	(0.623)	(0.276)			
–	–	1.000	–1.027	–0.072	–0.755			
			(0.038)	(0.716)	(0.317)			
1.000	–	–	1.000[b]	0.106	1.480			
			(–)	(0.717)	(0.300)			
–	1.000	–	0.000[b]	–0.181	1.509	2.428	3	0.488
			(–)	(0.610)	(0.255)			
–	–	1.000	–1.000[b]	0.010	–0.850			
			(–)	(0.699)	(0.292)			
1.000	–	–	1.000[b]	0.000[b]	1.477			
			(–)	(–)	(0.298)			
–	1.000	–	0.000[b]	0.000[b]	1.514	3.186	6	0.785
			(–)	(–)	(0.256)			
–	–	1.000	–1.000[b]	0.000[b]	–0.850			
			(–)	(–)	(0.291)			

Franc/mini-ECU case[a] — Test statistics

EX^{eu}_{ch}	$TRER_{ch,gdp}$	$PF^{eu}_{ch,cpi}$	PTF^{eu}_{ch}	INT^{eu}_{ch}	ytt_{ch}	χ^2	d.f.	P-value
1.000	–	–	0.975	1.256	1.806			
			(0.077)	(0.968)	(0.320)			
–	1.000	–	–0.088	0.220	2.175	N.A.	–	–
			(0.072)	(0.906)	(0.300)			
–	–	1.000	–0.944	–0.349	–1.369			
			(0.083)	(1.039)	(0.344)			
1.000	–	–	1.000[b]	1.266	1.788			
			(–)	(0.973)	(0.320)			
–	1.000	–	0.000[b]	0.215	2.122	3.834	3	0.280
			(–)	(0.922)	(0.303)			
–	–	1.000	–1.000[b]	–0.358	–1.334			
			(–)	(1.042)	(0.342)			
1.000	–	–	1.000[b]	0.000[b]	1.921			
			(–)	(–)	(0.314)			
–	1.000	–	0.000[b]	0.000[b]	2.144	5.842	6	0.441
			(–)	(–)	(0.289)			
–	–	1.000	–1.000[b]	0.000[b]	–1.371			
			(–)	(–)	(0.324)			

Notes:
a. *Numbers in parentheses are estimated standard errors.*
b. *Restricted.*

$$PRER_{ch}^{y} = \eta \cdot E_{ch}^{y} + u_{ch}^{y}, \qquad (3.11)$$

And

$$TRER_{ch} = (\eta - 1) \cdot E_{ch}^{y} + u_{ch}^{y}. \qquad (3.12)$$

Estimates of the final-form multipliers $\delta\, TRER_{ch} / \delta\, E_{ch}^{y}$ (with three lags) based on equation (3.12) with E_{ch}^{y} defined on the French franc, DM, yen and pound sterling, as well as the US dollar, indicate that $TRER_{ch}$ and E_{ch}^{y} are orthogonal to one another in all cases; these results are reported in Table 3.9. As $\delta\, PRER_{ch}^{y} / \delta\, E_{ch}^{y} = 1 + \delta\, TRER_{ch} / \delta\, E_{ch}^{y}$ evidently E_{ch}^{y} is confined to $PRER_{ch}^{y}$.

Table 3.9 Orthogonality tests: Swiss true real exchange rates, 1973:02–1991:04

F-F Multiplier		Price level	FF	DM	Yen	Pound	Dollar
	{	DEF	−0.15	0.16	0.01	−0.02	0.07
		P-value	0.46	0.48	0.91	0.87	0.37
$\delta TRER_{ch} / \delta E_{ch}^{y}$							
	{	CPI	−0.17	0.26	−0.04	−0.00	0.04
		P-value	0.33	0.17	0.72	0.97	0.60

Table 3.10 Percent measurement error in the Swiss PPP real exchange rate, 1973:02–1991:04

Variable form	Price level	*Vis-à-vis* the:					
		FF	DM	Yen	Pound	Dollar	Average
	{ DEF	39.64	47.25	62.99	56.09	76.81	56.56
Levels:	*t*-statistic	3.70	4.08	7.21	8.67	7.47	–
	CPI	47.91	69.64	89.54	68.60	83.62	71.86
	t-statistic	4.35	6.07	18.76	11.79	10.43	–
:	{ DEF	77.66	67.78	89.40	90.83	93.78	83.89
1st DIF	*t*-statistic	10.88	13.21	20.14	32.85	36.22	–
	CPI	81.35	75.46	91.88	92.91	94.99	87.32
	t-statistic	13.08	17.47	23.46	36.33	41.48	–

The variance of the measurement error content of $PRER_{ch}^y$ might appear to be $\sigma_{P,E} = (\sigma_P^2 - \sigma_{P,T})$, where σ_P^2 is the variance of $PRER_{ch}^y$ and $\sigma_{P,E}$ ($\sigma_{P,T}$) is its covariance with E_{ch}^y ($TRER_{ch}$) but, as $\sigma_{P,T}$ clearly can be negative, that concept of the error is faulty as it can exceed the variance of $PRER_{ch}^y$. However, since OLS estimates of the residuals of equations (3.11) and (3.12), $\hat{u}_{ch}^y$, are common to $PRER_{ch}^y$ and $TRER_{ch}$, and are orthogonal to E_{ch}^y, they constitute the *verity* in $PRER_{ch}^y$, and thus the error component in the variance of $PRER_{ch}^y$ is defined as $(\sigma_P^2 - \sigma_{P,\hat{u}}) = \hat{\eta} \cdot \sigma_{P,E}$ where $\hat{\eta}$ is an OLS estimate of η. The *relative* error is $\hat{\eta} \cdot \sigma_{P,E} / \sigma_P^2 = r_{P,E}^2 \leq 1$, estimates of which appear in Table 3.10. As expected, the error levels are lower for Swiss PPP real exchange rates *vis-à-vis* European currencies, but in general the error content is appallingly high: the estimates range from 40 to 95 per cent and the simple average is 75 per cent. The error is particularly high when those real rates are defined on consumer prices or are first differenced; indeed, the first differences of $PRER_{ch}^y$ are hopelessly contaminated with measurement error. Moreover, despite the high stability of the SF/DM *nominal* exchange rate, from 47 to 75 per cent of the variance of the corresponding real exchange rate is measurement error.

4.0 THE MAIN FINDINGS

Turning first to the behavior of the Swiss nominal exchange rate *vis-à-vis* the US dollar and the 'mini-ECU', the main conclusions are as follows:

1. The simple 'commodity-currency' approach was highly successful in tracking the post-1973 behavior of both the Swiss franc/US dollar and the Swiss franc/mini-ECU nominal exchange rates.
2. In the Swiss case at least, the answer to the first question posed at the outset of this article is in the affirmative: the Swiss floating exchange rate fully insulates the Swiss economy from external price shocks. The exchange rate response is similar for exports and imports: a 10 per cent rise in either price index induces a revaluation of approximately 5 per cent.
3. Despite large fluctuations in the Swiss PPP real exchange rates since 1973, long-run purchasing power parity was not rejected.

4. The Swiss nominal exchange rate was found to be highly sensitive to the external terms of trade.
5. Swiss monetary policy has been independent of external inflation; the modest Swiss inflation since 1973 is strictly home grown.
6. Interest rate parity could be rejected for both the franc/dollar and the franc/mini-ECU exchange rate; in the franc/dollar case, however, a rise in Swiss interest rates results in a small but statistically significant appreciation of the Swiss franc.
7. The empirical evidence is consistent with weak foreign exchange market efficiency (as defined in this article) for both the Swiss franc/dollar and the Swiss franc/mini-ECU nominal exchange rates.

Concerning real exchange rates, the principal findings are the following:

1. Theory alone indicates that, even if the true real exchange rate of Country X is 'real' (that is, orthogonal to shocks to nominal variables), the PPP real exchange rate between Countries X and Y will be 'real' only if those two countries completely dominate the world markets for Country X's traded goods. *If the domination is only partial, that PPP real exchange rate will be contaminated with measurement error.*
2. In the Swiss case, the answer to the second question posed at the outset of this article is clearly in the negative: the behavior of the Swiss PPP real exchange rate does not accurately reflect that of her true real rate. While the *Swiss true* real exchange rate is orthogonal to all relevant nominal variables in both the short run and the long, orthogonality was strongly rejected for the *Swiss PPP real exchange rates, which respond strongly to shocks to nominal variables. Since these rates are 'real' in name only, they are unreliable for analytical purposes and misleading for macroeconomic policy evaluation.*
3. As predicted by Cassel (1922, p. 154), deviations of Swiss PPP real exchange rates from her true real rate arise from fluctuations in relative prices that introduce measurement error. Indeed, it was found that from 40 to 90 per cent of the total variance in the Swiss real exchange rates *vis-à-vis* the US dollar, French franc, DM, pound sterling and yen was measurement error, the simple average being 64 per cent. When first differenced, the range was 68–95 per cent and the average was 86 per cent. Even in the SF/DM case, measurement error is from 47 to 75 per cent. In view of the inordinate emphasis that has been placed on PPP real exchange rates as indicators of failed macroeconomic policies, one wonders how much mischief may have been wrought by blind obedience

to simple measurement error.[33]

4. Swiss real exchange rates were found to be highly sensitive to the terms of trade; indeed, the terms of trade have been the main source of shocks to the Swiss true real rate.

5. The US and the four major European countries appear to dominate world markets for Swiss tradeable, with the latter having the larger share of that market power. The distribution of that market power between those two blocs was found to be very similar for that Swiss imports and exports.

4.1 Concluding Comments

The paradox posed by the evident orthogonality of the Swiss true real exchange rate despite the high variability of her PPP real rate is explained by measurement error in PPP real rates. Consider a hypothetical 10 per cent depreciation of the mini-ECU *vis-à-vis* all currencies; from equation (3.4) it follows that PTF_{ch}^{us} declines by 7 per cent, causing the franc to depreciate by 7 per cent so neither the Swiss price level nor her true real exchange rate are affected. But the franc/dollar PPP real rate, $PRER_{ch}^{us} = EX_{ch}^{us} + P_{us} - P_{ch}$, depreciates by 7 per cent, a depreciation that may persist for a prolonged period of time.

As was hypothesized at the outset, the behavior of Swiss PPP real exchange rates does not warrant rejection of the theory underlying purchasing power parity; quite to the contrary. While movements in the nominal exchange rate in response to external price shocks are directly and immediately transmitted to the PPP real exchange rate, it is precisely those movements that insulate the Swiss true real rate from those shocks; in that sense, floating exchange rates perform an important neutrality function.

ACKNOWLEDGEMENTS

The author is indebted to members of workshops and seminars at the Universities of Chicago and Western Australia, Monash University, the Graduate Institute of International Studies (Geneva), the Universidad Catolica de Chile and the Universidad Torcuato Di Tella and especially Ken Clements, John Devereux, Hans Genberg, James Lothian, Lester Telser and Michael Woodford for valuable comments. Financial support from the Swiss National Science Foundation also is gratefully acknowledged.

APPENDIX 1: EXCHANGE RATES AND PRICES OF TRADED GOODS

Ignoring transport costs, tariffs and other barriers to trade, the 'law of one price' for internationally traded good q states that:

$$P_q^j = P_q^j + EX_i^j \qquad (3.13)$$

where P_q^j is the (natural logarithm of the) price of good q in currency i, and EX_i^j is the (natural logarithm of the) price of currency j in terms of currency i.[34] With no loss of generality, set $i = X$; that is the currency of Country X will be the reference currency.[35] The excess demand for good q in Country j, $D^{j,q}$, is a function of its real price and a vector, Z_q^j, of all other relevant variables (that is the market 'fundamentals' in Country j):

$$D^{q,j} = D^{q,j} [(P_q^j - P_j), Z_q^j]$$
$$= D^{q,j} [(P_q^x - EX_x^j - P_j), Z_q^j] \qquad (3.14)$$

where P_j is the (natural logarithm of the) price level in the country j. As:

$$P_q^x - EX_x^j - P_j = (P_q^x - P_x) - (P_j + EX_x^j - P_x)$$
$$\equiv P_q^{x,R} - PRER_x^j$$

the excess demand for good q in Country j can be written as a function of the natural logarithm of the ratio of its real price in Country X to the PPP real exchange rate between Country X and j:

$$D^{q,j} = D^{q,j} [(P_q^{x,R} - PRER_x^j), Z_q^j]$$

In a world of M countries, there are M such excess demand equations which must sum to zero:

$$\sum_j^M D^{q,j} = [(P_q^{x,R} - PRER_x^j), Z_q^j] = 0$$

and hence in principle there is a solution for $P_q^{x,R}$ in terms of the $PRER_x^j$ and the Z_q^j. By differentiating the summation totally and rearranging:

$$dP_q^{x,R} = \sum_j^M (D_1^{q,j} / D_1^q) \cdot d(PRER_x^j) - (D_2^{q,j} / D_1^q) \cdot dZ_q^j$$

where $D_1^{q,j} \equiv \partial (D^{q,j}) / \partial (P^{x,R} - PRER_x^j) < 0$, $D_2^{q,j} = \partial (D^{q,j}) / \partial Z_q^j$, and $D_1^q \equiv \sum_j^M D_1^{q,j}$, and a local linear approximation is obtained by integration:

$$P_q^{x,R} = \sum_j^M \vartheta_j^q \cdot PRER_x^j + F(Z_q) \tag{3.15}$$

where $\vartheta_j^q \equiv D_1^{q,j} / D_1^q \geq 0$ and $F(Z_q)$ is the integral of $-\sum_j^M (D_2^{q,j} / D_1^q) \cdot \partial Z_q^j$. The ϑ_j^q are non–negative fractions that sum to unity and $F(Z_q)$ captures the Z_q^j vectors (the fundamentals – which are assumed to be orthogonal to $PRER_x^j$).

The ϑ_j^q coefficients measure the relative market power possessed by each country and, as such, have no logical relation to international trade patterns. In the limiting case when $\vartheta_j^q = 0$, country j is a price taker in the world market for good q as its real exchange rate *vis à vis* country X has no effect on the real price of good q in currency X. At the other extreme, if $\vartheta_j^q = 1$, country j is a price maker; any change in its real exchange rate causes an equiproportionate change in the real price of good q in country X.

Equation (3.15) can be generalized to a real price index for any subset of traded goods; that index is defined as $PT_x^R \equiv \sum_q^N w_q \cdot P_q^{x,R}$, where the w_q are non-negative weights that sum to unity. Combining that price index with equation (3.15), we obtain:

$$PT_x^R \equiv \sum_q^N w_q \cdot \left[\sum_j^M \vartheta_j^q \cdot PRER_x^j + F(Z_q) \right]$$

$$= \sum_j^M \Theta_x^j \cdot PRER_x^j + G(Z_x) \tag{3.16}$$

where the $\Theta_x^j \equiv \sum_q^N w_q \cdot \vartheta_q^j$, which sum to unity, have the same interpretation as the ϑ_q^j; they measure the relative market power possessed by Country j over the prices of the subset of goods traded internationally by Country X. The term $G(Z_x) \equiv \sum_q^N w_q \cdot F(Z_q)$ captures the global fundamentals for those goods.

Equation (3.16) can be defined on nominal prices by adding P_x to both sides of equation (3.16):

$$PT_x = \sum_j^M \Theta_x^j \cdot (P_j + EX_x^j) + G(Z_x).$$

That equation also can be expressed in the currency of, say, Country Y by use of the identity $EX_x^j - EX_x^y \equiv EX_y^j$ and the property that $\sum_j^M \Theta_x^j = 1$:

$$PTF_x^y = \sum_j^M \Theta_x^j \cdot (P_j + EX_y^j) + G(Z_x) \qquad (3.17)$$

where $PTF_x^y = PT_x - EX_x^y$; this expression appears as equation (3.4) in the text.

APPENDIX 2: TERMS-OF-TRADE ENDOGENEITY

It is evident from Appendix 1 that equation (3.17) can be decomposed into an equation imports and another for exports. As the Θ s for imports and exports are unlikely to be identical, the terms of trade may be endogenous in that they are be affected by shocks to the PF_j^y variables, causing bias in the estimates of equations (3.3) and (3.7)–(3.9) in which ytt_{ch} and/or TT_{ch} appear. To determine if ytt_{ch} is endogenous, an ad hoc equation was parameterized as follows (3.18) and estimated by NLLS–ROB for each price level measure (def, cpi and ppi). The φ_k indicate the long-run response of ytt_{ch} to permanent shocks to the price level variables (such as, $\delta ytt_{ch} / \delta P_{us} = \varphi_{us} = b(1)/a(1)$). The results, summarized in Table 3.11, indicate that all three currency blocks possess positive but differential market power over dollar prices of Swiss importables and exportables; positive shocks to the US and European price levels worsen the Swiss terms of trade, while positive shocks to the Swiss price level improve them.

$$
\begin{aligned}
\Delta ytt_{ch,t} = -\sum_{i=1}^{3} & \left[\left(\sum_{j=0}^{i} a_j \right) \cdot \Delta ytt_{ch,t-i} + \left(\sum_{j=0}^{i} b_j \right) \cdot \Delta P_{us,t-i} \right. \\
& \left. + \left(\sum_{j=0}^{i} c_j \right) \cdot \Delta PF^{us}_{eu,t-i} + \left(\sum_{j=0}^{i} d_j \right) \cdot \Delta PF^{us}_{ch,t-i} \right] \\
& + a(1) \cdot (ytt_{ch,t-4} + \varphi_{us} \cdot P_{us,t-4} + \varphi_{eu} \cdot PF^{us}_{eu,t-4} \\
& + \varphi_{ch} \cdot PF^{us}_{ch,t-4}
\end{aligned}
\tag{3.18}
$$

Table 3.11 Endogeneity tests on y_{tt}; Switzerland, 1974:01–1991:04

	Ψ_{us}	t-statistic [a]	P-value
US price level:			
GDP deflator	−0.1441	−7.0278	0.0000
Consumer prices	−0.0971	−4.0464	0.0002
Producer prices	−0.1128	−8.5365	0.0000
European price level:	Ψ_{eu}	t-statistic	P-value
GDP deflator	−0.0297	−1.6785	0.0994
Consumer prices	0.0047	0.2557	0.7992
Producer prices	−0.0332	−2.2844	0.0265
Swiss price level:	Ψ_{ch}	t-statistic	P-value
GDP deflator	0.0479	2.7588	0.0080
Consumer prices	0.0312	1.7353	0.0887
Producer prices	0.0639	3.7779	0.0004

Notes: Computed using robust standard errors with four lags and a damp factor of 0.75 for the GDP deflator, and 0.85 for consumer and producer price.

REFERENCES

Cassel, G. (1922), *Money and Foreign Exchange After 1914,* London: Constable.
Devereux, J. and M. Connolly (1994), 'Commercial policy, the terms of trade and the real exchange rate revisited', *Journal of Development Economics,* **50**, pp. 81–99.

Dickey, D.A., Jansen, D.W. and D.L. Thorton (1991), 'A primer on cointegration with an application to money and income', *Federal Reserve Bank of St. Louis Review*, **73**, pp. 58–78.

Diebold, F.X., Husted, S. and M. Rush (1991), 'Real exchange rates under the gold standard, *Journal of Political Economy'*, **99**, pp. 1252–1271.

Dornbusch, R. (1974), 'Tariffs and nontraded goods', *Journal of International Economics*, **4**, pp. 177–185.

Edwards, S. (1989), *Real Exchange Rates, Devaluation, and Adjustment: Exchange Rate Policy in Developing Countries*, Cambridge, MA: MIT Press.

Evans, M.D. and J.R. Lothian (1993), 'The response of exchange rates to permanent and transitory shocks under floating exchange rates', *Journal of International Money and Finance*, **12**, pp. 563–586.

Fama, E.F. (1984), 'Forward and spot exchange rates', *Journal of Monetary Economics*, **14**, pp. 319–338.

Fischer, S. (1986), *Indexation, Inflation, and Economic Policy*, Cambridge, MA: MIT Press.

Freebairn, J. (1990), 'Is the $A a commodity currency', in K. Clements and J. Freebairn (eds), *Exchange Rates and Australian Commodity Exports*, Centre for Policy Studies, Monash University, and Economic Research Centre, The University of Western Australia, Melbourne and Perth, pp. 6–30.

Frenkel, J. (1981), 'The collapse of purchasing power parity during the 1970s', *European Economic Review*, **16**, pp. 145–165.

Genberg, H. (1978), 'Purchasing power parity under fixed and flexible exchange rates', *Journal of International Economics*, **8**, pp. 247–276.

Gruen, D.W.R. and J. Wilkinson (1994), 'Australia's real exchange rate – is it explained by the terms of trade or by real interest rate differentials?', *Economic Record*, **70**, pp. 204–219.

Hansen, H. and K. Juselius (1995), *CATS in RATS: Cointegrating Analysis of Time Series*, Evanston, IL: ESTIMA.

Hansen, L.P. (1982), 'Large sample properties of generalized method of moments estimators', *Econometrica*, **50**, pp. 1029–1054.

Huizinga, J. (1987), 'An empirical investigation of the long run behavior of real exchange rates', in Brunner, K. and A. Meltzer (eds), *Carnegie–Rochester Conference Series on Public Policy*, vol. 27, Amsterdam: North-Holland Publishing Company, pp. 149–214.

Jones, R.W. and D.D. Purvis (1983), 'International differences in response to common external shocks: the role of purchasing power parity', in E. Classen and P. Salin (eds), *Recent Issues in the Theory of Flexible Exchange Rates*, Amsterdam: North-Holland Publishing Company, pp. 33–55.

Lothian, J.R. and M.P. Taylor (1996), 'Real exchange rate behavior: the recent float from the perspective of the past two centuries', *Journal of Political Economy*, **104**, pp. 488–509.

Michaely, M. (1981), 'Foreign aid, economic structure and dependence', *Journal of Development Economics*, **9**, pp. 313–330.

Mussa, M. (1979), 'Empirical regularities in the behavior of exchange rates and theories of the foreign exchange market', in K. Brunner and A. Meltzer (eds),

Carnegie–Rochester Conference Series on Public Policy, vol. 11, North-Holland Publishing Company: Amsterdam, pp. 9–57.

Mussa, M. (1986), 'Nominal exchange rate regimes and the behavior of real exchange rates: evidence and implications', in K. Brunner and A. Meltzer (eds), *Carnegie–Rochester Conference Series on Public Policy*, vol. 25, Amsterdam: North-Holland Publishing Company, pp. 117–113.

Neary, P.J. (1988), 'Determinants of the equilibrium exchange rate', *American Economic Review*, **78**, pp. 210–215.

Ostry, J.D. (1988), *The Balance of Trade, Terms of Trade, and Real Exchange Rate*, International Monetary Fund Staff Paper, 35, pp. 541–573.

Ridler, D. and C.A. Yandle (1972), *A Simplified Method for Analyzing the Effects of Exchange Rate Changes on Exports of a Primary Commodity*, International Monetary Fund Staff Paper, 19, pp. 559–575.

Saidi, N. and A. Swoboda (1983), 'Nominal and real exchange rates: issues and some evidence', in E. Claassen and P. Salin (eds), *Recent Issues in the Theory of Flexible Exchange Rates*, Amsterdam: North-Holland Publishing Company, pp. 3–27.

Salter, W.E.G. (1959), 'Internal and external balance: the role of price and expenditure effects', *Economic Record*, **35**, pp. 226–238.

Sjaastad, L.A. (1980), 'Commercial policy, "true tariffs" and relative prices', in J. Black and B. Hindley (eds), *Current Issues in Commercial Policy and Diplomacy*, London: Macmillan, pp. 26–51.

Sjaastad, L.A. (1985), 'Exchange rate regimes and the real rate of interest', in M. Connolly and J. McDermott (eds), *The Economics of the Caribbean Basin*, New York: Praeger Publishers, pp. 135–164.

Sjaastad, L.A. and F. Scacciavillani (1996), 'The price of gold and the exchange rates', *Journal of International Monetary Finanace*, **15**, pp. 879–897.

Stockman, A. (1988), 'Real exchange-rate variability under pegged and floating nominal exchange-rate systems: an equilibrium theory', in K. Brunner, and A. Meltzer (eds), *Carnegie–Rochester Conference Series on Public Policy*, vol. 29, Amsterdam: North-Holland Publishing Company, pp. 259–294.

Theil, H. and J.C.G. Boot (1962), 'The final form of econometric equation systems, *Review of International Statistics*, **30**, pp. 136–152.

White, H. (1980), 'A heteroscedasticity-consistent covariance matrix estimator and a direct test for heteroscedasticity', *Econometrica*, **48**, pp. 817–838.

NOTES

1 See Frenkel (1981) for an early study of the departures from PPP in the 1970s.
2 Edwards' huge compilation of real exchange rate data is a prime example of the PPP real exchange rate approach to testing purchasing power parity (Edwards, 1989).
3 Huizinga (1987) and others find evidence of mean reversion in PPP real exchange rates during the post-Bretton Woods period, and Diebold et al. (1991) also find mean reversion under the gold standard. Evans and Lothian (1993) find both temporary and permanent influences on real exchange rates during the post-Bretton Woods period, and Lothian and

Taylor (1996) find strong evidence of mean reversion in both the US dollar/sterling and French franc/sterling real exchange rates during the past two centuries.

4   The highly variable relative prices during the post-Bretton Woods era arising from singular events (the oil prices shocks) and from higher inflation rates also may affect exchange rates. See Fischer (1986) for evidence on the relation between inflation and relative price dispersion.

5   Mussa (1979), for example, claimed that 'the natural logarithm of the spot exchange rate follows approximately a random walk' and, in Mussa (1986), he argued that 'short-term changes in nominal exchange rates and in real exchange rates show substantial persistence during subperiods when the nominal exchange rate is floating'.

6   Final-form multipliers were first defined by Theil and Boot (1962).

7   While largely an oral tradition, the Australian 'commodity-currency' approach to exchange rate determination is clearly enunciated in Freebairn (1990) and Gruen and Wilkinson (1994).

8   Salter's point that the level of expenditure relative to income also affects the equilibrium value of *PNT* relative to *PT* suggests a third variable (Salter, 1959). Michaely (1981) finds broad empirical support for that effect, but its magnitude varies over time. While the Salter effect is ignored in the development of the nominal exchange rate model, it was tested in the empirical work and found to be not significant in the particular case under study.

9   For succinct treatments of the effect of the terms-of-trade on the relative price of non-traded goods, see Neary (1988) and Devereux and Connolly (1994); for one that admits inter-temporal substitution as well, see Ostry (1988).

10 Note that, by combining $PT = IMP + \Omega \cdot TT$ with equation (3.2), one obtains:

$$PNT_t = C(L) \cdot (IMPt + \Omega \cdot TT_t) + D(L) \cdot ytt_t$$

which is very similar to the 'omega' equation, $PNT - EXP = \omega \cdot (IMP - EXP)$, introduced by Sjaastad (1980) to quantify the 'incidence' of protection. The incidence parameter, $\delta PNT / \delta IMP = \omega$, summarizes the substitution effect noted by Dornbusch (1974). From the homogeneity postulate [C(1) = 1] and the above equation it follows that $\delta PNT / \delta IMP = (1 - \Omega)$ and hence $\omega = 1 - \Omega$

11 See Sjaastad and Scacciavillani (1996) for an application of this approach to a particular commodity (gold).

12 As shown in Sjaastad (1980), trade restrictions distort the exchange rate/price level relationship. Combining the price level with equation (3.2) yields:

$$P_t = \{1 - w \cdot [1 - C(L)]\} \cdot [EX_t + IMPF_t + \Omega \cdot TT_t + (1 - \Omega) \cdot \tau_t] + w \cdot D(L) \cdot ytt_t$$

where $\tau = ln(1 + t)$ and t is a uniform tariff. With *IMPF, TT* and *ytt* held constant, $\delta (P - EX)/\delta_\tau = (1 - \Omega)$ which, in the absence of complementarity, is a positive fraction. As most estimates of Ω are between 0.25 and 0.5, import protection depresses the exchange rate relative to the price level.

13 The mini-ECU price of the dollar, $ex^\$_{ECU}$, was defined as:

$$ex^\$_{ECU,t} = [GDP^\$_{FRA,t} \cdot (ex^\$_{FF,t}/e\,\bar{x}^\$_{FF}) + GDP_{DEU,t} \cdot (ex^\$_{DM,t}/e\,\bar{x}^\$_{DM})$$
$$+ GDP_{ITA,t} \cdot (ex^\$_{LIT,t}/e\,\bar{x}^\$_{LIT}) + GDP_{GBR,t} \cdot (ex^\$_{\pounds,t}/e\,\bar{x}^\$)]/GDP_{EU,t}$$

where $e\,\overline{x}_j^{\$}$ is the period-average price of the US dollar in terms of currency j, GDP_j is the gross domestic product of country j and GDP_{EU} is the combined GDP of the four major European countries; all measures of GDP are in DM.

14 Import and export implicit prices indices are from TIME SERIES DATA EXPRESS, EconData Pty Ltd, Canberra, Australia and are identified as CHE.SA.EXPIPI and CHE.SA.IMPIPI. All other data are from the ESTIMA RATS-OECD database.

15 All estimates were by ESTIMA RATS386 version 4.2. Unit-root tests were made by DFUNIT.SRC with four lags and a trend for variables in level form.

16 Lags were added until estimates of $\alpha(1)$, $\beta(1)$ and $\gamma(1)$ stabilized, which occurred at the fifth lag (coinciding with the Schwarz Information Criterion). For NLLS–RON, the 'damp' factor was set to produce positive definite VCV matrices; for NLLS–GMM, it was set at unity to obtain Newey–West estimates. The instruments were a constant, lagged ΔEX, ΔTT, Δytt, INT, the three versions of lagged $TRER$, and the residuals of a regression of ytt and TT on $IMPF$. A trade-balance variable was dropped as tests of a joint zero restriction on its coefficients was not rejected at the 35 per cent level.

17 As $\Delta IMPF = \Delta IMP - \Delta EX$, the implicit presence of $-\Delta EX$ on the right hand side of equation (3.3`) may bias the estimate of β_o downward. Replacing ΔEX on the left-hand side with $\Delta IMP - \Delta IMPF$ eliminates any spurious correlation:

$$
\begin{aligned}
\Delta IMP_{ch,t} &= -\sum_{i+1}^{N-1}[\overline{\alpha}_i \cdot \Delta EX^{us}_{ch,t-i} - \overline{\beta}_i \cdot (\Delta IMP_{ch,t-i} + \Omega \cdot \Delta TT_{ch,t-i})] \\
&\quad + (\beta_0 + 1) \cdot \Delta IMPF^{us}_{ch,t} + (\beta_0 \cdot \Omega) \cdot \Delta TT_{ch,t} + \overline{\gamma}(L) \cdot \Delta ytt_{ch,t} \\
&\quad + \alpha(1) \cdot EX^{us}_{ch,t-N} + \beta(1) \cdot PTF^{us}_{ch,t-N} \\
&\quad + \gamma(1) \cdot ytt_{ch,t-N} + \rho_{INT,0} \cdot \Delta INT^{us}_{ch,t}
\end{aligned}
$$

Estimates of this equation were identical with those reported in Table 3.2.

18 Estimates of equation (3.3A) with zero to four lags on PTF (the Akaike and the Schwarz Information Criteria indicate zero lags) produced results very similar to those reported for five lags in panel D of Table 3.2.

19 EX, $IMPF$ and INT are defined on the Deutsche mark. A zero restriction on the INT coefficients is not rejected at the 33 per cent (28 per cent) level. The instruments were a constant, TT, ytt, INT, lagged ΔEX, all versions of $PRER$ (one lag), and the residuals of a regression of ytt and TT on $IMPF$.

20 Edwards (1989), for example, defines the real exchange rate as the ratio of the foreign-currency price of traded goods to the domestic-currency price of non-traded goods, but in his empirical analysis, he uses the usual PPP version, with the obligatory apology that 'unfortunately, it is not possible to find an exact empirical counterpart to the [true] analytical construct' (p. 87).

21 High short-run correlations between nominal and PPP real exchange rates are well known; concerning his 'second important regularity', Mussa (1986) noted that 'during subperiods when the nominal exchange rate is floating, there is strong correlation between short-term movements in the real exchange rate and short-term movements in the nominal exchange rate' (p. 131).

22 For both the subperiod 1973:01–1980:02 (dollar depreciation) and the subperiod 1980:03–1991:04, the correlations between EX and $PRER$ increased relative to the period as a whole,

while those between *EX* and *TRER* decreased. When first differenced, the results were very similar to the period as a whole.

23   The Θ_x^k sum to unity over $k \neq X$: $\sum_{k\neq x}^{M} \theta_x^k = \sum_{k\neq x}^{M} \left[\Theta_x^k /(1 - \Theta_x^x) \right] = 1$; also Θ_x^x is defined as $\Theta_x^x /(1 - \Theta_x^x)$ even though it is not a proper member of the Θ_x^j set.

24   In a somewhat different but equally relevant context, Saidi and Swoboda (1983) argue that 'different weights (in national price indices) for different commodity groups, whether traded or non-traded, induce deviations from PPP when relative prices change; these variations will be persistent as long as relative prices changes persist' (p. 13).

25   Nonetheless, PPP can still hold in the long run [that is PPP real exchange rates will be mean reverting as found by Huizinga (1987) and others] even if $\Phi = -1$ as a permanent shock to, say, P_z may eventually induce an adjustment in EX_y^z such that PF_z^y returns to its original level.

26   This may explain why PPP real exchange rates often differ according to the choice of reference country Y; that choice determines the size of Θ_x^y and hence the degree to which $PRER_x^y$ is contaminated with measured error.

27   Unit roots are rejected for all versions of *TRER*; see Panel B of Table 3.4. Since *TRER* defined on producer prices behaves oddly and as the coefficient of determination of the PPI version was negative, that version was not included in the analysis. The instruments were a constant, *PTF*, two versions of (*PRER* – *TRER*) and *PRER* (with five lags), *TRER* defined on producer prices, the forward premium, the residuals of a regression of *ytt* on *PTF*, and *ytt* (with six lags).

28   The instruments were a constant, the US and European price levels, and the residuals of a regression of *ytt* on the Swiss/US PPP real exchange rates.

29. Unit roots were rejected at the 3 per cent level for all versions of the franc/dollar PPP real exchange rtes (see Table 3.4). The instruments for the NLSYSTEM–GMM estimates were ΔPTF, *INT*, *ytt* (with six lags), both versions of $TRER_{ch}$ and $PRER_{eu}^{us}$ and the residuals of a regression of $\Delta PRER_{eu}^{us}$ on *ytt*.

30   Devereux and Connolly (1994) report similar results in their study of four Latin-American countries.

31   Since $TRER_{ch} = PTF_{ch}^y - PTF_{ch}^y$ and all three variable appeared in the analysis, $TRER_{ch}$ and PF_{ch}^y had to be defined on different price levels.

32   Similar results (not reported) were found for the franc/dollar case with $TRER_{ch}$ defined on CPI_{ch} and PF_{ch}^{us} on DEF_{ch} and, for the franc/mini-ECU case, with PF_{ch}^{eu} defined on DEF_{ch} and $TRER_{ch}$ on CPI_{ch}.

33   Had Edwards (1989) encountered the Swiss case, he may well have found episodes of 'real exchange rate misalignment' to be attributed to 'inconsistent' macroeconomic policies when, in reality, no such misalignments had occurred.

34   This approach apparently was first employed by Ridler and Yandle (1972) in a study of the effect of exchange rates on commodity prices. The model presented in this appendix first appeared in Sjaastad (1985).

35   As the interest is in currency blocs rather than countries, there is no one-to-one correspondence between countries and currencies.

4. Purchasing Power Parity and International Competitiveness

Meher Manzur

Purchasing power parity (PPP) gives the relationship between exchange rates and national price levels. The absolute PPP states that the exchange rate is equal to the ratio of domestic to foreign prices. According to the relative PPP, the change in the exchange rate is equal to the inflation differential. As a central concept in international finance, PPP has useful wide-ranging applications. This chapter deals with one such application. The objective, in part, here is to investigate the relative efficacy of PPP in the measurement of international competitiveness. The thrust is empirical and the analysis is carried out using the data from selected East Asian economies.[1]

The East Asians are viewed as highly competitive internationally. Over the last two decades, they have recorded an astonishing and sustained economic growth that has improved the living standards of more people, more rapidly than at any other time or place in history. According to the competitiveness index of the Global Competitiveness Report 1996, four out of the top ten economies in the world are from this region. These are Singapore, Hong Kong, Taiwan and Malaysia. Even though Japan does not make the top ten, it ranks highly among the G7 and the OECD countries. Korea occupies the twentieth position, ahead of countries like Germany, Sweden, France and Belgium. A pertinent issue is whether we have a decent measure of international competitiveness that is consistent with the success story of this region. How successful is PPP in this regard?

International competitiveness has traditionally been defined in terms of movements in the real exchange rates.[2] Real exchange rates are defined as nominal exchange rates adjusted for inflation. However, the true real exchange rate for any country is defined as the ratio of its traded to non-traded goods prices reflecting the internal relative price structure in the economy. Note that it does not explicitly involve the nominal exchange rate. The empirical counterpart of the true real exchange rate is based on purchasing power parity (PPP) which explicitly involves the nominal rate, and usually is written as $r_{it} = s_{it}p_{1t}/p_{it}$, where s_{it} is the domestic currency cost of \$US1, p_{1t} is the US price level and p_{it} is the price level of the country i ($i=2, ..., n$) in terms of local currency.[3] When there is a nominal depreciation of the currency of the country i, s_i rises; if prices remain unchanged, the real rate r_i also rises and this represents a real depreciation. Similarly, if foreign prices (p_1) increase relative to price at home (p_i) there is again a real depreciation. Thus an increase in r_i is interpreted as a real depreciation, one which improves the competitiveness of the country's exports.

PPP, or some variants of it, is commonly used to calculate real exchange rates as an index of international competitiveness. In some cases, (for example, the Morgan Guaranty estimate) this calculation is given a multilateral flavour by defining in terms of weighted averages of several PPP-based real exchange rates. Whether bilateral or multilateral, the PPP real exchange rate is likely to be infected with measurement errors. As Sjaastad (1998) demonstrates, the PPP real exchange rate would deviate from the true real exchange rate unless the foreign currency price index for the home country's traded goods and the overall price level of the foreign country are perfectly correlated. In general, of course, there is no reason to expect such perfect correlation between the two (also see Manzur, 1991). Sjaastad (1998) also highlights a second source of measurement error in the bilateral PPP exchange rate that arises when third countries dominate the world markets for the home country's traded goods.[4] Yet another problem is the use of one reference country, such as the USA, that gives rise to asymmetry (see Manzur, 1993).

The objective of this chapter is to re-examine the relative usefulness of PPP in the measurement of international competitiveness. In this pursuit, we first introduce an alternative measure of real exchange rates as an indicator of international competitiveness. The measure, which we call 'basket approach', is applied to the data for selected East Asian countries, namely, Japan, Korea, Malaysia, Thailand and Singapore. This new measure is then compared with the conventional form of real exchange rates based on PPP using time-series econometrics.

The chapter is organised as follows. The basket approach is discussed in Section 2. The data and preliminary results are given in Section 3. The results indicate that the PPP-based real exchange rates tend to understate the measure of competitiveness for these countries. In the next section, we employ two types of unit-root and cointegration tests. The empirical results confirm that basket real exchange rates have significant influence on export competitiveness, while PPP real exchange rates do not. Some concluding remarks are made in the last section.

1.0 THE BASKET APPROACH

Following Sjaastad (1990), we introduce a new measure of real exchange rates, which we call 'basket' real exchange rates. This basket approach to real exchange rates involves defining all prices and exchange rates on an appropriately-weighted 'basket' of currencies instead of a single currency. This method is likely to be free from the measurement errors inherent in the PPP approach as discussed earlier.

Let s_{it} be the cost of \$US1 at time t in terms of the currency of country i ($i = 1, ..., n$). We define the basket of n currencies as containing x_i units of currency i. The US dollar value of x_i is x_1/s_{it}, so that the cost of the basket in US dollars is given by:

$$\sum_{i=1}^{n} x_i \frac{1}{s_{it}} = \sum_{i=1}^{n} \frac{x_i}{\bar{s}_i} \frac{\bar{s}_i}{s_{it}},$$

where s_i is the period average of s_{it}. The term $x_i/\bar{s}_i$ is in dollars at the period average exchange rate. It is thus the 'dollar quantity' of currency i in the basket and $\sum_{i=1}^{n}(x_i/s_i) = M$ (say) is the overall dollar size of the basket, again a quantity measure. We use average exchange rate to avoid fluctuations associated with quarterly exchange rates. Dividing the cost of the basket by its size M, we obtain the US dollar price of the basket:

$$usb_t = \sum_{i=1}^{n} w_i \frac{\bar{s}_i}{s_{it}},$$

where $w_i = (x_i/\bar{s}_i)/M$ is the weight given to currency i, with $\sum_{i=1}^{n} w_i = 1$. The ith currency price of the basket is given by:

$$sb_{it} = usb_t s_{it}.$$

Letting E_{it} be the logarithm of sb_{it} and C_{it} (the logarithm of) the price level (CPI) in country i, we obtain the ith price level measured in terms of the currency basket,

$$Cb_{it} = C_{it} - E_{it},$$

and for the world,

$$WCb_t = \sum_{i=1}^{n} w_i Cb_{it},$$

We define the real exchange rate for country i as the world cost of the basket relative to its cost in i:

$$s_{it}^r = WCb_t - Cb_{it}, \qquad (4.1)$$

where s_{it}^r is the basket measure of real exchange rates for country i ($i = 1,...,n$).

2.0 THE DATA AND THE RESULTS

The data used in this study are quarterly observations of nominal exchange rates and consumer price indices (CPI) for the period starting from the first quarter of 1973 to the fourth quarter of 1996. For the weights (w_i), we use exports. All data are from the International Monetary Fund's (IMF) International Financial Statistics CD-ROM data disk, and contained in a separate appendix available on request.

We calculate the basket real exchange rate changes using equation (4.1). The PPP real exchange rates are calculated using the following:

$$Dr_{it} = Ds_{it} + Dp_{1t} - Dp_{it}, \qquad (4.2)$$

where D is the log-change operator ($D_{xt} = \log x_t - \log x_{t-1}$), r_{it} is the real exchange rate, s_{it} is the domestic currency cost of one US dollar, p_{1t} is the US price level and p_{it} is the price level of country i ($i = 2, ..., n$) in terms of the domestic currency.

For the purpose of comparison, the two series are plotted together against time in Figures 4.1 to 4.5.

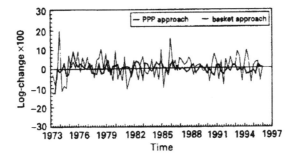

Figure 4.1 Real exchange rates: basket vs PPP method, 1973(1)–1996(1), Singapore

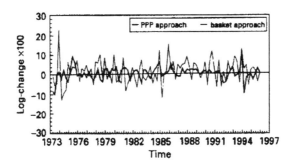

Figure 4.2 Real exchange rates: basket vs PPP method, 1973(1)–1996(1), Malaysia

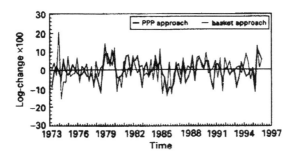

Figure 4.3 Real exchange rates: basket vs PPP method, 1973(1)–1996(1), Japan

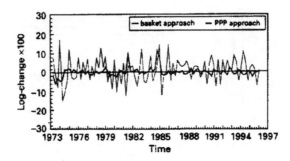

*Figure 4.4 Real exchange rates: basket vs PPP method, 1973(1)–1996(1),
Thailand*

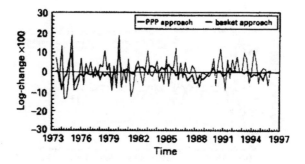

*Figure 4.5 Real exchange rates: basket vs PPP method, 1973(1)–1996(1),
Korea*

Here, a positive (negative) value represents a real depreciation
(appreciation). From the figures, it can be seen that the two approaches of
real exchanges rates diverge largely in all cases. For all countries, the basket
measure of real exchange rates tends to be larger in magnitude for the
quarterly changes compared to the PPP measure. This implies that real
exchange rates are more volatile when we use the basket measure as opposed
to the PPP measure. This also implies that the PPP real exchange rates have a
tendency to understate the measure of competitiveness. That is, the
competitiveness of the traded goods sectors for these countries is
significantly more than that implied by PPP.

Real exchange rates are closely linked to the export competitiveness of a
country. A real depreciation reduces the cost to foreigners of a bundle of
goods denominated in domestic currency, and may increase foreign demand

for domestically produced goods. In what follows, we employ cointegration analysis to see if this relationship holds for the countries under study.

3.0 COINTEGRATION TESTS

Following Engle and Granger (1987), we conduct the cointegration test in two steps. The first step is to examine the order of difference for the variables. If a series has a stationary, inevitable and stochastic ARMA representation after differencing d times, it is said to be integrated of order d, and denoted as I(d). A necessary condition for cointegration is that the two series be integrated of the same order d with d ≥ 1. For our purpose, we examine the variables for d = 0 or 1. That is, for any variable z, we test the the null hypothesis that $z_t \sim I(1)$, or equivalently, u_t is stationary where

$$u_t = \Delta z_t = z_t - z_{t-1}, \tag{4.3}$$

$$u_t = \Delta z_t = z_t - z_{t-1} = \beta_0 + \alpha_0 t + \alpha_1 z_{t-1} + \sum_{i=1}^{p} \beta_i \Delta z_{t-1} + \varepsilon_t. \tag{4.4}$$

To do this we apply the Dickey–Fuller (1979, 1981) unit root test procedure based on the OLS regression

The variable p is chosen to achieve white noise residuals, ε_t. Testing the null hypothesis of the presence of a unit root in z_t [that is, the series is I(1)] is equivalent to testing the hypothesis that $\alpha_1 = 0$ in equation (4.4). If α_1 is significantly less than zero, the null hypothesis of a unit root is rejected. The test statistics used is the usual t-ratio, but the distribution is not the t-distribution under the null hypothesis (see Tiku and Wong 1998). For robustness, we use both the Dickey–Fuller (DF) and augmented Dickey–Fuller (ADF) tests. To check whether z_t is a random walk with or without drift, we employ Φ_2 and Φ_3 found in Dickey and Fuller (1981). Note that all variables in this section are in log form.

The unit-root test results are given in Table 4.1. As can be seen, all variables, namely, exports (x_i), basket real exchange rates (s_i^r) and PPP real exchange rates (s_i^p) for $i = 1, ..., 5$ countries, are I(1), except exports, for Japan and Korea which we cannot reject to be I(0) if we use the DF, Φ_2 and Φ_3 statistics, but I(0) is rejected under ADF. As such, we cannot conclude exports to be I(1) or I(0) for these two countries. As a further check, we run the tests on all variables in their first differences and the results (not reported here) indicate that the variables are all stationary (that is, I(0)) in their first differences.

Table 4.1 DF–ADF unit root: Singapore, Malaysia, Japan, Thailand and Korea, 1973(1)–1996(4)

Country	DF	ADF	Φ_2	Φ_3
Exports				
Singapore	−2.939	−2.429	*15.881	*5.137
Malaysia	−2.712	−1.881	*10.490	3.872
Japan	*−3.563	−1.362	*7.516	*8.513
Thailand	−2.826	−2.054	*5.757	*3.994
Korea	*−4.696	−2.047	4.397	*11.838
Basket real exchange rates				
Singapore	−0.306	−3.111	0.890	*3.850
Malaysia	−2.305	−0.423	2.086	*2.939
Japan	−2.006	−2.531	1.077	2.368
Thailand	−2.631	−3.076	1.352	*3.697
Korea	−2.839	−3.144	0.776	*4.216
PPP real exchange rates				
Singapore	−1.147	−1.378	0.484	0.712
Malaysia	−2.229	−0.378	0.229	2.485
Japan	−1.617	−2.315	0.878	1.637
Thailand	−1.571	−2.106	0.026	1.237
Korea	−1.374	−1.937	0.370	1.124

Notes: The p-value is less than 0.05. The critical value for DF and ADF is −3.458 at 0.05 level of significance.

It is to be pointed out that the Dickey–Fuller unit root tests can be quite sensitive to structural (or regime) changes. Structural breaks will bias the Dickey–Fuller unit root tests (and other classical tests, such as Phillips–Perron, 1988) toward the nonrejection of a unit root. Perron (1989) shows how it is possible to incorporate a known structural change into the tests for unit roots. Caution needs to be exercised since it is always possible to argue that structural change has occurred; each year has something different about it than the previous year. As an extension, Perron and Vogelsang (1992) shows how to test for a unit root when the precise date for structural break is unknown. Furthermore, there is also a substantial literature concerning the power of the classical tests and the presence of the deterministic regressors in the estimating equations (see Leamer, 1986; Zellner, 1988). As Sims (1988) demonstrates, an alternative is to take a Bayesian approach and avoid specific hypothesis testing altogether.

For our purpose, we check the time-series plots of our data, but can see nothing in the form of any structural breaks. Nevertheless, we employ the Bayesian approach – the Sims test as a measure of a stronger type of unit root tests. This test is based on Bayesian posterior odds ratios given by a weighted average of the likelihood function over all points consistent with the null hypothesis, divided by a similar function for the alternative hypothesis, with weights derived from the prior distribution of the parameters. Thus the Sims test is different from the classical tests and is arguably a better test for the presence of unit roots in economic time series (Whitt, 1992; also see Manzur and Ariff 1995 for an application).

Using all the series in levels, we run Bayesian tests in RATS 4.31 with alpha = 0.8 (as suggested by Sims) where alpha is the prior probability on the stationary values of the autoregressive coefficient. The results from the procedure is given in Table 4.2. The first is the t-squared which is used as the test statistic. The 'Schwarz limit' and the 'Small sample limit' are the asymptotic and small sample Bayesian 'critical valucs' for the test statistic. The 'marginal alpha' is the value of alpha at which the posterior odds for and against the unit root are even. A small value indicates that the data evidence is strongly against the unit-root hypothesis. As can be seen, the test statistic falls between the Schwarz limit and the small sample limit for all the variables. Thus the test fails to reject the unit-root hypothesis for the large sample. However, the basket exchange rate result for Japan does not seem to be very strong, which is consistent with our DF–ADF results in Table 4.1.

The next step is to estimate the cointegrating parameter in the following equation:

$$x_{it} = \alpha + \beta \, s_{it}^j + e_t \qquad j = r, p, \tag{4.5}$$

where x_{it} is exports, s_{it}^r, is the basket real exchange rate and s_{it}^p, is PPP real exchange rate for country i. The most common tests for stationarity of estimated residuals are Cointegrating Regression Dickey–Fuller (CRDF) and Augmented Dickey–Fuller (CRADF) tests which are based on the OLS regression

$$\Delta \hat{e}_t = \gamma \, {}_{i=1}^p \hat{e}_{t-1} + \sum \gamma_1 \Delta \hat{e}_{t-i} + \xi_t, \tag{4.6}$$

where $\hat{e}_t$ are residuals from the cointegrating regression and p is chosen to achieve empirical white noise residuals. The null hypothesis of noncointegration is rejected if the t-ratio is less than the relevant critical value.

The results of cointegration tests based on equations (4.5) and (4.6) are given in Table 4.3. As can be seen, exports and basket real exchange rates are cointegrated except for Japan. The Japanese result may stem from our unit root results in Tables 4.2 and 4.3.

Table 4.2 Sims unit root tests: Singapore, Malaysia, Japan, Thailand and Korea, 1973(1)–1996(4)

Country	Squared t	Schwarz limit	Small sample limit	Marginal alpha
Exports				
Singapore	3.040	9.860	3.863	0.8579
Malaysia	1.289	9.357	3.360	0.9185
Japan	6.112	9.042	3.045	0.4632
Thailand	0.316	8.980	2.984	0.9382
Korea	4.024	8.560	2.563	0.6584
Basket real exchange rates				
Singapore	0.554	7.364	1.367	0.8573
Malaysia	0.023	8.091	2.094	0.9185
Japan	4.029	5.875	−0.122	0.3342
Thailand	0.211	7.527	1.531	0.8855
Korea	0.997	6.742	0.745	0.7791
PPP real exchange rates				
Singapore	1.427	7.030	1.033	0.7666
Malaysia	0.824	7.852	1.856	0.8701
Japan	2.191	7.543	1.546	0.7434
Thailand	1.210	7.526	1.529	0.8243
Korea	1.958	7.319	1.322	0.7443

Notes: See text for definition.

However, we reject exports and PPP real exchange rates to be cointegrated for all the five countries. Consequently, the results for the cointegration regression relation between exports and PPP real exchange rates cannot be used (see Granger and Newbold, 1974). Similarly, the cointegration regression relation between exports and basket real exchange rates cannot be used for Japan. This also can explain why its R^2 value is quite small.[5]

The cointegration results reported are based on Engle and Granger (1987). Although this procedure is easily implemented, it may have several important defects (see, for example, Stock, 1987; Johansen, 1988; Stock and Watson, 1988). Fortunately, several methods have been developed that avoid the problems inherent in the Engle and Granger procedure. For comparison purposes, we now employ the Johansen (1991) procedure, based on Johansen and Juselius (1990) which is widely recognised as having good asymptotic properties.

Table 4.3 Engle and Granger cointegration tests: Singapore, Malaysia, Japan, Thailand and Korea, 1973(1)–1996(4)

Country	Model	R^2	CRDF	CRADF
Basket real exchange rates				
Singapore	$x_{1t} = 22.62 + 3.55s^r_{1t}$	0.8421	-3.649^b	-3.423^b
Malaysia	$x_{2t} = 16.34 + 2.19s^r_{2t}$	0.8847	-3.635^b	-2.802
Japan	$x_{3t} = 10.69 - 0.14s^r_{3t}$	0.0006	-2.491	-1.796
Thailand	$x_{4t} = 12.05 - 3.26s^r_{4t}$	0.8921	-3.350^a	-2.703
Korea	$x_{5t} = 0.30 - 3.90s^r_{5t}$	0.6013	-3.290^a	-3.640^b
PPP real exchange rates				
Singapore	$x_{1t} = 8.11 + 1.14s^p_{1t}$	0.0137	-1.485	0.612
Malaysia	$x_{2t} = 4.87 + 4.46s^p_{2t}$	0.6985	-2.371	-1.819
Japan	$x_{3t} = 22.58 - 2.36s^p_{3t}$	0.6406	-1.755	-2.624
Thailand	$x_{4t} = -11.23 + 6.06s^p_{4t}$	0.3638	-1.261	-1.198
Korea	$x_{5t} = 27.24 - 2.78s^p_{5t}$	0.0765	-1.697	-1.126

Notes:
a The P-value is less than 0.10. The critical value for CRDF and CRADF is –3.090 at 0.10 level of significance.
b The P-value is less than 0.05. The critical value for CRDF and CRADF is –3.403 at 0.05 level of significance. See text for definition of the variables in the model.

Results using the Johansen procedure are reported in Table 4.4 (we use Eviews 3 for this purpose). The test assumes no trend in the series with an intercept in the cointegration relation, and uses four lags in levels. The eigenvalues are presented in the first column, for which the second column gives the LR test statistic:

$$Q_{r=} - T \sum_{i=r+1}^{k} \log(1 - \lambda_i).$$

Table 4.4 Johansen cointegration tests: exports and basket real exchange rates, 1973(1)–1996(4)

Eigenvalue	Likelihood ratio	5% critical value	1% critical value	Hypothesised no of CE(s)
Singapore				
0.2056	21.1211	15.41	20.04	None[b]
0.0045	0.4013	3.76	6.65	At most 1
Malaysia				
0.2719	14.5589	15.41	20.04	None
0.0371	1.5513	3.76	6.65	At most 1
Japan				
0.3832	19.4957	15.41	20.04	None[a]
0.0042	0.1674	3.76	6.65	At most 1
Thailand				
0.2410	24.9452	15.41	20.04	None[b]
0.0014	0.1268	3.76	6.65	At most 1
Korea				
0.3342	17.3731	15.41	20.04	None[a]
0.0168	0.6962	3.76	6.65	At most 1

Notes:
a Denotes rejection of the hypothesis at 5 per cent significance level.
b Denotes rejection of the hypothesis at 1 per cent significance level.

For $r = 0, 1, \ldots, k-1$ where the ith largest eigenvalue λ_i is the so-called trace statistic and is the test of $Hi(r)$ against $Hi(k)$. To determine the number of cointegrating relations r, we can proceed sequentially from $r = 0$ to $r = k-1$ until we fail to reject. The first rows under each country test the hypothesis of no cointegration, and the second rows under each country test the hypothesis of one cointegrating relation. As can be seen, the trace statistic does not reject the hypothesis for all countries at the 1 per cent and 5 per cent levels. For Malaysia, the result is not very strong, but still significant at the 10 per cent level. The results for exports and PPP real exchange rates are reported in Table 4.5. As can be seen, the cointegration relation is decisively rejected for all five countries.

Table 4.5 Johansen cointegration tests: exports and PPP real exchange rates, 1973(1)–1996(4)

Eigenvalue	Likelihood ratio	5% critical value	1% critical value	Hypothesised no of CE(s)
Singapore				
0.0816	8.3661	15.41	20.04	None[b]
0.0048	0.4498	3.76	6.65	At most 1
Malaysia				
0.0283	3.9112	15.41	20.04	None
0.0142	1.2970	3.76	6.65	At most 1
Japan				
0.0822	11.3754	15.41	20.04	None[a]
0.0359	3.3989	3.76	6.65	At most 1
Thailand				
0.0627	6.7708	15.41	20.04	None[b]
0.0104	0.9417	3.76	6.65	At most 1
Korea				
0.0530	7.1870	15.41	20.04	None[b]
0.0225	2.1209	3.76	6.65	At most 1

Notes:
a Denotes rejection of the hypothesis at 5 per cent significance level.
b Denotes rejection of the hypothesis at 1 per cent significance level

As a follow-up of the preceding cointegration results, we now investigate the causal link between basket real exchange rates and exports. This obviously has significant implications as to the discussion of influence of real depreciation on export competitiveness. For our purpose, we use the standard Granger (1969) approach. This approach is based upon the prediction error: X is said to Granger cause Y if Y can be forecast better using past Y and past X than just past Y. The results of the Granger causality tests are reported in Table 4.6. We use a lag length of six. Note that in general it is better to use more rather than fewer lags, since the theory is couched in terms of the relevance of all past information. (We tried alternative lag lengths with very similar results.) The reported F-statistics are the Wald statistics for the joint hypothesis. In Table 4.6, we present the pairwise causality test results for exports and basket real exchange rates. The corresponding results for exports and PPP real exchange rates are also reported in the table in parentheses. As can be seen, for Malaysia and Thailand, we cannot reject the hypothesis that exports do not Granger cause basket real exchange rates but we do reject the hypothesis that basket real exchange rates do not Granger cause exports for all countries. It appears that Granger causality runs both ways between basket real exchange rates and exports for Singapore, Japan and Korea. Interestingly, except for Singapore and Korea, there appears no causality between PPP real exchange rates and exports, and for Singapore and Korea, the causality appears to run one-way from exports to PPP real exchange rates but not the other way. We also employed the alternative routines as suggested by Sims (1972) and the results (not reported here) are very similar.

Table 4.6 Granger causality test: exports, PPP and basket real exchange rates, 1973(1)–1996(4)

Null hypothesis	F-statistics	Probability
Singapore		
B(P) does not Granger cause X	7.8938 (1.4306)	0.0000 (0.2138)
X does not Granger cause B(P)	2.4973 (2.5671)	0.0895 (0.0255)
Malaysia		
B(P) does not Granger cause X	3.1160 (0.8458)	0.0089 (0.5387)
X does not Granger cause B(P)	1.5728 (0.6548)	0.1671 (0.6862)
Japan		
B(P) does not Granger cause X	4.1888 (0.4068)	0.0184 (0.6670)
X does not Granger cause B(P)	1.5894(1.5769)	0.0210 (0.2123)
Thailand		
B(P) does not Granger cause X	2.2764 (1.6503)	0.0452 (0.1459)
X does not Granger cause B(P)	1.5547 (0.5180)	0.1725 (0.7929)
Korea		
B(P) does not Granger cause X	5.9423 (1.7394)	0.0038 (0.1231)
X does not Granger cause B(P)	5.4393 (5.0711)	0.0060 (0.0020)

Notes: B = Basket real exchange rates, P = PPP real exchange rates, X = exports. Figures in parentheses corresponding to pairwise causality results for PPP real exchange rates and exports.

4.0 CONCLUSION

Among the several indicators of price competitiveness, the use of PPP real exchange rate as an index of international competitiveness is conventional. However, this measure is infected with several measurement problems. In this chapter, we demonstrate a new measure of real exchange rate – the 'basket' approach – which tends to perform better than the PPP measure.

Using the basket approach, the results indicate that all the countries included in this study, on average, experience real depreciation in their currencies over the sample period. This implies that there is an improvement in these nations' export competitiveness. On the other hand, all the countries except Malaysia, on average, experience real appreciation in their currencies under the PPP approach. Thus, under the PPP method, all the countries except Malaysia would have seen deterioration in their price competitiveness. Since the Asian countries have been experiencing excellent growth in exports for the past decades, it follows that the basket approach tends to reflect the change in the real exchange rate better than that based on the PPP approach. In addition, for all countries, the basket measure of real exchange rates tends to be greater in magnitude for the quarterly changes when compared with the PPP measure. This suggests that the PPP real exchange rates may have a tendency to understate the measure of competitiveness for these Asian countries.

This result is interesting and provides support to the well-known Balassa (1964) hypothesis. According to Balassa, productivity growth in the sector producing non-traded goods (or services) is slower than that pertaining to traded goods. This causes the relative price of nontraded goods to be higher in more affluent countries. The result is that the actual value of the currency of an affluent country will be systematically above its PPP level. The results also provide support to the widely held notion that the currencies of the countries under study are overvalued. This notion seems to be a direct result of measuring real exchange rates using PPP.

Note that over a period as long as 1973–1996, there may be a very strong correlation between imports and exports, particularly since both have grown strongly during that period. One might expect, then, that we would obtain similar results if we replaced the export variable with an import variable. This would imply that there is a worsening in the competitiveness of import-competing industries in these nations. This is not, however, consistent with the Balassa effect. One possibility to avoid this problem is to use trade balance data rather than exports. Unfortunately, a clean data set on trade balance for the sample used in this chapter is very difficult to obtain. In future research, it may be useful to revisit the issue with data on trade balance.

ACKNOWLEDGEMENTS

The author is grateful to Larry Sjaastad for constructive comments, and to Alan Wong and Inn–Chau Chee for help.

REFERENCES

Balassa, B. (1964), 'The purchasing power parity: a reappraisal', *Journal of Political Economy*, **72**, pp. 584–596.

Bian, G. and W.K. Wong (1997), 'An alternative approach to estimate regression coefficients', *Journal of Applied Statistical Science*, **6**, pp. 21–4.

Dickey, D. and W. Fuller (1979), 'Distribution of the estimators for autoregressive time series with a unit root', *Journal of the American Statistical Association*, **74**, pp. 427–431.

Dickey, D. and W. Fuller (1981), 'Likelihood ratio statistics for autoregressive time series with unit roots', *Econometrica*, **49**, pp. 1057–1072.

Dwyer, J. (1991), 'Issues in the measurement of Australia's competitiveness', *Supplement to Economic Record*, pp. 53–59.

Engle, R. and C.W.J. Granger (1987), 'Cointegration and error correction: representation, estimation and testing', *Econometrica*, **55**, pp. 251–276.

Granger, C.W.J. (1969), 'Investigating causal relations by econometric models and cross-spectral model', *Econometrica*, **37**, pp. 424–438.

Granger, C.W.J. and P. Newbold (1974), 'Spurious regression in economics', *Journal of Econometrics*, **2**, pp. 111–120.

Leamer, E. (1986), 'A Bayesian analysis of the determinants of inflation', in P.A. Belsey and E. Kuh (eds), *Model Reliability*, Cambridge, MA: MIT Press, pp. 62–89.

Johansen, S. (1988), 'Statistical analysis of cointegration vectors', *Journal of Economic Dynamics and Control*, **12**, pp. 231–254.

Johansen, S. (1991), 'Estimation and hypothesis testing of cointegration vectors in Gaussian vector autoregressive models', *Econometrica*, **59**, pp. 1551–1580.

Johansen, S. and K. Juselius (1990), 'Maximum likelihood estimation and inference on cointegration with application to the demand for money', *Oxford Bulletin of Economics and Statistics*, **52**, pp. 169–209.

Manzur, M. (1990), 'An international comparison of prices and exchange rates: a new test of purchasing power parity', *Journal of International Money and Finance*, **9**, pp. 75–91.

Manzur, M. (1991), 'Purchasing power parity and relative price variability: the missing link?', *Australian Economic Papers*, **30**, pp. 128–147.

Manzur, M. (1993), *Exchange Rates, Prices and World Trade: New Methods, Evidence and Implications*, London and New York: Routledge.

Manzur, M. and M. Ariff (1995), 'Purchasing power parity: new methods and extensions', *Applied Financial Economics*, **5**, pp. 19–26.

Manzur, M., Wong, W.K. and Inn–Chau Chee (1999), 'Measuring international competitiveness: experience from East Asia', **31**, pp. 1383-1391.

Perron, P. (1989), 'The great crash, the oil price shock, and the unit root hypothesis', *Econometrica*, **57**, pp. 1361–1401.

Perron, P. and T. Vogelsang (1992), 'Nonstationary and level shifts with an application to purchasing power parity', *Journal of Business and Economic Statistics*, **10**, pp. 301–320.

Phillips, P. and P. Perron (1988), 'Testing for a unit root in time series', *Biometrika*, **75**, pp. 270–301.

Sjaastad, L.A. (1990), 'Exchange rates and commodity prices: the Australian case', in K. Clements and J. Freebairn (eds), *Exchange Rates and Australian Commodity Exports*, Melbourne and Perth: Centre for Policy Studies, Monash University and Economic Research Centre, The University of Western Australia, pp. 81–147.

Sjaastad, L.A. (1998), 'On exchange rates, nominal and real', *Journal of International Money and Finance*, **17**, pp. 407–439.

Sims, C.A. (1972), 'Money, income and causality', *American Economic Review*, pp. 540–552.

Sims, C.A. (1988), 'Bayesian skepticism on unit root econometrics', *Journal of Economic Dynamics and Control*, **12**, pp. 463–474.

Stock, J. (1987), 'Asymptotic properties of least-squares estimators of cointegrating vectors', *Econometrica*, **55**, pp. 1035–1056.

Stock, J. and M. Watson (1988), 'Testing for common trends', *Journal of the American Statistical Association*, **83**, pp. 1097–1107.

Tiku, M.L. and W.K. Wong (1998), 'Testing for a unit root in an AR(1) model using three and four moment approximations: symmetric distributions', *Communications in Statistics: Simulation and Computation*, **27**, pp. 185–198.

Tiku, M.L., Wong, W.K. and G. Bian (1999), 'Time series models with asymmetric innovations', *Communications in Statistics: Theory and Methods*, **28**, pp. 315–341.

Whitt, J. Jr. (1992), 'The long-run behaviour of the real exchange rate: a reconsideration', *Journal of Money, Credit and Banking*, **24**, pp. 72–82.

Wong, W.K. and R.B. Miller (1990), 'Analysis of ARIMA-noise models with repeated time series', *Journal of Business and Economic Statistics*, **8**, pp. 243–250.

Zellner, A. (1988), 'Bayesian analysis in econometrics', *Journal of Econometrics*, **37**, pp. 27–50.

NOTES

1   This chapter is based on Manzur et al (1999).
2   See Dwyer (1991) for more details on definitions of international competitiveness.
3   See Chapter 2 in this volume for more details on PPP. Also see Manzur (1990) and Manzur and Ariff (1995).
4   Sjaastad (1998) reports that during the 1973:1–1991:4 period, more than two-thirds of the variance in (first-differenced) franc/dollar and franc/mini-ECU PPP real exchange rates changes was measurement error arising from shocks to the US and European price levels

and/or the mini-ECU/dollar exchange rate. He concludes that since these rates are 'real' in name only, they are unreliable for analytical purposes and misleading for macroeconomic policy evaluation.

5   See Wong and Miller (1990), Tiku et al. (1999) and Tiku and Wong (1998) for more information about the property of time series and unit root test, and Bian and Wong (1997) for more information about regression properties.

5. The World Real Interest Rate

Li Lian Ong, Kenneth W. Clements and H.Y. Izan

How do we determine if two regions share the same market? What about two countries which may or may not be neighbours? A useful way of thinking about this problem is to invoke some form of the 'law of one price' whereby regions/countries are part of one market if the prices of relevant commodities/assets are more or less the same once appropriate adjustments have been made. Such adjustments would take into account differing currencies and, possibly, impediments to price equalization which are approximately constant over time. Under this approach, the basic mechanism which equalizes prices is one of arbitrage – agents buy where the price is low and sell where high. A related mechanism which prevents prices within the same market from diverging is expectations. The expectation that pricing anomalies will soon be eliminated can itself rapidly bring about price equalization without any physical movement of goods or assets. Application of these ideas in international finance include the celebrated (but controversial) conditions of purchasing power parity, the link between exchange rates and prices, and the various forms of interest rate parity, the relationship between interest rates and exchange rates.

This chapter deals with a particular version of interest rate parity, namely the equalization of real interest rates in different countries. Such equalization has profound effects. If interest rates in real terms are the same internationally, then the cost of borrowing is independent of where that borrowing occurs and in what currency the loan is denominated. Moreover, the equalization of real rates means that the role of monetary policy within any one country is very much circumscribed; in the limit, monetary policy can only affect domestic interest rates via its influences on the world interest rate. A world with highly mobile capital and integrated financial markets would seem to be not inconsistent with these implications of the equalization of real interest rates.

We begin with a brief review of the basic interest rate parity conditions.

1.0 PARITY CONDITIONS

1.1 Covered Interest Rate Parity

The theory of covered interest rate parity (CIRP) is 'a relationship between the premium (or discount) on a forward contract for foreign exchange and the differential in interest rates on securities that are identical in all respects except for the currency of denomination' (Frenkel and Levich, 1975, p. 337). This theory thus provides a link between domestic and foreign interest rates, and the spot and forward exchange rates. It is synonymous with covered arbitrage of nominal interest rates. When interest rates on comparable securities are used, tests give strong support to covered interest rate parity.[1]

1.2 Uncovered Interest Rate Parity

The uncovered interest rate parity (UIRP) condition entails uncovered arbitrage of nominal interest rates so that the interest differential equals the expected change in the spot exchange rate.[2] If the foreign exchange market is efficient, then the forward rate is an unbiased predictor of the future spot rate ('speculative efficiency', Bilson, 1981). Note that efficiency here means that participants in the foreign exchange market exhibit rational expectations and risk neutrality. CIRP plus speculative efficiency jointly imply UIRP. Uncovered interest parity is contentious and a large body of research has investigated whether or not investors demand a risk premium to compensate for an unhedged exposure to exchange-rate uncertainty. In general, as this research has yielded contradictory results, this issue is still unsettled.[3]

1.3 Real Interest Rate Equality

The final parity condition relates to the equality of inflation-adjusted interest rates in different countries. Like UIRP, this is also an uncovered relationship between interest rates. As shown in Section 2 below, ex ante relative purchasing power parity and UIRP imply real interest rate equality (RIRE). In what follows, we provide a brief overview of previous research on RIRE.

The bilateral tests of Hodrick (1979) on ex ante real interest rates in the US and other OECD countries indicate that the evidence is not inconsistent with the hypothesis of RIRE. Mishkin (1984), in turn, explores the multi-lateral performance of short-term real interest rates in the Euromarket for seven OECD countries. Unlike Hodrick, he is able to decisively reject the hypothesis of equality of real interest rates in these countries. The joint hypothesis of UIRP and ex ante relative PPP is also strongly rejected by Mishkin. Cumby and Obstfeld (1984) carry out tests of UIRP, ex ante relative PPP, as well as bilateral tests of ex ante RIRE between the US and five other OECD countries. With the exception of the US$–Deutsche mark exchange rate, they also reject the hypothesis of UIRP. Furthermore, the expected exchange rate changes appear to be poor and biased predictors of relative inflation rates, thereby calling into question relative PPP. Cumby and Obstfeld also reject real interest rate equality in almost all cases.

Mark (1985) incorporates the effects of taxes into his analysis of RIRE but finds little support for the hypothesis of net-of-tax real rate equality. Similarly, Cumby and Mishkin (1986) find that although a significant positive correlation exists between real interest rate movements in the US and seven major industrialized countries, international linkages are less than complete. They also find no evidence that real rates are more closely linked within Europe than with the US.[4]

Dutton (1993) argues that for the purposes of international comparisons, real interest rates should be defined in terms of traded goods prices alone; as non-traded goods are poorly arbitraged internationally, the prices of these goods should be excluded from the computation of real returns. Consequently, Dutton uses price indices constructed from the traded goods component of the CPI for the major OECD countries to deflate nominal interest rates; her results provide broad support for the equality hypothesis.

In a pioneering study, Gagnon and Unferth (1995) estimate the common component of real interest rates for all major countries, which they interpret as the world real interest rate. Their data consist of real interest rates of nine OECD countries over the 1977–1993 period. The authors argue that their study differs from previous ones in that they: (i) focus on countries and time period with the most liberal domestic and international capital markets; (ii) allow for a constant risk premium across countries; and (iii) treat all countries symmetrically, whereas previous studies focus on bilateral parity relationships between the US and selected partner countries.

Our objective in this study is to illustrate how stochastic index-number methodology (see, for example, Selvanathan and Prasada Rao, 1994) can be used to measure the world real interest rate and test the hypothesis of RIRE. According to the stochastic approach to measuring inflation, each commodity price change is viewed as containing some information about the true (or underlying) rate of inflation, as well as some commodity-specific noise. This leads naturally to a signal-extraction problem of how to combine the noisy prices in such a way so as to yield an estimate of the rate of inflation which possesses some desirable statistical properties. In addition to a point estimate, this approach also leads to a standard error of inflation which, under certain conditions, increases when there is more variability in relative prices. This attractive result agrees with intuition that in times of large changes in relative prices, the meaning of the overall rate of inflation becomes more ambiguous. The availability of this standard error means that confidence intervals can be constructed for the underlying rate of inflation, and other inference procedures can be employed. It seems to us that this type of information would be highly valued by financial markets. It is for these reasons that advocates of the stochastic approach would like to see government agencies publish standard errors for inflation on a routine basis.

This chapter is organized as follows. In Section 2, we demonstrate the conditions under which real interest rates are equalized internationally. Section 3 sets out stochastic index-number methodology. In Section 4, we show how Gagnon and Unferth's (1995) model can be reinterpreted in terms of the stochastic approach. Extensions of the basic idea to deal with differing country sizes, the distinction between traded and non-traded goods, the 'true' real interest rate are contained in Sections 5 and 6. The conclusion follows in Section 7.

2.0 WHEN ARE REAL INTEREST RATES EQUALIZED INTERNATIONALLY?

In this section, we set out sufficient conditions for the equalization of real interest rates internationally. We begin by defining the relative version of PPP, whereby the change in the exchange rate is equal to the inflation differential:

$$\log(S_t/S_{t-1}) = \log(P_t/P_{t-1}) - \log(P_t^* / P_{t-1}^*),$$

where S is the spot exchange rate, and P and $P*$ are the price levels at home and abroad. Let this PPP relationship hold ex ante or in an expected sense.[5] Thus if E_t represents expectations conditional on information available at time t, then for any horizon of k periods,

$$E_t[\log(S_{t+k}/S_t)] = E_t[\log(P_{t+k}/P_t) - \log(P^*_{t+k}/P^*_t)] . \qquad (5.1)$$

In words, the expected depreciation of the exchange rate reflects the expected inflation differential.

Under UIRP, the nominal interest differential between similar k-period bonds denominated in different currencies $(R_{kt} - R^*_{kt})$ must equal the expected change in the exchange rate over the holding period k:

$$R_{kt} - R^*_{kt} = E_t[\log(S_{t+k}/S_t)] , \qquad (5.2)$$

where $R_{kt} = \log(1 + n_{kt})$ and $R^*_{kt} = \log(1 + n^*_{kt})$. The variables n_{kt} and n^*_{kt} represent the k-period nominal interest rates for the domestic country and the foreign country at time t, respectively. Substituting equation (5.2) into equation (5.1), we obtain $R_{kt} - R^*_{kt} = E_t[\log(P_{t+k}/P_t) - \log(P^*_{t+k}/P^*_t)]$, which could also be rearranged as $R_{kt} - E_t[\log(P_{t+k}/P_t)] = R^*_{kt} - E_t[\log(P^*_{t+k}/P^*_t)]$. Accordingly, if we define $r_{kt} \equiv R_{kt} - E_t[\log(P_{t+k}/P_t)]$ and $r^*_{kt} \equiv R^*_{kt} - E_t[\log(P^*_{t+k}/P^*_t)]$ as the domestic and foreign ex ante real rate, we have the result that

$$r_{kt} = r^*_{kt} .$$

Thus under ex ante relative PPP and URIP, ex ante real interest rates are equalized internationally.

3.0 INDEX NUMBERS AS MEANS

Government agencies typically measure inflation by collecting data on individual prices and then combining those in the form of some index-number formula. This approach is deterministic as it involves no uncertainty, the result being that the inflation rate 'is what it is' – no more, no less.

An alternative approach is to view inflation as a signal-extraction problem, so that the individual prices contain information on the underlying rate of inflation, but this information is contaminated with 'noise'. The problem then becomes how to combine the individual prices so that the effects of noise are minimized. The solution involves some form of averaging of the prices.

Under certain conditions, these averages coincide with popular index-number formulae used in the conventional approach. Although they are familiar, these measures of inflation have very different foundations from those employed by government agencies. The foundations are statistical, so that uncertainty plays a prominent and explicit role. For example, not only do we obtain a point estimate of inflation, but also a standard error, so that confidence intervals for the underlying rate of inflation can be constructed. This is known as the stochastic approach to index numbers.

The stochastic approach has recently been rehabilitated by Clements and Izan (1987) and Selvanathan and Prasada Rao (1994).[6] As this will be used later in the chapter to measure the world interest rate, we now set out the elements of this approach to illustrate the principles involved. For convenience, the measurement of inflation will be used here.

3.1   The Basic Idea

Let there be n consumer goods with prices in period t, P_{1t} ,..., P_{nt}, and $p_{it} = (P_{it}/P_{i,t-1})$ let be the ith price for this period in terms of last period's value. Note that $p_{it} = 1 + g_{it}$, with $g_{it} = (P_{it} - P_{i,t-1})/P_{i,t-1}$ the growth rate in the ith price. Consider the following statistical model for the evolution of p_{it}:

$$p_{it} = \gamma_t + \varepsilon_{it}, \qquad (5.3)$$

where γ_t is an unknown parameter and ε_{it} is an error term, such that

$$E[\varepsilon_{it}] = 0, \quad \text{cov}[\varepsilon_{it}, \varepsilon_{jt}] = \sigma_t^2 \delta_{ij}, \qquad (5.4)$$

where δ_{ij} is the Kronecker delta which takes the value 0 if $i \neq j$ and 1 if $i = j$. equation (5.3) holds for $i = 1,..., n$ prices, so the parameter γ_t is interpreted as (one plus) the expected value of the growth rate common to all prices, that is, $E(p_{it}) = 1 + E(g_{it}) = \gamma_t$. In other words, each price increases at the same rate except for a zero-mean random component. Accordingly, γ_t could also be interpreted as the underlying rate of inflation.

The second member of equation (5.4) for $i \neq j$ states that the random components are uncorrelated over commodities. If we take γ_t to the left–hand side of equation (5.3), we obtain $p_{it} - \gamma_t = \varepsilon_{it}$. The left-hand side of this equation is the growth in the ith price relative to the common growth rate, or the growth in the relative price of good i. Accordingly, the error term ε_{it} is the ith relative price change.

Next, consider the n price changes p_{1t} ,..., p_{nt} . Under the assumptions in equation (5.4), the average of these n price changes provide the best linear unbiased estimator (BLUE) of the rate of inflation, γ_t , in equation (5.3):

$$\hat{\gamma}_t = \frac{1}{n}\sum_{i=1}^{n} p_{it} \ .$$

The sampling variance of $\hat{\gamma}_t$ is

$$\text{var}\,\hat{\gamma}_t \ = \ \frac{1}{n}\sigma_t^2,\tag{5.5}$$

where σ_t^2 can be estimated unbiasedly by

$$\hat{\sigma}_t^2 = \frac{1}{n-1}\sum_{i=1}^{n}\left(p_{it} - \hat{\gamma}_t\right)^2 \ .$$

This expression is a measure of the variability in relative prices in that, when relative prices are unchanged, $p_{it} = \hat{\gamma}_t\,(i = 1 ,..., n)$ and $\hat{\sigma}_t^2 = 0$; and when there is greater change in relative prices, $\hat{\sigma}_t^2$ increases.

The above perspective on the measurement of inflation illustrates the intuitive result that when there is more dispersion in relative prices, it is more difficult to obtain a precise estimate of the underlying rate of inflation. The sampling variance expression in equation (5.5) increases with relative price variability, and thus provides a natural formalization of intuition.

3.2 The Weighted Case

The preceding approach can be improved upon by attributing more weight to those commodities which are more important in the consumer's budget. Let $q_{i,t-1}$ be the quantity demanded of good i in period $t - 1$, so that $P_{i,t-1}\,q_{i,t-1}$ is the expenditure on i and $M_{t-1} = \sum_{i=1}^{n} P_{i,t-1}q_{i,t-1}$ is the total expenditure on all goods. Consequently, $w_{i,t-1} = \left(P_{i,t-1}q_{i,t-1}\right)/M_{t-1}$ is the share of total expenditure devoted to i, or the budget share of good i.

We replace equation (5.4) with

$$E[\varepsilon_{it}] = 0, \quad cov[\varepsilon_{it}, \varepsilon_{jt}] = \frac{\lambda_t^2}{w_{i,t-1}} \delta_{ij}, \tag{5.6}$$

where λ_t^2 is a constant with respect to commodities. Thus, the variance of the relative price of i is $\lambda_t^2 / w_{i,t-1}$ and is inversely proportional to $w_{i,t-1}$. This means that the variability of a relative price falls as the commodity becomes more important in the consumer's budget. Clements and Izan (1987) justify this assumption on the basis that as a commodity becomes more important in the overall economy, there is less scope for its relative price to change.

Equation (5.6) means that generalized least squares (LS) is appropriate, which we shall implement in the form of weighted LS. We multiply both sides of equation (5.3) by $\sqrt{w_{i,t-1}}$ to give

$$y_{it} = \gamma_t x_{i,t-1} + u_{it}, \tag{5.7}$$

where $y_{it} = p_{it}\sqrt{w_{i,t-1}}$, $x_{i,t-1} = \sqrt{w_{i,t-1}}$ and $u_{it} = \varepsilon_{it}\sqrt{w_{i,t-1}}$.

It follows from equation (5.6) that

$$cov[u_{it}, u_{jt}] = w_{i,t-1}cov[\varepsilon_{it}, \varepsilon_{jt}] = \lambda_t^2\delta_{ij},$$

so that $var[u_{it}] = \lambda_t^2$, which is common for all commodities. Under the stated assumptions, we can thus apply LS to equation (5.7) to obtain the BLUE of γ_t:

$$\hat{\gamma}_t = \frac{\sum_{i=1}^{n} y_{it} x_{i,t-1}}{\sum_{i=1}^{n} x_{i,t-1}^2} = \sum_{i=1}^{n} w_{i,t-1} p_{it}. \tag{5.8}$$

where the second step follows from $\sum_{i=1}^{n} x_{i,t-1}^2 = \sum_{i=1}^{n} w_{i,t-1} = 1$. Equation (5.8) is a Laspeyres' price index. The variance of $\hat{\gamma}_t$ is given by

$$\text{var}\,\hat{\gamma}_t = \frac{\lambda_t^2}{\sum_{i=1}^{n} x_{i,t-1}^2} = \frac{\lambda_t^2}{\sum_{i=1}^{n} w_{i,t-1}} = \lambda_t^2 \,.$$

An unbiased estimator of λ_t^2 is given by

$$\hat{\lambda}_t^2 = \frac{1}{n-1}\sum_{i=1}^{n}\left(v_{it} - \hat{\gamma}_t x_{i,t-1}\right)^2 = \frac{1}{n-1}\sum_{i=1}^{n} w_{i,t-1}\left(p_{it} - \hat{\gamma}_t\right)^2,$$

which we write as

$$\text{var}\,\hat{\gamma}_t = \frac{\Pi_t}{n-1},$$

where $\Pi_t = \sum_{i=1}^{n} w_{i,t-1}\left(p_{it} - \hat{\gamma}_t\right)^2$ is a weighted variance of relative price changes.[7] This demonstrates that the variance of the price index $\hat{\gamma}_t$ is proportional to the degree of relative price variability across commodities. Consequently, the same basic result emerges, but in a weighted form.

3.3 Systematic Changes in Relative Prices

In the previous sub-sections, relative price changes are all assumed to be zero on average, that is the error term in equation (5.3), which represents the ith relative price change, has zero expectation. Following Clements and Izan (1987), we now extend our analysis to allow for systematic changes in relative prices.

We redefine p_{it} as the sum of the common trend in all prices, γ_t, a commodity-specific component, β_i, and a zero-mean random component, ζ_{it}:

$$p_{it} = \gamma_t + \beta_i + \zeta_{it}, \quad i = 1, ..., n; \ t = 1, ..., T, \tag{5.9}$$

where T is the number of time periods. As before, γ_t is the underlying rate of inflation. The parameter $\beta_i = E(p_{it} - \gamma_t)$ is the expected change in the ith relative price. We assume that ζ_{it} is independent over commodities and time and that its variance is inversely proportional to the corresponding budget-share:

$$\text{cov}[\zeta_{it}, \zeta_{jt}] = \frac{\eta_t^2}{w_{i,t-1}} \delta_{ij},$$

where η_t^2 is a constant with respect to commodities.

Since any increase in γ_t for each t by any number k and a corresponding decrease in β_i for each i by the same k would not affect the right-hand side of equation (5.9), we need to impose a normalisation in order to identify the model. Clements and Izan (1987) set a budget share–weighted average of the β_i's to zero:

$$\sum_{i=1}^{n} w_{i,t-1} \beta_i = 0. \qquad (5.10)$$

Although there are an infinite number of normalizations equation (5.10) has the attraction of permitting a simple, intuitive interpretation, namely, a budget share–weighted average of the relative price changes is zero.

We proceed as before and multiply both sides of equation (5.9) by $\sqrt{w_{i,t-1}}$ to obtain

$$y_{it} = \gamma_t x_{it} + \beta_i x_{it} + \zeta'_{it} \qquad (5.11)$$

where $\zeta'_{it} = \zeta'_{it} \sqrt{w_{i,t-1}}$. The LS estimators of equation (5.11), constrained by equation (5.10), are

$$\hat{\gamma}_t = \sum_{i=1}^{n} w_{i,t-1} p_{it}, \quad \hat{\beta}_i = \sum_{t=1}^{T} \phi_t (p_{it} - \hat{\gamma}_t) \qquad (5.12)$$

where $\phi_t = (1/\eta_t^2)/\sum_{s=1}^{T}(1/\eta_s^2)$. It is apparent that $\hat{\gamma}_t$ is the Laspeyres' index, as before, while the estimator of the systematic component of the change in the relative price, $\hat{\beta}_i$, is a weighted average of the relative price changes $(p_{it} - \hat{\gamma}_t)$ over all T periods. The weights ϕ_t are inversely proportional to η_t^2, which, in turn, is proportional to the error variance in period t. This means that less weight is accorded to those observations with a higher variance.[8]

The variances of the estimators in equation (5.12) are

$$\text{var }\hat{\gamma}_t = \eta_t^2, \text{ var }\hat{\beta}_i = \frac{1}{\sum\limits_{t=1}^{T}(1/\eta_t^2)}\left(\frac{1}{w_{it-1}}-1\right) \tag{5.13}$$

Here, we see that the variance of $\hat{\gamma}_t$ increases with η_t^2, which, in turn, rises with relative price variability. Therefore, we once again find that the variance of the estimator of overall price index is higher the larger the relative price movements. The variance of $\hat{\beta}_i$ is proportional to the difference between $1/w_{i,t-1}$ and a constant term, which means that this variance increases as $w_{i,t-1}$ falls.[9]

4.0 APPLICATION TO INTEREST RATES

Recall that in equation (5.9) we defined the price relative p_{it} as the sum of the common trend in all prices, γ_t, a commodity-specific component, β_i, and a zero-mean random component, ξ_{it}. Consider a similar model for real interest rates whereby each country's rate is the sum of the common component in all countries' real interest rates, a country-specific component and a zero-mean random component. Accordingly, we replace the commodity subscript i in equation (5.9) with a country subscript $c(c = 1,...,C$ countries) and the price relative p with the real interest rate r :

$$r_{ct} = \gamma_t + \beta_c + \xi_{ct}. \tag{5.14}$$

If we reparameterise β_c as $\mu + \alpha_c$, equation (5.14) then becomes

$$r_{ct} = \gamma_t + \mu + \alpha_c + \xi_{ct}. \tag{5.15}$$

As before, the parameters of equation (5.15) are not identified. Consider the following normalizations:

$$\sum_{c=1}^{C}\alpha_c = 0, \ \sum_{t=1}^{T}\gamma_t = 0. \tag{5.16}$$

This is an alternative to the normalization in equation (5.10). The interpretation of equation (5.15) is as follows. Since r represents the change in a bond price, it is completely analogous to the price relative p, which is defined as $1 + g$, with g the rate of growth of the nominal price in question. The parameters $\mu + \gamma_t$ are the common components in all interest rates in the world, which is analogous to the overall rate of inflation in the case of prices. The parameter α_c is the country effect, which, as countries now play the role of commodities, is analogous to the relative price change before. This country effect tells us whether the interest rate in a particular country deviates from the world rate.

To proceed further, consider a variable x_{ct} ($c = 1,...,C$; $t = 1,...,T$) and let $x_{.t} = (1/C)\sum_{c=1}^{C} x_{ct}$ be the average over the c subscript and $x = (1/T)\sum_{t=1}^{T} x_{.t}$ be the average of x_{ct} over both subscripts. Thus, if we average equation (5.15) over $c = 1,...,C$, we obtain $r_{.t} = \gamma_t + \mu + \zeta_{.t}$, which follows from the first member of normalization equation (5.16). Next, we average the above over $t = 1,..., T$, so that $r = \mu$, which follows from the second member of equation (5.16) and the assumption $E(\zeta_{it}) = 0$. This means that μ is interpreted as the average real interest rate across all countries and time periods. In this sense, μ is the 'world' interest rate.

Gagnon and Unferth (1995) implement equation (5.15) as a dummy variable regression. The parameter γ_t is estimated as the coefficient of a dummy variable that takes the value '1' in period t and '0' in other periods, the parameter μ is the regression constant and α_c is estimated as the coefficient of a dummy variable that takes the value '1' for country c and '0' for other countries.[10] Clearly, Gagnon and Unferth's estimates can be reinterpreted in terms of stochastic index numbers. Gagnon and Unferth's data consist of annual real interest rates for Belgium, Britain, Canada, Denmark, Germany, Holland, Japan, Switzerland and the US, for the period September 1977–December 1993.[11] Thus, $C = 9$ countries and $T = 16$ periods when annual data are used. The authors define the real interest rate r as the nominal interest rate observed in the last month of period $t - 1$ minus the percentage change in the consumer price index from $t - 1$ to t; accordingly, r is an ex post real interest rate. Their results for annual data are given in the left-hand panel of Table 5.1, while Figure 5.1 shows the estimated country effects, α_c, and the world real interest rate in year t, $\mu + \gamma_t$, together with its 95 per cent confidence interval.[12] The right-hand panel of Table 5.1 will be discussed later. We see from the left-hand panel that the country effects for all countries except Britain and Canada are significant. This suggests that there are significant departures of domestic interest rates from the world rate. Thus, these results imply a rejection of the hypothesis of strict RIRE. Panel (B) of Figure 5.1 indicates that the real rate for the world varies substantially over time and the width of the 95 per cent confidence interval averages 1.3

per cent.

*Table 5.1 Estimate of the world interest rate model: annual data,
1978–1993*

Coefficient	Gagnon and Unferth's results			OLS results		
	Estimate	t-stat	% level of sig.	Estimate	t-stat	% level of sig.
Intercept, μ	4.24 (0.08)	53.00	0.1	4.23 (0.14)	30.97	0.10
Country Effects α_c						
Belgium	1.50 (0.24)	6.25	0.00	1.50 (0.39)	3.90	0.10
Britain	0.37 (0.24)	1.54	–	0.38 (0.39)	0.98	–
Canada	0.32 (0.24)	1.33	–	0.33 (0.39)	0.85	–
Denmark	2.07 (0.24)	8.63	0.10	2.08 (0.39)	5.38	0.10
Germany	–0.67 (0.24)	–2.79	1.00	–0.67 (0.39)	–1.73	10.00
Holland	0.47 (0.24)	1.96	10.00	0.48 (0.39)	1.24	–
Japan	–0.98 (0.24)	–4.08	0.10	–0.98 (0.39)	–2.54	5.00
Switzerland	–2.58 (0.24)	–10.75	0.10	–2.64 (0.39)	–6.83	0.10
US	–0.49 (0.24)	–2.04	5.00	–0.49 (0.39)	–1.26	–
Time Effects γ_t						
1978	–2.50 (0.32)	–7.81	0.10	–2.49 (0.53)	–4.71	0.10
1979	–4.60 (0.32)	–14.38	0.10	–4.60 (0.53)	–8.69	0.10
1980	–1.86 (0.32)	–5.81	0.10	–1.85 (0.53)	–3.50	0.10
1981	–0.93 (0.32)	–2.91	1.00	–0.93 (0.53)	–1.75	10.00
1982	2.22 (0.32)	6.94	0.10	2.23 (0.53)	4.21	0.10
1983	0.84 (0.32)	2.63	1.00	0.85 (0.53)	1.60	–
1984	0.60 (0.32)	1.88	10.00	0.61 (0.53)	1.16	–
1985	0.96 (0.32)	3.00	1.00	0.97 (0.53)	1.83	10.00
1986	1.99 (0.32)	6.22	0.10	1.88 (0.53)	3.56	0.10
1987	0.31 (0.32)	0.97	–	0.32 (0.53)	0.61	–
1988	–0.42 (0.32)	–1.31	–	–0.41 (0.53)	–0.78	–
1989	–0.62 (0.32)	–1.94	10.00	–0.62 (0.53)	–1.17	–
1990	0.94 (0.32)	2.94	–	0.95 (0.53)	1.79	10.00
1991	1.63 (0.32)	5.09	0.10	1.64 (0.53)	3.10	1.00
1992	1.37 (0.32)	4.28	0.10	1.37 (0.53)	2.60	1.00
1993	–0.08 (0.32)	–0.25	–	0.08 (0.53)	0.15	–

Notes:

a The coefficient estimates and standard errors are to be divided by 100.

*b The level of significance in the last column shows the probability of incorrectly rejecting
the null hypothesis that the individual country or time effects are not significantly different
from zero. Where '–' is indicated, the null hypothesis cannot be rejected at any level less
than 10 per cent.*

c Standard errors within parentheses.

Exchange Rates, Interest Rates and Commodity Prices

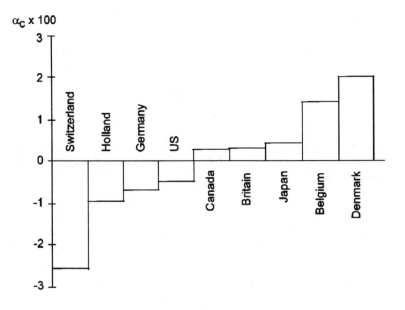

(A) Country effects

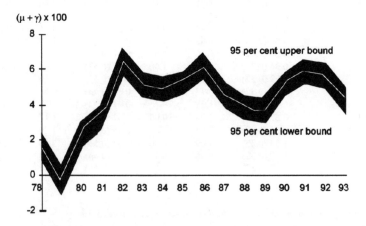

(B) World interest rate and 95 per cent confidence interval

Figure 5.1 Gagon and Unferh's estimates of the world interest rate model: annual data, 1978–1993

Gagnon and Unferth (1995) estimate their model by multivariate LS, with the covariance matrix of the residuals restricted to be scalar. This procedure yields the same coefficient estimates as ordinary least squares (OLS); however, the standard errors are computed differently.[13] As there is no compelling reason to employ multivariate LS, we re-estimate by OLS using the same data for comparison purposes.

We write equation (5.15) as a dummy variable regression:

$$r_{ct} = \mu + \sum_{s=1}^{T} \gamma_s d_{cts} + \sum_{d=1}^{C} \alpha_d z_{ctd} + \zeta_{ct} ,$$

where $d_{cts} = 1$ if $t = s$, 0 otherwise; and $z_{ctd} = 1$ if $c = d$, 0 otherwise. Using constraint equation (5.16) in the form $\alpha_c = -\sum_{c=1}^{C-1} \alpha_c$, $\gamma_T = -\sum_{t=1}^{T-1} \gamma_t$ in the above, we obtain:

$$r_{ct} = \mu + \sum_{s=1}^{T-1} \gamma_s d_{cts} - \left(\sum_{s=1}^{T-1} \gamma_s \right) d_{ctT} + \sum_{d=1}^{C-1} \alpha_d z_{ctd} - \left(\sum_{d=1}^{C-1} \alpha_d \right) z_{ctC} + \zeta_{ct} ,$$

or

$$r_{ct} = \mu + \sum_{s=1}^{T-1} \gamma_s d'_{cts} + \sum_{d=1}^{C-1} \alpha_d z'_{ctd} + \zeta_{ct} , \tag{5.17}$$

where $d'_{cts} = d_{cts} - d_{ctT}$; and $z'_{ctd} = z_{ctd} - z_{ctC}$.

We use Gagnon and Unferth's data to estimate equation (5.17) by OLS and the results are contained in the right-hand panel of Table 5.1. Note that the estimates of the coefficients are virtually identical (as expected), while the standard errors increase so that the country and time effects are less significant. Now we find that the country effects for Holland and the US, in addition to Britain and Canada, are insignificant. However, Gagnon and Unferth's rejection of the strict hypothesis of RIRE still holds, as the α_cs for Belgium, Denmark, Japan and Switzerland are significant.

5.0 A WEIGHTED EXTENSION

The significance of the country effects in Gagnon and Unferth's results imply a rejection of the hypothesis of a common real interest rate for the world. It could, however, be that their result is an artifact of equation (5.17), whereby equal importance is assigned to each country's influence on the world interest rate. In applying unweighted LS to determine the world real interest rate, the same weight is given to interest rates in the US as, say, those of Denmark. Intuitively, we would expect the US, which on average makes up 50 per cent of total GDP and contributes 30 per cent of the total trade of our sample countries, to exert more influence on world interest rates than Denmark, which makes up 1 per cent of GDP and 2 per cent of total trade. Therefore, in this section we explore an alternative approach whereby countries exert differing influences on the world real interest rate, depending on their overall economic influence and integration with the rest of the world. This leads to a weighted world interest rate model which can be regarded as an application of weighted stochastic index-number methodology, as discussed above.

To estimate equation (5.17) by weighted LS, it is appropriate to weight the observations for country c by the square root of some measure of the relative size of that country. The idea is that there is likely to be more variability in the interest rates in smaller countries, just as there is likely to be more variability in the relative price of less important commodities, as discussed in Clements and Izan (1987). Of course, giving less weight to smaller countries in this context can be justified directly without any appeal to the variability of interest rates. Let $w_{c,t-1}$ be a weight for country c (the definition of this weight will be specified subsequently). We then multiply both sides of equation (5.17) by $\sqrt{w_{c,t-1}}$ to yield

$$y_{ct} = \gamma_t x_{ct} + \mu x_{ct} + \alpha_c x_{ct} + \zeta'_{ct} , \qquad (5.18)$$

where $y_{ct} = r_{ct}\sqrt{w_{c,t-1}}$, $x_{ct} = \sqrt{w_{c,t-1}}$ and $\zeta'_{ct} = \zeta_{ct}\sqrt{w_{c,t-1}}$. The corresponding normalizations are

$$\sum_{c=1}^{C}\alpha_c x_{ct} = 0, \quad \sum_{t=1}^{T}\gamma_t x_{ct} = 0 \qquad (5.19)$$

The LS estimators of equation (5.18), constrained by equation (5.19), are the analog of equation (5.12). Similarly, their sampling variances are the analog of equation (5.13) so that the variance of the estimated time component $\hat{\gamma}_t$ increases with real interest rate volatility, while the variance of the country component α_c increases as the country 'size' falls.

We employ two different sets of weights: (i) the share of each country's total trade (exports plus imports) in total world trade; and (ii) the share in world GDP.[14] The trade weighting scheme is used as it measures the degree of integration of the country in question with the world economy, while the GDP weights represent economic influence in terms of the contribution to world income.[15] Our sample countries are Britain, Canada, Denmark, Germany, Japan, Holland and the US.[16] As Belgium and Switzerland are now omitted, we re-estimate the unweighted equation (5.15) for the seven OECD countries. A comparison of Table 5.2 with the right-hand panel of Table 5.1 reveals that the country effects are again significant for Denmark, Germany and Japan, with Britain, Canada, Holland and the US remaining insignificant.

Table 5.2 Estimates of the world interest rate model for seven OECD countries: annual data, 1978–1993

Coefficient	Estimate	t–statistic	% level of significance
Intercept, μ	4.39 (0.17)	26.44	0.10
Country effects, α_c			
Britain	0.22 (0.41)	0.53	–
Canada	0.17 (0.41)	0.41	–
Denmark	1.92 (0.41)	4.71	0.10
Germany	–0.83 (0.41)	–2.04	5.00
Holland	0.32 (0.41)	0.77	–
Japan	–1.14 (0.41)	–2.80	1.00
US	–0.65 (0.41)	–1.59	–
Time effects, γ_t			
1978	–3.06 (0.64)	–4.76	0.10
1979	–4.78 (0.64)	–7.43	0.10
1980	–2.27 (0.64)	–3.53	0.10
1981	–0.78 (0.64)	–1.21	–
1982	2.50 (0.64)	3.89	0.10
1983	1.14 (0.64)	1.78	10.00
1984	0.82 (0.64)	1.28	–
1985	1.11 (0.64)	1.72	10.00
1986	1.87 (0.64)	2.91	1.00
1987	0.31 (0.64)	0.49	–
1988	–0.45 (0.64)	–0.70	–
1989	–0.24 (0.64)	–0.37	–
1990	0.96 (0.64)	1.49	–
1991	1.69 (0.64)	2.63	1.00
1992	1.18 (0.64)	1.83	10.00
1993	0.00 (0.64)	0.00	–

Notes: See notes to Table 5.1.

Table 5.3 Estimates of the weighted world interest rate model: annual data, 1978–1993

Coefficient	Estimate	t-statistic	% level of significance
Weighted by GDP			
Intercept, μ	0.99 (0.07)	15.26	0.10
Country effects, α_c			
Britain	0.93 (0.52)	1.79	10.00
Canada	−0.06 (0.64)	−0.09	–
Denmark	−3.50 (1.08)	−3.23	1.00
Germany	0.75 (0.30)	2.45	5.00
Holland	−1.65 (0.84)	−1.96	10.00
Japan	1.15 (0.32)	3.57	0.10
US	2.37 (0.22)	10.81	0.10
Time effects, γ_t			
1978	−4.29 (0.57)	−7.51	0.10
1979	−5.51 (0.57)	−9.65	0.10
1980	−2.81 (0.57)	−4.92	0.10
1981	1.40 (0.57)	2.46	5.00
1982	4.34 (0.57)	7.60	0.10
1983	1.77 (0.57)	3.09	1.00
1984	1.90 (0.57)	3.32	0.10
1985	1.79 (0.57)	3.14	1.00
1986	2.98 (0.57)	5.21	0.10
1987	−0.85 (0.57)	−1.49	–
1988	−0.26 (0.57)	−0.46	–
1989	0.12 (0.57)	0.22	–
1990	−0.59 (0.57)	−1.03	–
1991	1.37 (0.57)	2.39	5.00
1992	−0.11 (0.57)	−0.19	–
1993	−1.25 (0.57)	−2.18	5.00
Weighted by trade			
Intercept, μ	1.34 (0.07)	20.08	0.10
Country effects, α_c			
Britain	0.76 (0.44)	1.73	10.00
Canada	−0.08 (0.51)	−0.16	–
Denmark	−2.88 (0.83)	−3.47	0.10
Germany	0.74 (0.31)	2.37	5.00
Holland	0.22 (0.50)	0.43	–
Japan	−0.05 (0.38)	−0.12	–
US	1.30 (0.29)	4.41	0.10

Time effects, γ_t

1978	−3.75 (0.62)	−6.07	0.10
1979	−5.14 (0.62)	−8.34	0.10
1980	−2.40 (0.62)	−3.89	0.10
1981	0.27 (0.62)	0.43	−
1982	3.46 (0.62)	5.61	0.10
1983	1.19 (0.62)	1.93	10.00
1984	1.36 (0.62)	2.21	5.00
1985	1.34 (0.62)	2.17	5.00
1986	2.65 (0.62)	4.29	0.10
1987	−0.16 (0.62)	−0.26	−
1988	−0.49 (0.62)	−0.80	−
1989	0.06 (0.62)	0.10	−
1990	0.18 (0.62)	0.29	−
1991	1.50 (0.62)	2.43	5.00
1992	0.64 (0.62)	1.03	−
1993	−0.70 (0.62)	−1.14	−

Notes: See notes to Table 5.1.

We now apply the weighted equation (5.18) to the data for the seven countries. The results for both GDP and trade weights are presented in Table 5.3. The country effects are now significant for Germany, Japan and the US, where GDP weights are used, and significant for Denmark, Germany, Japan and the US when trade weights are applied. It is also interesting to note that the time effects are mostly insignificant for the latter half of the sample for both sets of weights; this same pattern occurred previously. The estimates of the average real rate for the world are quite stable at a little over 4 per cent per annum, whether or not weighting is used. A comparison of the Table 5.3 results with those in Table 5.2 reveals that there is only one major effect of employing country weights – the country effect for the US becomes significant. However, the conclusion from this section must be that weighting countries does not seem to appreciably affect the tests of RIRE.

6.0 FURTHER EXTENSIONS

So far, we have tested for RIRE using annual data. We now re-estimate equation (5.18) using quarterly data to test for the short-term validity of RIRE. In doing so, we find that country effects are similar to those using annual data, that is α_c, for Germany, Japan and the US are significant when GDP weights are used, while those for Denmark, Germany, Japan and the US are significant when trade weighting is applied. The significance of the time effects are similar to the annual estimates.[17]

Table 5.4 Estimates of the world interest rate model for seven OECD countries: annual data deflated by WPI, 1978–1993

Coefficient	Estimate	t-stat	% level of significance
Unweighted			
Intercept, μ	6.13(0.38)	16.07	0.10
Country effects, α_c			
Britain	1.47 (0.93)	1.58	–
Canada	–0.45 (0.93)	–0.48	–
Denmark	1.33 (0.93)	1.43	–
Germany	–1.10 (0.93)	–1.18	–
Holland	0.43 (0.93)	0.46	–
Japan	–0.77 (0.93)	–0.82	–
US	–0.91 (0.93)	–0.98	–
Time effects, γ_t			
1978	–2.71 (1.48)	–1.84	10.00
1979	–12.43 (1.48)	–8.42	0.10
1980	–3.80 (1.48)	–2.57	5.00
1981	–2.93 (1.48)	–1.99	5.00
1982	2.59 (1.48)	1.75	10.00
1983	0.23 (1.48)	0.15	–
1984	–0.65 (1.48)	–0.44	–
1985	4.54 (1.48)	3.08	1.00
1986	8.82 (1.48)	5.98	0.10
1987	–0.28 (1.48)	–0.19	–
1988	–2.46 (1.48)	–1.67	10.00
1989	–1.25 (1.48)	–0.85	–
1990	2.44 (1.48)	1.65	–
1991	5.15 (1.48)	3.49	0.10
1992	1.69 (1.48)	1.14	–
1993	1.06 (1.48)	0.72	–
Weighted by GDP			
Intercept, μ	6.06 (0.62)	9.73	0.10
Country effects, α_c			
Britain	1.47 (1.16)	1.28	–
Canada	–0.43 (1.38)	–0.31	–
Denmark	1.42 (2.72)	0.52	–
Germany	–1.04 (0.66)	–1.57	–
Holland	0.15 (1.85)	0.08	–
Japan	–0.75 (0.85)	–0.89	–
US	–0.83 (0.73)	–1.13	–

Time effects, γ_t

1978	−4.77 (1.23)	−3.86	0.10
1979	−11.08 (1.23)	−8.89	0.10
1980	−3.76 (1.23)	−3.04	1.00
1981	0.76 (0.53)	0.62	–
1982	3.74 (1.23)	3.03	1.00
1983	2.49 (1.23)	2.01	5.00
1984	1.85 (1.23)	1.50	–
1985	3.78 (1.24)	3.06	1.00
1986	6.73 (1.24)	5.45	0.10
1987	−0.64 (1.23)	−0.52	–
1988	−1.37 (1.23)	−1.11	–
1989	−1.70 (1.23)	−1.38	–
1990	−0.16 (1.23)	−0.13	–
1991	3.78 (1.23)	3.07	1.00
1992	0.19 (1.23)	0.15	–
1993	0.17 (1.23)	0.14	–

Weighted by Trade

Intercept, μ	6.12 (0.49)	12.36	0.10

Country effects, α_c

Britain	1.5 (1.00)	1.50	–
Canada	−0.49 (1.16)	−0.42	–
Denmark	1.42 (2.15)	0.66	–
Germany	−1.05 (0.70)	−1.49	–
Holland	0.27 (1.14)	0.23	–
Japan	−0.73 (0.09)	−0.81	–
US	−0.93 (0.75)	−1.24	–

Time effects, γ_t

1978	−3.89 (1.40)	−2.78	1.00
1979	−11.95 (1.40)	−8.56	0.10
1980	−3.33 (1.40)	−2.38	5.00
1981	−1.38 (1.40)	−0.99	–
1982	3.30 (1.40)	2.37	5.00
1983	0.94 (1.40)	0.68	–
1984	0.49 (1.40)	0.35	–
1985	4.07 (1.40)	2.92	1.00
1986	8.00 (1.40)	5.73	0.10
1987	−0.44 (1.40)	−0.32	–
1988	−2.24 (1.40)	−1.60	–
1989	−1.37 (1.40)	−0.98	–
1990	1.36 (1.40)	0.97	–
1991	4.35 (1.40)	3.12	1.00
1992	1.38 (1.40)	0.99	–
1993	0.70 (1.40)	0.50	–

Notes: See notes to Table 5.1.

To determine whether capital market intervention affects interest rate equalization, we extend the sample to include countries that have more restricted capital markets, namely, Austria, France, Italy, Norway and Sweden (OECD, 1990). Surprisingly, we find that all five 'restricted' countries generally do not have significant country effects, except for France when trade weights are used.[18] The country effects for the 'unrestricted' economies are similar to earlier estimates, but are now more significant.

We also analyze the effects of using the WPI as an alternative to the CPI to derive real interest rates. Dutton (1993) argues that because the prices of non-traded goods are poorly arbitraged, real interest rates should be defined in terms of the prices of traded goods alone for the purposes of international comparisons. Since the WPI is made up of mainly traded goods, we re-estimate using annual real interest rates defined in terms of the WPI for the seven OECD countries with free capital markets.[19] The results are presented in Table 5.4.

In this table, there are three sets of results: (i) unweighted; (ii) weighted by GDP; and (iii) weighted by trade. Comparing the unweighted results with those obtained with the CPI (Table 5.2), we see that using the WPI has the effect of making all the country coefficients insignificant, whereas in Table 5.2, three of the seven country coefficients are significant.

This means that RIRE now holds, contradicting Gagnon and Unferth's (1995) findings with the CPI. Similar results of insignificant country effects emerge in the unweighted WPI case when we use quarterly data for (i) the seven countries; and (ii) the 12 countries (the additional five have restricted capital markets).[20]

Next, we compare the GDP-weighted results, given in the middle panel of Table 5.4, with those in the left-hand panel of Table 5.3. Since GDP weights are used in both cases, this comparison involves only the WPI (Table 5.4) against the CPI (Table 5.3). The country effects are now insignificant in all cases, while previously, three were significant. We thus conclude that here also the WPI results are more supportive of RIRE.[21] Finally, regarding the trade weights, we compare the results in the far right-hand panel of Table 5.4 with those in the right panel of Table 5.3. As can be seen, the effect of moving from the CPI to the WPI is to reduce the number of significant country coefficients from four to none.[22]

The main finding thus far is as follows. When real rates are defined in terms of the WPI, which excludes many goods that do not enter into international trade, none of the country effects are significant. In other words, there is now more support for the hypothesis that real rates are equalized internationally. This result seems to hold on both a quarterly and annual basis.

Table 5.5 Estimates of the true real interest rate with relative price changes for seven OECD countries: annual data, 1978–1993

Coefficient	Estimate	t-statistic	% level of significance
Intercept, μ	4.33 (0.19)	22.79	0.10
Country effects, α_c			
Britain	0.18 (0.41)	0.43	–
Canada	0.19 (0.41)	0.46	–
Denmark	1.94 (0.41)	4.76	0.10
Germany	–0.82 (0.41)	–2.01	5.00
Holland	0.31 (0.41)	0.77	–
Japan	–1.15 (0.41)	–2.83	1.00
US	–0.64 (0.41)	–1.57	–
Time effects, γ_t			
1978	–3.07 (0.65)	–4.76	0.10
1979	–4.52 (0.76)	–5.94	0.10
1980	–2.22 (0.65)	–3.42	0.10
1981	–0.71 (0.66)	–1.08	–
1982	2.50 (0.65)	3.87	0.10
1983	1.18 (0.65)	1.82	10.00
1984	0.87 (0.65)	1.34	–
1985	0.99 (0.67)	1.48	–
1986	1.64 (0.74)	2.21	5.00
1987	0.33 (0.65)	0.52	–
1988	–0.39 (0.65)	–0.60	–
1989	–0.20 (0.65)	–0.31	–
1990	0.91 (0.65)	1.39	–
1991	1.57 (0.67)	2.35	5.00
1992	1.16 (0.65)	1.79	10.00
1993	–0.02 (0.65)	–0.04	–
Relative Price Changes, λ	1.03 (0.05)	19.56	0.10

Notes: See notes to Table 5.1.

Consider now a more formal comparison between the CPI and the WPI. Let the 'true' rate of inflation be a weighted average of the growth rates of the CPI and WPI, π^{CPI} and π^{WPI}:

$$\pi = \lambda(\pi^{CPI}) + (1 - \lambda)(\pi^{WPI}),$$

where λ is the weight given to the CPI. The real interest rate in terms of the true deflator (or the 'true' real rate) is then $r = i - \pi$, or $r = i - [\lambda(\pi^{CPI}) + (1 - \lambda)(\pi^{WPI})]$. Alternatively, we could write it as $r = r^{WPI} - \lambda(\pi^{CPI} - \pi^{WPI})$, where $r^{WPI} = i - \pi^{WPI}$ is the real rate defined in terms of the WPI. It then follows that if we use the true real rate, equation (5.15) becomes

$$r_{ct}^{WPI} = \gamma_t + \mu + \alpha_c + \lambda\left(\pi_{ct}^{CPI} - \pi_{ct}^{WPI}\right) + \xi_{ct.} \qquad (5.20)$$

This equation shows that the unknown weight λ can be estimated as a coefficient. Equation (5.20) also reveals that λ has the additional interpretation as the response of the WPI real rate to relative prices, $\partial r^{WPI} / \partial\left(\pi^{CPI} - \pi^{WPI}\right)$, which is reminiscent of the Tobin–Mundell effect.[23]

Estimates of equation (5.20) using annual data are presented in Table 5.5. Interestingly, we find that the results are very similar to those in Table 5.2, where CPI real interest rates are used. The WPI real rate appears highly responsive to relative price changes, with λ insignificantly different from 1. This indicates that the true real rate is very similar to the CPI real rate. Similar results to those using quarterly CPI-deflated interest rates are obtained when we re-estimate equation (5.20) with data for: (i) the seven countries; and (ii) the 12 countries including those with restricted capital markets. For these cases, the estimated CPI weight λ remains high at 0.92 and 0.93, respectively.[24]

We thus conclude that the true rate of inflation is largely based on CPI prices, where 'true' is interpreted in terms of the appropriate deflator for the real interest rate. It appears that while the WPI real rate is equalized internationally, neither the CPI real rate nor the true real rate is equalized. Another interpretation of our results is that the goods and services that enter into the calculation of the CPI are very different from the mainly tradable goods that are used in deriving the WPI.

7.0 SUMMARY AND CONCLUSION

The integration of world capital markets would tend to equalize the cost of borrowing funds, in real terms, across countries. Recent research has investigated the extent to which this in fact occurs, by examining departures of domestic interest rates from those prevailing in the world. While earlier research tests whether pairs of countries have the same interest rates, in a pioneering study, Gagnon and Unferth (1995) introduce a methodology which applies to all major countries simultaneously. Their approach is to regress interest rates across countries and over time on dummy variables for each period and each country. Interest rates in a given country are then said to exhibit departures from the world rate if the coefficient of the dummy variable for that country is significant.

Another recent area of research is what is known as 'stochastic index numbers' (Clements and Izan, 1987; Selvanathan and Prasada Rao, 1994). When applied to prices, the underlying rate of inflation is treated as an unknown parameter to be estimated from the individual price data. Each individual price contains noisy information on the underlying rate of inflation and the effect of the noise is minimized by employing some type of averaging of the individual prices. The attractiveness of this approach is that it leads not only to a point estimate of inflation, but also a standard error. This standard error increases with the degree of relative price variability, which agrees with the intuitive notion that, in some sense, inflation is less well-defined when there is substantial variation in relative prices.

In this chapter, we combine these two areas of research. We show that Gagnon and Unferth's model of real interest rates for the world can be interpreted as an application of the stochastic approach to index numbers. Additionally, we extend their approach by weighting countries to recognize their differing importance in the world economy, in terms of their shares in income and trade. It turns out, however, that weighting per se does not substantially affect the results.

As non-traded goods are poorly arbitraged, it can be argued that for international comparisons, real interest rates should be expressed in terms of traded goods only. We investigated whether our tests are sensitive to the choice of the price index used to deflate nominal interest rates. We used the Wholesale Price Index, which comprises a high proportion of traded goods, as the deflator. In contrast to earlier results which use the CPI, we are unable to reject the hypothesis that real rates are equalized internationally.

ACKNOWLEDGEMENTS

The authors would like to thank Joseph Gagnon for providing the data and for his helpful comments, to Robert Brooks, Richard Levich, Jason Mitchell, and in particular, James Lothian and Anthony Selvaranthan for their helpful suggestions and comments.

REFERENCES

Bilson, J.F.O. (1981), 'The 'speculative efficiency' hypothesis', *Journal of Business*, **54**, pp. 435–451.

Clements, K.W. and H.Y. Izan (1987), 'The measurement of inflation: a stochastic approach', *Journal of Business and Economic Statistics*, **5**, pp. 339–350.

Click, R.W. (1996), 'Contrarian MacParity', *Economics Letters*, **53**, pp. 209–212.

Crompton, P. (1996), *A Reconsideration of the New Stochastic Approach to Index Numbers*, Discussion Paper, No. 96:42, Department of Economics, The University of Western Australia.

Cumby, R.E. (1988), 'Is it risk? Explaining deviations from uncovered interest parity', *Journal of Monetary Economics*, **22**, pp. 279–299.

Cumby, R.E. (1996), *Forecasting Exchange Rates on the Hamburger Standard: What You See is What You Get with McParity*, NBER Working Paper Series, No. 5675, National Bureau of Economic Research.

Cumby, R.E. and F.S. Mishkin (1986), 'The international linkage of real interest rates: the European–US connection', *Journal of International Money and Finance*, **5**, pp. 5–23.

Cumby, R.E. and M. Obstfeld (1984), 'International interest rate and price level linkages under floating exchange rates: a review of recent evidence', in J.F. O'Bilson and R. Marston (eds), *Exchange Rate Theory and Practice*, Chicago: University of Chicago Press, pp. 121–151.

Diewert, W.E. (1995), *On the Stochastic Approach to Index Numbers*, Discussion Paper, No. 95–31, Department of Economics, University of British Columbia, Vancouver.

Domowitz, I. and C. Hakkio (1985), 'Conditional variance and the risk premium in the foreign exchange market', *Journal of International Economics*, **19**, pp. 47–66.

Dooley, M. and P. Isard (1980), 'Capital controls, political risk, and deviations from interest-rate parity', *Journal of Political Economy*, **88**, pp. 370–384.

Dutton, M.M. (1993), 'Real interest rate parity: new measures and tests', *Journal of International Money and Finance*, **12**, pp. 62–77.

Edison, H.J. and B.D. Pauls (1993), 'A re-assessment of the relationship between real exchange rates and real interest rates, 1974–1990', *Journal of Monetary Economics*, **31**, pp. 165–187.

Evans, M.D.D. and K.K. Lewis (1995), 'Do long-term swings in the dollar affect estimates of the risk premium?', *Review of Financial Studies*, **8**, pp. 709–742.

Fama, E.F. (1984), 'Forward and spot exchange rates', *Journal of Monetary Economics*, **14**, pp. 319–338.

Frenkel, J.A. (1982), 'In search of the exchange risk premium: a six currency test assuming mean-variance optimisation', *Journal of International Money and Finance*, **1**, pp. 255–274.

Frenkel, J.A. (1988), 'Recent estimates of time-variation in the conditional variance and in the exchange risk premium', *Journal of International Money and Finance*, **7**, pp. 115–125.

Frenkel, J.A. and R.M. Levich (1975), 'Covered interest arbitrage: unexploited profits?', *Journal of Political Economy*, **83**, pp. 325–338.

Frenkel, J.A. and R.M. Levich (1977), 'Transaction costs and interest arbitrage: tranquil vs. turbulent periods', *Journal of Political Economy*, **85**, pp. 1209–1226.

Frenkel, J.A. and A.K. Rose (1995), 'A panel project on purchasing power parity: mean reversion within and between countries', *Journal of International Economics*, **40**, pp. 209–224.

Gagnon, J.E. and M.D. Unferth (1995), 'Is there a real world interest rate?', *Journal of International Money and Finance*, **14**, pp. 845–855.

Hakkio, C.S. (1984), 'A re-examination of purchasing power parity: a multi-country and multi-period study', *Journal of International Economics*, **17**, pp. 265–277.

Hansen, L.P. and R.J. Hodrick (1983), 'Risk averse speculation in the forward foreign exchange market: an econometric analysis of linear models', in J.A. Frenkel (ed.), *Exchange Rates and International Macroeconomics*, Chicago: University of Chicago Press, pp. 113–142.

Hodrick, R.J. (1979), *Some Evidence on the Equality of Expected Real Interest Rates across Countries*, Working Paper, No. 8, 79–80, Graduate School of Industrial Administration, Carnegie–Mellon University.

Hodrick, R.J. and S. Srivastava (1984), 'An investigation of risk and return in forward foreign exchange', *Journal of International Money and Finance*, **3**, pp. 5–29.

Hsieh, D.A. (1984), 'Tests of rational expectations and no risk premium in forward exchange rates', *Journal of International Economics*, **17**, pp. 173–184.

Lewis, K. (1995), 'Puzzles in international financial markets', in G. Grossman, and K. Rogoff (eds), *Handbook of International Economics*, vol. 3, Amsterdam: North-Holland.

Mark, N.C. (1985), 'Some evidence on the international inequality of real interest rates', *Journal of International Money and Finance*, **4**, pp. 189–208.

Mishkin, F.S. (1984), 'Are real interest rates equal across countries: an empirical investigation of international parity conditions', *Journal of Finance*, **39**, pp. 1345–1357.

Mundell, R.A. (1963), 'Inflation and real interest', *Journal of Political Economy*, **71**, pp. 280–283.

Mussa, M.L. and M. Goldstein, (1993), *The Integration of World Capital Markets. Changing Capital Markets: Implications for Monetary Policy*, Proceedings of the Federal Reserve Bank of Kansas City Symposium, Jackson Hole, pp. 245–313.

OECD, (1990), *Liberalisation of Capital Movements and Financial Services in the OECD Area*, Paris: Organisation for Economic Co-operation and Development.

Ong, L.L. (1997), 'Burgernomics: The economics of the Big Mac standard', *Journal of International Money and Finance*, **16**, pp. 865–878.

Pakko, M.R. and P.S. Pollard (1996), 'For here or to go? Purchasing power parity and the Big Mac', *Federal Reserve Bank of St. Louis Review*, **78**, pp. 3–21.

Piggott, C.A. (1993), 'International interest rate convergence: a survey of the issues and evidence', *Federal Reserve Bank of New York Quarterly Review*, **18**, pp. 24–37.

Pope, P.F. and D.A. Peel (1991), 'Forward foreign exchange rates and risk premia – a reappraisal', *Journal of International Money and Finance*, **10**, pp. 443–456.

Popper, H. (1990), *International Capital Mobility: Direct Evidence from Long-Term Currency Swaps*, International Finance Discussion Paper, No. 386, Board of Governors of the Federal Reserve System.

Rogoff, K. (1996), 'The purchasing power parity puzzle', *Journal of Economic Literature*, **34**, pp. 647–668.

Selvanathan, E.A. and D.S. Prasada Rao (1994), *Index Numbers: A Stochastic Approach*, London: Macmillan.

Selvanathan, E.A., Prasada Rao, D.S. and H.E. Doran (1997), *Estimation of General and Commodity-Specific Rates of Inflation Using Linear Time-Varying Constraints*, paper presented at the Australasian Economic Society Meeting, Melbourne.

Theil, H. (1975), *Theory and Measurement of Consumer Demand*, Two vols. Amsterdam: North-Holland Press.

Tobin, J. (1965), 'Money and economic and economic growth', *Econometrica*, **33**, pp. 671–684.

NOTES

1   See also Frenkel and Levich (1977); Dooley and Isard (1980); Popper (1990) and Mussa and Goldstein (1993).

2   A related concept is real uncovered interest rate parity which links real interest differentials and real exchange rates. See Edison and Pauls (1993) for some recent evidence.

3   Hansen and Hodrick (1983); Fama (1984); Hodrick and Srivastava (1984); Hsieh (1984) and Cumby (1988) find support for the existence of such premia; however, Frenkel (1982) and Domowitz and Hakkio (1985) find otherwise. Pope and Peel (1991) suggest that the foreign exchange market is possibly inefficient, while Evans and Lewis (1995) show that systematic forecast errors can explain some of the deviations from uncovered interest rate parity, which also points in the direction of inefficiency. For surveys, see Frenkel (1988) and Lewis (1995).

4   See Mussa and Goldstein (1993) and Piggott (1993) for further discussions on the convergence of real interest rates.

5   In contrast to older results, recent evidence on PPP is fairly supportive, at least for longer-term horizons (Rogoff, 1996) and especially for hamburgers (Click, 1996; Cumby, 1996; Pakko and Pollard, 1996; Ong, 1997).

6   These authors provide references to previous literature on the subject. See Diewert (1995) for a critical review of the methodology. Other recent contributions to this area include Crompton (1996) and Selvanathan et al. (1997).

7   This variance is closely related to the Divisia variance of prices (Theil, 1975).

8   See Clements and Izan (1987) for details of the derivation of equation (5.12).

9   See Clements and Izan (1987) for details of the derivation of equation (5.13).

10   Another perspective of Gagnon and Unferth's approach is that of a panel regression, whereby data are pooled over countries and time. The panel regression approach has two advantages over pure time-series regressions. It reduces the amount of time-series data required, but still provides sufficient data for powerful tests; moreover, it increases the volatility in the data by exploiting cross-sectional variation (see Hakkio, 1984 and Frenkel and Rose, 1995).

11   These countries are identified by the OECD as having relatively open and unrestricted financial markets (see OECD, 1990).

12 The parameter μ is the overall average real rate and γ^t is the deviation at time t from this average. The standard errors underlying the confidence interval are calculated as the square roots of (var μ + var γ^t) as cov $(\mu, \gamma^t) = 0$.

13 We are grateful to Joseph Gagnon for clarifying these issues, as well as supplying the interest rate and inflation data used in this chapter.

14 GDP and trade data are obtained from the International Financial Statistics of the International Monetary Fund.

15 The two sets of weights reveal some interesting patterns and contrasts. Not surprisingly, we find that the three major economies of the US, Germany and Japan have the highest GDP and trade weights. However, while Japan is second richest in terms of GDP, its trade is less than that of Germany. Also of note is that there is more cross-country dispersion in the GDP shares than in the trade shares. The GDP share for the US increased during the first half of the 1980s, but has since fallen, while the opposite is true for Germany. Japan's share of world GDP has increased since the mid-1980s. Similarly, the US share of total world trade increased during the 1980s, while German trade fell. Japan's trade share increased in the early 1980s, but has remained constant since.

16 We are unable to include the full set of countries used by Gagnon and Unferth (1995) as the data for Belgium and Switzerland are incomplete.

17 These estimates are available on request. Results for the unweighted model with quarterly data show significant country effects for Denmark, Japan and the US, compared to Denmark, Germany and Japan for annual data.

18 Detailed results are available on request.

19 The WPI data are also provided by Joseph Gagnon.

20 Detailed results are available on request.

21 We also use GDP weights and the WPI with (1) quarterly data; and (2) the 12 countries. For (1), the findings are similar with those using annual data, with all country effects being insignificant. For (2), again all country effects are insignificant.

22 We also use trade weights and the WPI with (1) quarterly data; and (2) the 12 countries. As with the GDP weights, we find that all country effects are insignificant in both cases.

23 See Mundell (1963) and Tobin (1965).

24 Detailed results are available on request.

6. Term Structure of Interest Rates: Experience from the G7 Countries

Meher Manzur

The term structure of interest rates refers to interest rates that differ only in their length to maturity. The most durable explanation of the term structure is the expectations theory. This theory states that the expected returns on bonds of different maturities are equalised, or that they differ by constant term premia. According to this theory, the long rates are given by the current and expected short rates, implying that the spread between long rates and short rates reflects the market's forecast of changes in short rates.

Interest in the term structure is historical. The reason is that an understanding of what drives the term structure is central to understanding monetary policy and its transmission mechanism. The topic has attracted increased interest in recent times due to its close link with the valuation of interest rate derivatives. Unfortunately, the determinants of the term structure remain poorly understood. Existing literature on this topic provides mixed evidence. A vast majority of previous studies indicate that the term structure contains no useful information in predicting short term interest rates, a finding that may result from substantial fluctuations in the term premium for long term bonds (see, for example, Shiller *et al*, 1983; Mankiw and Summers, 1984). More recent research using more formal tests now favours a different view. It shows that the term structure contains information for the very short run and the long run, but is not reliable at predicting movements of interest rates over the intermediate term, the time in between (see, for example, Fama, 1984; Fama and Bliss, 1987; Stambaugh, 1988; Froot, 1989; Campbell and Shiller, 1991). Thus, the evidence is still far from conclusive and clear-cut. The whole area needs a new way of thinking about the issues and this study is an attempt in that direction.[1]

The purpose of this chapter is to re-examine the various forms of expectations theory of the term structure of interest rates in a multi-country context, using data from the Group of Seven (G7) countries. Given the G7 countries comprises world's major economies, an examination of the interest rate behaviour in these countries is expected to provide a basis for a general explanation of the term structure. Furthermore, ever-increasing integration of financial markets and massive flow of capital across countries imply a closer interaction of interest rates and exchange rates. Consequently, the basic factors driving the interest and exchange rate movements – government policy, cyclical factors, inflation and other market forces – all have important international dimensions. From this perspective, a multi-country approach could be promising.

The chapter is organised as follows. Section 2 discusses the methodology employed in this chapter. Data and some preliminary analyses are contained in Section 3, followed by empirical results in Section 4. In Section 5, further analyses are carried out in an attempt to explain the existence and variation of the term premium. Finally, Section 6 presents a few concluding comments.

1.0 METHODOLOGY

There are a number of different approaches that can be used to test the validity of the expectations hypothesis. See Nelson (1979) for a brief review of literature on this. For our purpose, we use the simplest and most common version. This version postulates that the holding period returns on securities that differ only in their terms to maturity are the same, after allowing for a constant term premium. Under this hypothesis, the current yield spread should predict the expected change in both long and short rates, such that they are positively related.

We denote the short-term and long-term interest rate as r_t and R_t, respectively. Here, r_t is the one-period yield on a short-term money instrument, such as the 3-month Treasury bill rate. This yield is considered as a one-period yield maturing over three months. R_t is the yield on a coupon-paying, long-term government bond, which is defined as the discount rate at which the present value of the coupon payments and the terminal value of the bond equates the price of the said bond.

The long-term government bond can be approximated by a consol, that is, an infinite-life security paying fixed coupons every period, as used in Mankiw (1986). This facilitates the calculation of the holding return of the long-term bond between period t and the next, denoted by H_t. This holding period return is calculated by:

$$H_t = \frac{P_{t+1} - P_t + C}{P_t} \tag{6.1}$$

where P_t and P_{t+1} are the price of the consol at period t and $t+1$, respectively, and C is the coupon payments received each period. Given the price of an infinite coupon-paying instrument to be $P_t = C/R_t$, substituting this relationship into equation (6.1) yields:

$$H_t = R_t - \left(\frac{R_{t+1} - R_t}{R_{t+1}} \right) \tag{6.2}$$

Given this holding period return of the long bond, the excess holding return between the long and short bonds is $E_t = H_t - R_t$, where E_t denotes the excess holding return. Another variable of interest in this study is the yield spread, denoted by Y_t, and defined as the long rate minus the short rate, or $Y_t = R_t - r_t$. When the spread is positive, this means that the yield curve is upward sloping as the long rate exceeds the short rate. The change in the short and long rate is simply their first differences.

1.1   Testing Expectations Hypothesis: Forecasting Excess Returns

The expectations hypothesis of the term structure requires the term premium, defined as the expected difference between the holding return on a long bond and the holding return on the short-term instrument, to be constant through time. The term premium is thus defined as the expected excess holding period return, or $\theta \equiv E_t (H_t - r_t)$, conditional upon the information available at time t. This premium represents the extra return expected for holding the long bond rather than the short-term instrument. This can be expressed in terms of yields of equation (6.2) and becomes:

$$R_t - r_t \equiv \left(\frac{E_t R_{t+1} - R_t}{E_t R_{t+1}} \right) + \theta_t \tag{6.3}$$

where the yield spread is seen here as reflecting both expected change in the long rate plus the term premium. Removing the expectation from equation (6.33), the excess holding return can now be written as the sum of the term premium and an expectation error, or

$$H_t - r_t \equiv \theta + v_{t+1} \tag{6.4}$$

where θ is the constant term premium and v_{t+1} is the expectations error. The expectation error is the difference between the actual and expected returns on the long bond; it represents the 'news' about the long rate, and forms the unanticipated component of the excess holding return (see Mankiw, 1986).

To make this hypothesis operational, one can invoke that expectations are rational, that is, the expectation error is not forecastable with currently available information (see Mankiw, 1986). This implies that the excess holding return, or $H_t - r_t \equiv \theta + v_{t+1}$ is not forecastable using variables known at time t. Given this joint hypothesis, one can employ a generic test for the expectations theory by regressing the excess return on any variable (X_t) known at time t with the regression model:

$$H_t - r_t = \alpha + \beta X_t + v_{t+1} \tag{6.5}$$

and tests the null hypothesis that $\beta = 0$ for expectations hypothesis to hold. If $\alpha = 0$ is also statistically significant, we can further deduce that the result points to the pure form of expectations hypothesis with no term premium. In what follows, the possible candidates to replace X_t in equation (6.5) will be discussed.

An obvious candidate to replace X_t in equation (6.5) would be the lagged values of the excess return. The reason is that lagged values of the expectations error, v_{t+1} are known at time t, the excess return should be serially uncorrelated under the expectations theory. This requirement implies that the currently available information cannot be utilised to forecast excess returns (see Mankiw, 1986). One way to test this implication is to check for serial correlation in the excess return. For expectations hypothesis to hold, the estimated autocorrelations should not be significant.

Another variable to consider for equation (6.5) is the yield spread. The reason is that the spread between the long and the short rate reflects both the expected change in the long rate and the term premium. Recall from equation (6.3), that the spread $(R_t - r_t)$ is a constant risk premium, plus an optimal forecast of changes in future interest rates. Consequently, the yield spread can be used to replace X_t in equation (6.5). Thus, the regression model for this test is:

$$H_t - r_t = \alpha + \beta (R_t - r_t) + \varepsilon_{t+1} \tag{6.6}$$

Under expectations hypothesis, the spread would have a predicted coefficient of zero, such that the yield spread should not forecast the excess return using information available at time t.

1.2   Testing Expectations Hypothesis: The Predictive Power of the Spread

This type of test for expectations theory centres on the use of yield spread between the long and short rate (or the yield curve) to forecast the change in subsequent long or short rates. A standard test of this phenomenon is to regress the change in long or short rate on the yield spread to see if the spread accurately predicts changes in their respective subsequent rate.

As discussed earlier, a rise in the long rate relative to the short rate implies the expectation of higher short rates in the future, according to the expectations hypothesis. Thus, if the market makes correct predictions on average, future short rates would subsequently tend to rise, generating a positive correlation of the change in short rates with the earlier spread. This idea is tested by regressing the change in the one period ahead short rate on the yield spread, or

$$r_{t+1} - r_t = \alpha + \beta(R_t - r_t) + \varepsilon_{t+1} \qquad (6.7)$$

and test whether $\beta > 0$. However, Mankiw (1986) noted that test of the null hypothesis does not follow exactly from the theory, as the short rate need not rise in the immediate succeeding period. Nevertheless, if the coefficient for the yield spread, or β, is positive and significant, one could argue that expectations theory holds. By the same token, we can regress the change of long rate on the yield spread and see if these two variables are positively correlated.

2.0 DATA AND PRELIMINARY ANALYSIS

We use quarterly observations for the G7 countries, namely, the United States, Japan, the United Kingdom, Germany, France, Canada and Italy for the period 1975(3) to 1998(4). The idea is to focus on the recent flexible exchange rate regime. All data are from Datastream International database. The short rate is the 3-months Treasury bill rates of the countries under study, while the long rate is the yield on their respective long-term government bond. For the Japanese series, we use the discount rate as a proxy for the T-bill rate, as the 3-months T-bills are only issued by the Bank of Japan as recent as September 1989. A more detailed description and listing of the data is contained in a separate appendix available upon request.

2.1 Preliminary Analysis

As this study focuses on the multi-country experience, a natural starting point is to examine the correlation of the various series across the G7 countries. The cross-country correlation coefficients of various bond yield measures are given in Table 6.1. As can be seen, the levels of the short rates are reasonably correlated across the seven countries (with all correlation coefficients above 0.5), but not so for their quarterly change. A notable exception is the correlation between the US and Canada, which has a correlation coefficient of 0.72.

The change in the short rate is a better indication of interest rate movement across countries. As can be seen, the observed correlations are poor, implying that there was substantial independence in the rate movements across G7 countries. The cross-country correlations of the excess holding returns and the yield spreads also exhibit substantial independent variation. The exceptions are the US–Canada and Germany–France correlation coefficients both falling in the region of their lower 7th decile. This may not be surprising as these two pairs of countries are historically closely linked to each other.

Table 6.2 presents the means and standard deviations of various interest rate measures of the G7 countries. As can be observed, the yield spread is positive for all countries indicating that the yield curves are generally upward sloping (as long rates typically exceed their short rates). However, these series exhibit substantial volatility, with standard deviation of the yield spread exceeding 1 per cent for all countries, except Japan. The mean figures for the change in short and long rates are all negative, indicating a downward trend in the rates across all countries. The positive means of the excess returns for all countries indicate that the long bonds outperformed the short-term securities (to a varying degree from less than 1 per cent to 2.06 per cent), although only by a very small magnitude in Italy.

2.2 Test of Stationarity

We run a series of tests of stationarity of the data. The standard Augmented Dicky–Fuller and the Bayesian Sims tests produced mixed results (not reported here).

Table 6.1 Correlation matrix of bond yield measures: G7 countries, 1975(3)–1998(4)

Country	US	Japan	UK	Germany	France	Canada	Italy
Short Rate							
US	1						
Japan	0.575	1					
UK	0.669	0.755	1				
Germany	0.509	0.634	0.571	1			
France	0.689	0.762	0.629	0.766	1		
Canada	0.883	0.707	0.809	0.672	0.811	1	
Italy	0.573	0.755	0.563	0.645	0.886	0.703	1
Change In Short Rate							
US	1						
Japan	0.146	1					
UK	0.153	0.290	1				
Germany	0.318	0.371	0.304	1			
France	0.248	0.242	0.209	0.503	1		
Canada	0.720	0.127	0.239	0.515	0.391	1	
Italy	0.075	0.028	0.197	0.211	0.290	0.171	1
Excess Holding Return							
US	1						
Japan	−0.069	1					
UK	0.160	0.549	1				
Germany	0.099	0.345	0.360	1			
France	−0.099	0.202	0.249	0.664	1		
Canada	0.719	0.138	0.452	0.351	0.285	1	
Italy	−0.198	0.344	0.345	−0.015	0.232	0.151	1
Yield Spread							
US	1						
Japan	−0.077	1					
UK	0.163	0.558	1				
Germany	0.091	0.350	0.361	1			
France	−0.118	0.182	0.241	0.661	1		
Canada	0.720	0.113	0.450	0.342	0.271	1	
Italy	−0.212	0.334	0.333	−0.021	0.229	0.138	1

As a final check, we employ the test introduced by Im *et al.* (1997) (IPS henceforth). This test involves reordering of seven countries into a set that could be considered as a panel. The main advantage of the use of panels in the context of unit root and cointegration tests is the considerable improvement in the power of this test. This test has the advantage of allowing for different parameter estimates and autocorrelation structures amongst the various series across the panel. However, Hansen and King (1998), among others, raise some concerns about this approach.

Table 6.2 Summary statistics of bond yield measures: G7 countries, 1975(3)–1998(4)

	US	Japan	UK	Germany	France	Canada	Italy
Short Rate	6.95	3.89	9.70	5.61	8.97	8.97	12.65
	(2.81)	(2.18)	(3.03)	(2.04)	(3.22)	(3.50)	(3.91)
Change in Short Rate	−0.02	−0.08	−0.04	−0.02	−0.04	−0.03	−0.08
	(0.93)	(0.52)	(1.16)	(0.58)	(0.95)	(1.19)	(1.55)
Long Rate	8.61	5.91	10.53	7.27	9.59	9.91	12.71
	(2.03)	(2.13)	(2.48)	(1.27)	(2.86)	(2.32)	(3.79)
Change in Long Rate	−0.02	−0.08	−0.09	−0.05	−0.06	−0.05	−0.08
	(0.54)	(0.49)	(0.76)	(0.40)	(0.55)	(0.66)	(0.80)
Excess Holding Return	1.67	2.06	0.87	1.68	0.63	0.95	0.06
	(1.52)	(0.78)	(1.97)	(1.14)	(1.25)	(1.80)	(1.87)
Yield Spread	1.66	2.02	0.83	1.66	0.62	0.93	0.06
	(1.50)	(0.78)	(1.98)	(1.14)	(1.24)	(1.77)	(1.85)

Notes: Standard deviations are shown in parentheses.

The IPS panel test statistic is constructed from the average ADF t-statistics, or

$$\bar{t}_{NT} = \left(\frac{1}{N}\right)\sum_{i=1}^{N} t_{iT} \qquad (6.9)$$

where t_{iT} is the ADF t-statistic from country i. IPS show that $\bar{t}_{NT}$ is normally distributed under the null hypothesis, and they provide Monte Carlo estimates of its mean and variance. These values can be used to convert $\bar{t}_{NT}$ into a standard normal ψ_i statistic that can be compared against conventional critical values. The test statistic is thus revised to:

$$\psi_i = \frac{\sqrt{N}\left\{\bar{t}_{NT} - \frac{1}{N}\sum_{i=1}^{N} E\left[t_{iT}(p_i,0)\right]\right\}}{\sqrt{\frac{1}{N}\sum_{i=1}^{N} Var\left[t_{iT}(p_i,0)\right]}} \qquad (6.10)$$

where N is the number of panels (countries), $\bar{t}_{NT}$ is the average ADF t-statistic in equation (6.9), and values for $E\left[t_{iT}(p_i,0)\right]$ and $Var\left[t_{iT}(p_i,0)\right]$ are obtained from the results of the Monte Carlo simulation carried out by IPS.

Table 6.3 presents the test statistics and their t-distribution critical values (at 5 per cent confidence interval) of the series tested. Thus the null hypothesis that a series is non-stationary can be rejected if the test statistic exceeds the critical value. The results indicate that all variables except the long rate in the regression models in Section 2 are stationary. However, the long rate in its first difference was found to be stationary.

Table 6.3 IPS panel tests for unit roots: G7 countries, 1975(3)–1998(4)

Series	Ψ_i Statistics	T-distribution C.V. (5%)	Series Stationary?
R_t	−0.54	1.99	No
r_t	−2.74	1.99	Yes
$R_{t+1} - R_t$	−5.09	1.99	Yes
$r_{t+1} - r_t$	−6.37	1.99	Yes
$H_t - r_t$	−2.86	1.99	Yes
$R_t - r_t$	−3.46	1.99	Yes

3.0 EMPIRICAL RESULTS

As discussed in Section 2, the first test was the regression of excess return on its lagged values. The excess return should be serially uncorrelated under the expectations hypothesis. Table 6.4 gives the first five autocorrelations. The results indicate that the first five autocorrelations of excess holding return are significant for all countries. Thus, this test appears to reject the expectation hypothesis.

We now estimate equation (6.6) using OLS, and the results are given in Table 6.5.

Table 6.4 Autocorrelations of excess holding returns: G7 countries,
1975(3)–1998(4)

Lag	USA	Japan	UK	Germany	France	Canada	Italy
1	0.89	0.68	0.91	0.93	0.79	0.86	0.69
	(0.00)	(0.00)	(0.00)	(0.00)	(0.00)	(0.00)	(0.00)
2	0.75	0.47	0.77	0.82	0.55	0.70	0.42
	(0.00)	(0.00)	(0.00)	(0.00)	(0.00)	(0.00)	(0.00)
3	0.68	0.32	0.62	0.70	0.41	0.58	0.31
	(0.00)	(0.00)	(0.00)	(0.00)	(0.00)	(0.00)	(0.00)
4	0.60	0.16	0.49	0.57	0.32	0.46	0.25
	(0.00)	(0.00)	(0.00)	(0.00)	(0.00)	(0.00)	(0.00)
5	0.53	0.02	0.38	0.45	0.24	0.37	0.09
	(0.00)	(0.00)	(0.00)	(0.00)	(0.00)	(0.00)	(0.00)

Notes: Figures in parenthesis are the significance level for the Ljung–Box Q-statistic.

As can be seen, the coefficients for the yield spread are very close to 1 for all countries. This is inconsistent with expectations theory. The results indicate that the spread between the long and short rate appears to be able to predict the excess holding return on the long-term bond.

Table 6.5 Regression of excess holding return on the yield spread: G7 countries, 1975(3)–1998(4)

Independent Variables	USA[a]	Japan	UK	Germany[a]	France[a]	Canada	Italy[a]
Constant[b]	−0.007	0.028	0.015	0.019	0.007	0.002	0.014
	(0.011)	(0.030)	(0.008)	(0.015)	(0.011)	(0.007)	(0.012)
Yield Spread[b]	1.007	0.999	0.998	0.994	1.006	1.007	1.010
	(0.005)	(0.014)	(0.004)	(0.007)	(0.006)	(0.003)	(0.004)
Summary Statistics							
R^2	0.999	0.983	0.999	0.998	0.998	0.999	0.999
D–W statistics	1.93	1.83	1.69	1.93	1.93	1.78	2.07
S.E.E.	0.06	0.10	0.07	0.05	0.05	0.06	0.06

Notes:
a Countries whose estimations are corrected for autocorrelation using the Cochrane–Orcutt procedure.
b Standard errors in parentheses.

If the assumption of rational expectations is maintained, this finding implies that the term premium varies through time and is positively correlated with this spread. The existence of a time-varying term premium constitutes a clear rejection of the expectations hypothesis theory. This result is consistent with Mankiw (1986), among others.

When the data are pooled across all G7 countries to capture the cross-country variation together with that of time-series, a single equation is estimated using the random coefficients model, which allows the coefficient of the yield spread to vary across countries. The coefficient on the yield spread was observed to be 1.004, and was statistically highly significant. This provides further evidence that the spread was significantly related to the excess holding return, such that a 1 per cent increase in the spread between the long and the short rate would produce an estimated excess return by slightly more than 1 per cent. Given that the standard deviation of the yield spread was large (see Table 6.2), these regressions indicate substantial variation in the term structure. Next we estimate equation (6.7) and the results are reported in Table 6.6.

Table 6.6 Regression of the change in one period ahead short rate on the yield spread: G7 countries, 1975(3)–1998(4)

Independent Variables	USA[a]	Japan[a]	UK[a]	Germany[a]	France[a]	Canada[a]	Italy[a]
Constant[b]	−0.166	−0.609	−0.195	−1.140	−0.304	−0.236	−0.110
	(0.183)	(0.190)	(0.177)	(0.378)	(0.192)	(0.200)	(0.280)
Yield Spread[b]	0.091	0.270	0.163	0.718	0.452	0.208	0.553
	(0.080)	(0.084)	(0.080)	(0.131)	(0.111)	(0.093)	(0.110)
Summary Statistics							
R^2	0.039	0.251	0.095	0.278	0.182	0.081	0.111
D-W statistics	1.90	2.05	1.92	2.14	1.88	1.95	1.84
S.E.E.	0.93	0.45	1.12	0.51	0.88	1.16	1.49

Notes:
a Countries whose estimations are corrected for autocorrelation using the Cochrane–Orcutt procedure.
b Standard errors in parentheses.

Note that a rise in the long rate relative to the short rate is due to the expectation of higher short rates in the future. Thus, future short rates would subsequently tend to rise, and we can expect a positive correlation of the change in short rates with the earlier spread, if the expectations hypothesis holds. The result indicates that coefficients on their yield spread are positive and significant for all countries except the USA. The pooled time-series cross-section regression provides similar results. Consequently, this test seems to provide support to the expectations hypothesis.

The corresponding results (not reported here) for the long rate are, however, negative. None of the coefficients, except Italy, was significant and all had wrong (negative) signs. One explanation could be that the short run movement of long rates does not obey the overall direction predicted by the expectations hypothesis due to long rates under-reacting to current short rates (or overreact to future short rates). See Campbell and Shiller (1991), and Hardouvelis (1994). Also see Fama (1984), Mankiw (1986), and Hardouvelis (1988) for alternative explanations.

Overall, the above results are somewhat mixed for the expectations hypothesis. Except for the regression of change of short rate on the yield spread, all other tests seem to reject the expectations theory. It should be noted that the explanatory power for the estimated equations is generally low (that is, low R^2) when measuring the predictive power of the yield spread. However, these mixed results are consistent with previous empirical work on the expectations model.

4.0 EXPLAINING THE TERM PREMIUM

In this section, we seek to explain the results. Note that the term premium signifies the extra return required by investors to compensate them for bearing the extra risk for holding a long bond over the short-term instrument. Following Fama (1976), Mishkin (1982) and Mankiw (1986), a risk variable can be included as a possible determinant of this time-varying term premium to see if they can explain the variation in the term premium. Given that risk is directly and positively related to the term premium, it is expected that the fluctuation in risk would be reflected in the yield spread between the long and short rate. Assuming this risk is observable, we could test the expectations theory by estimating the regression equation by including risk as an explicit variable as:

$$H_t - r_t = \alpha + \beta(R_t - r_t) + \gamma(RISK) + \varepsilon_t \qquad (6.11)$$

and see if β reduces to zero and γ becomes unity.

For the risk component to explain the variation of the term premium, this component must be positively correlated to the yield spread $(R_t - r_t)$, otherwise the addition of this risk variable as in equation (6.11) will not change β significantly (see Mankiw, 1986). Thus, another test of the hypothesis that risk explains the variation of the term premium is to estimate:

$$RISK_t = \alpha + \beta(R_t - r_t) + \varepsilon_t \tag{6.12}$$

and see if $\beta > 0$. If β is positive and significant, we can then conclude that the risk component may be the reason for the variation of the term premium.

Increased risk of capital loss is usually associated with greater interest rate volatility. Since the capital gain/loss of a long bond depends on its next period's price, or in terms of yield, on the next period's long rate, the more volatile the long rate means more risk in holding the long-term bond. Thus, higher interest rate volatility would be coupled with a higher term premium required by investors holding long bonds over short bonds.

Considering this measure of risk as ex post, or actual volatility, one can express it as the absolute value of percentage change in the price of the long bond:

$$VOL_t = \left| \frac{P_{t+1} - P_t}{P_t} \right| \tag{6.13}$$

or, express in terms of yields as:

$$VOL_t = \left| \frac{R_t - R_{t+1}}{R_{t+1}} \right| \tag{6.14}$$

Thus, one could test whether the interest rate volatility has any effect on the time-varying term premium by estimating:

$$VOL_t = \alpha + \beta(R_t - r_t) + \varepsilon_t \tag{6.15}$$

and test if or $\beta > 0$ and significant. The results of estimating equation (6.15) are presented in Table 6.7. As can be seen, the coefficients of the yield spread are negative in all cases except the UK, and statistically not different from zero for all seven countries. Thus, the results for this test seem to reject the hypothesis that the ex post volatility of interest rates explains the variation of the term premium. Similar results are obtained when the data are pooled across countries (not reported here).   Note that there is considerable controversy in the literature on the issue of measurement errors in risk (see Mankiw 1986).

Table 6.7 Regression of volatility of interest rates on the yield spread: G7 countries, 1975(3)–1998(4)

Independent variables	USA	Japan[a]	UK	Germany	France[a]	Canada	Italy[a]
Constant[b]	0.048	0.108	0.055	0.052	0.048	0.047	0.050
	(0.006)	(0.027)	(0.005)	(0.006)	(0.005)	(0.005)	(0.006)
Yield Spread[b]	−0.002	−0.015	0.001	−0.004	−0.002	−0.002	−0.000
	(0.003)	(0.012)	(0.002)	(0.003)	(0.003)	(0.002)	(0.003)
Summary Statistics							
R^2	0.008	0.111	0.001	0.021	0.029	0.012	0.029
D–W statistics	1.98	1.94	1.75	2.21	1.97	1.80	1.99
S.E.E.	0.04	0.07	0.04	0.03	0.04	0.04	0.05

Notes:
a Countries whose estimations are corrected for autocorrelation using the Cochrane–Orcutt procedure.
b Standard errors in parentheses.

4.1 Stock Market Development

According to the portfolio theory, the relevant measure of risk of an asset is the systematic (or non-diversifiable) risk. This is because an investor will not be compensated with a higher return for the diversifiable portion of the total risk. One possible explanation for the failure of the risk measure in the previous section to explain the variation of the term premium could be that it does not distinguish between the systematic and non-systematic risk.

To correct for this, Mankiw (1986) used consumption variability as well as the covariability with the stock market, to proxy for variation in the consumption beta and the market beta respectively. We now include the covariability with the stock market as a proxy for the market beta, and examine if it explains the time-varying term premium. Using the Capital Asset Pricing Model (CAPM), the time-varying term premium is given by:

$$\theta_t \equiv E_t (H_t - r_t) = A \, \text{cov} (H_t - r_t, ER_{m,t}) \qquad (6.16)$$

where $ER_{m,t}$ is the excess return on the stock market, A is the coefficient of relative risk aversion of a typical investor, and cov denotes the covariance conditional upon information at time *t*.

The actual stock market covariability at any time period *t* is defined as:

$$mcov_t = [(H_t - r_t) - (\overline{H_t - r_t})][ER_{m,t} - \overline{ER}_{m,t}] \tag{6.17}$$

where a bar over the variable indicates the sample mean of that series. The excess returns were calculated using the stock market returns (proxied by the quarterly discrete returns on the respective countries' leading stock indices)[2] less the risk-free rate (proxied by the 3-months Treasury bill rate). The market beta model suggests that the term premium is also proportional to the conditional expectation of *mcov*, or

$$\theta_t = AE_t(mcov_t) \tag{6.18}$$

Table 6.8 Regression of actual market covariability on the yield spread: G7 countries, 1975(3)–1998(4)

Independent Variables	USA	Japan	UK	Germany	France	Canada	Italy
Constant	6.281	−1.274	1.136	4.589	3.993	4.502	1.443
	(1.723)	(2.169)	(1.662)	(2.031)	(2.272)	(1.814)	(2.184)
Yield Spread	−2.845	0.853	−0.090	−2.150	−0.993	−1.603	−1.967
	(0.770)	(0.998)	(0.869)	(1.006)	(1.383)	(0.904)	(1.184)
Summary Statistics							
R^2	0.130	0.008	0.000	0.048	0.012	0.033	0.029
D–W statistic	1.95	1.98	2.41	1.97	1.93	1.77	2.06
S.E.E.	11.10	7.40	14.46	11.05	14.49	15.46	21.06

Notes: Standard errors in parentheses.

Thus, according to this model, the yield spread forecasts the excess holding return because it is proxying for variation in the market beta. To see if the variation in the market beta explains the variation in the term premium, the following regression is estimated:

$$mcov_t = \alpha + \beta(R_t - r_t) + \varepsilon_t \tag{6.19}$$

and test if $\beta > 0$ and significant.

Looking at the results of estimating equation (6.19) in Table 6.8, all countries except Japan have negative coefficients and only those for US and Germany are statistically significant. Note that these regressions have large standard error of estimation. The pooled regression (not reported here) also indicates a negative β, but statistically significant. Thus, it can be concluded that the role of market covariability measure to affect the time-varying term premium is far from clear-cut.

4.2 Exchange Rate Volatility

In a world of free movement of capital, the interest parity condition links the investor's return with the expected change in the exchange rate. Consequently, we can expect the volatility of the nominal exchange rate to affect the investor's expected return and, in turn, the changes in the term premium of bonds. Existing empirical work provides evidence to the covariance between asset returns and exchange rate, and the movements in risk premia on assets and the expected spot and forward foreign exchange rate (see Wolff, 1987). However, an explicit test of the link between the term premium and the exchange rate volatility is yet to be found in the existing literature.

Abstracting from this line of research, we now explore if nominal exchange rate volatility is any story. As before, we check for the link between the exchange rate volatility and the yield spread. Here, the exchange rate volatility is measured by the change of the current exchange rate from its previous period in logarithm form, or

$$VOL_t = \left(log\,X_t - log\,X_{t-1}\right) \times 100\% \qquad (6.20)$$

where X_t is the number of national currency units per US dollar at period t. These quarterly, end-period exchange rates are compiled from Datastream International. Because the US dollar is the base currency of the exchange rates series for the other six countries, the US is not included in this test. We estimate:

$$VOL_t = \alpha + \beta(R_t - r_t) + \varepsilon_t \qquad (6.21)$$

and test if $\beta > 0$ and significant. If the results are positive, then equation (6.6) can be re-estimated by including VOL_t as a regressor to see if the coefficient for the yield spread reduces to zero. The results are presented in Table 6.9. As can be seen, the results are mixed. The yield spread coefficients have wrong signs for Germany and Canada, and all of them, except for Japan, are statistically insignificant. For the pooled results (not reported here), the coefficient for the yield spread is positive, but statistically insignificant. Thus the link between the nominal exchange rate and term premium appears to be imprecise.

Table 6.9 Regression of nominal exchange rate volatility on the yield spread: G7 countries, 1975(3)–1998(4)

Independent Variables	Japan[a]	UK[a]	Germany[a]	France[a]	Canada[a]	Italy[a]
Constant[b]	−5.696	−0.115	0.206	0.097	0.518	0.909
	(1.964)	(0.694)	(1.206)	(0.829)	(0.277)	(0.794)
Yield Spread[b]	2.275	0.405	−0.450	0.182	−0.054	0.154
	(0.889)	(0.321)	(0.606)	(0.531)	(0.128)	(0.346)
Summary Statistics						
R^2	0.148	0.055	0.104	0.149	0.097	0.123
D–W	1.86	2.00	1.99	2.00	2.07	1.91
S.E.E.	5.22	5.07	4.72	4.54	1.62	4.91

Notes:
a Countries whose estimations are corrected for autocorrelation using the Cochrane–Orcutt procedure.
b Standard errors in parentheses.

Interestingly, replacing the nominal exchange rate volatility in equation (6.21) by purchasing power parity (PPP) real exchange rates makes no real difference to the results (not reported here).[3] This result, however, reinforces the phenomenon observed elsewhere that most of the real exchange rate changes come from the shocks to the nominal exchange rates (see Sjaastad, 1998).

5.0 CONCLUSION

This chapter provides a systematic analysis of various hypotheses regarding the term structure of interest rates, using the data from the G7 countries. More specifically, we provide explicit tests of the expectations hypothesis. The tests are conducted for individual countries, as well as jointly for all countries with data pooled together. Except for the ability of the yield spread to predict the change of future short rates, the tests, in general, tend to reject the expectations theory. This is consistent with the mainstream literature.

The failure of the expectations hypothesis is typically attributed to the existence of time-varying term premia. We employ tests involving interest rate volatility, stock market development, and the exchange rate volatility as possible determinants of this time-varying term premia. Empirical results indicate that these variables do not adequately explain the large variation in the term premium. This, again, is consistent with the existing literature.

While the results of this chapter are illuminating and insightful, several issues seem to remain unresolved. First, it may be possible that the cross-country correlation of various yield measures may provide some basis to explain the conflicting results reported in Table 6.5 and 6.6. This issue was not addressed in the present study and deserves further investigation. Second, most of the individual country regressions reported in this paper appeared to have a poor fit. When the data are pooled across countries using appropriate econometric procedures, the results did not change markedly. It may be possible in the future research to introduce new approaches to conduct the test both individually and simultaneously for all countries. Finally, linking the time-varying term premium with exchange rate developments is an innovation in this paper. It may be useful in future research to employ more formal approach in this regard.

REFERENCES

Campbell, J.Y. and R.J. Shiller (1991), 'Yield spreads and interest rate movements: A bird's eye view', *Review of Economic Studies*, **58**, May, pp. 495–514.

Fama, E.F. (1976), 'Inflation uncertainty and the expected returns on treasury bills', *Journal of Political Economy*, **84**(2), pp. 427–448.

Fama, E.F. (1984), The information in the term structure, *Journal of Financial Econometrics*, **3**, pp. 361–377.

Fama, E.F. and R. Bliss (1987), 'The information in long–maturity forward rates', *American Economic Review*, **77**, pp. 680–692.

Froot, K. A. (1989), 'New hope for the expectations hypothesis of the term structure of interest rates', *Journal of Finance*, **44**(2), pp. 283–305.

Hansen, P. and A. King (1998), 'Health care expenditures and GDP: panel data unit root test results–comments', *Journal of Health Economics*, **17**, pp. 377–381.

Hardouvelis, G. (1988), 'The predictive power of the term structure during recent monetary regimes', *Journal of Finance*, **43**, June, pp. 339–356.

Hardouvelis, G. (1994), 'The term structure spread and future changes in long and short rates in the G7 countries: Is there a puzzle?', *Journal of Monetary Economics*, **33**, April, pp. 225–283.

Im, K.S., Pesaran, M.H. and Y. Shin (1997), *Testing for Unit Roots in Panel Data*, Department of Applied Economics, University of Cambridge, Working Paper No. 9526, Dec. 1997, revision.

Mankiw, G.N. (1986), 'The term structure of interest rates revisited', *Brookings Papers of Economic Activities*, pp. 61–107.

Mankiw, G.N. and L.H. Summers (1984), 'Do long-term interest rates overreact to short-term interest rates?', *Brookings Papers of Economic Activities*, **1**, pp. 223–242.

Manzur, M. (1990), 'An international comparison of prices and exchange rates: A new test of purchasing power parity', *Journal of International Money and Finance*, **9**, pp. 75–91.

Manzur, M. and M. Ariff (1995), 'Purchasing power parity: New methods and extensions', *Applied Financial Economics*, **5**, pp. 19–26.

Manzur, M and D. Chow (1999), Term structure of interest rates: experience from the G7 countries, Working Paper Series, 99:15, December, School of Economics and Finance, Curtin Business School.

Mishkin, F.S. (1982), 'Monetary policy and short-term interest rates: An efficient markets-rational expectations approach', *Journal of Finance*, **37**, pp. 63–72.

Nelson, C.R. (1979), *Handbook of Financial Economics*, North-Holland Publishing Company.

Shiller, R.J., Campbell, J.Y. and K.L. Schoenholtz (1983), 'Forward rates and future policy: interpreting the term structure of interest rates', *Brookings Papers of Economic Activities*, **1**, pp. 173–188.

Sjaastad, L.A. (1998), 'On exchange rates, nominal and real', *Journal of International Money and Finance*, **17**, pp. 407–439.

Stambaugh, R.F. (1988), 'The information in forward rates: Implications for models of the term structure', *Journal of Financial Economics*, **21**, pp. 41–70.

Wolff, C. (1987), 'Forward foreign exchange rates, expected spot rates, and premia: A signal-extracting approach' *Journal of Finance*, **42**, pp. 395–406.

NOTES

1   This chapter is based on Manzur and Chow (1999).
2   In this test, the leading market indices used to compute the excess return on the stock market of each G7 countries are: S&P 500 Composite (USA), Nikkei 225 (Japan), FTSE 100 (UK), DAX (Germany), CAC–40 (France), TSE 300 (Canada), and MIB 30 (Italy). These quarterly end period data are compiled from Datastream International with full sample period of 1975 (3) to 1998 (4), except for the FTSE 100 and CAC–40, which are taken since 1978 (3) and 1987 (3), respectively, till 1998 (4).
3   See Manzur (1990), and Manzur and Ariff (1995) for innovations on PPP. Also see Chapter 2 in this volume.

7. Notes on Exchange Rates and Commodity Prices

Kenneth W. Clements and Meher Manzur

Prices of internationally traded commodities have been markedly volatile over the last two decades. As Maizels (1992) demonstrates, the world market price of sugar, for example, varied between 2.5 and 41 US cents per pound in the 1980s, and coffee ranged between 60 and 303 US cents per pound over the same period. 'Hard' commodities were similar, with aluminium prices swinging between 42 and 162 cents and copper between 58 and 159 cents (see, for more illustrations, Maizels, 1992). Note that commodity price volatility is even sharper and more pronounced in well-organised markets like the Chicago Board of Trade. Why are commodity prices so volatile?

The conventional approach is to explain this volatility in terms of demand–supply characteristics inherent in agricultural, energy and mineral commodities (variable supply, inelastic demand, and so on) and, in some cases, business cycles (see, for an overview, Sapsford and Morgan, 1994). Interestingly, a stylised fact is that commodity-price volatility echoes variability in exchange rates since the switch to floating by major currencies in the early 1970s. Whilst it is true that commodity prices and exchange rates are both asset prices that respond to news instantaneously, can something stronger be said about *causation*? Is exchange rate volatility *responsible* for the wide swings in commodity prices? Interestingly, this is the exact opposite to the question considered by Freebairn (in Chapter 9 of this volume), whereby the values of commodity currencies (such as, the Australian dollar) respond to changes in world commodity prices. In this chapter, we demonstrate that under the condition of purchasing power parity (PPP) holding for traded goods only, variations in exchange rates of dominant countries can be said to *cause* changes in the world commodity prices.

What follows are brief analytical notes on the interactions between exchange rates and commodity prices. The objective is to set the stage for further rigorous analysis on this topic to follow in subsequent chapters. The material in this chapter is largely based on an approach first used by Ridler and Yandle (1972), and subsequently further developed by Sjaastad (1985). A similar approach was also developed by Dornbusch (1987). The chapter is organised as follows. In the next section, we provide some illustrations of the issues using gold and iron-ore prices as examples. Section 2 presents a stylised model to determine the effects of exchange-rate changes on the internal and external prices of commodities. This is followed in Section 3 with a simple geometric exposition of the issues. Concluding comments are contained in the last section.

1.0 SOME ILLUSTRATIONS

We assume that PPP holds for individual commodities, but not for all goods (see Chapter 2 of this volume for more details on PPP). For illustration purposes, we first use the price gold as an example. Let p be the price of an ounce of gold in \$US, p^* be the DM price and s be the spot exchange rate, the \$US cost of 1 DM. Then, under PPP, we have

$$p = (1+x)sp^*,$$

where x represents transportation costs and the effects of any other barriers to trade in gold which cause a spread between the \$US price, p, and the DM price converted to \$US, sp^*. Let x be approximately constant, so that the PPP condition in change form is:

$$\hat{p} - \hat{p}^* = \hat{s} \qquad\qquad (7.1)$$

where a '^' indicates percentage change. In words, equation (7.1) states that the change in the \$US price of gold relative to its DM price equals the change in \$US/DM exchange rate (note that $\hat{s} > 0$ if the DM appreciates or the \$US depreciates). Now, consider a 10 per cent depreciation of the \$US relative to the DM, so that $\hat{s} = 10\%$. How is this 10 per cent relative-price change divided up between p and p^*? The possibilities are:

(i) $\hat{p} = 10\%$, $\hat{p}^* = 0$;

(ii) $\hat{p} = 0$, $\hat{p}^* = -10\%$; and

(iii) $\hat{p} > 0$, $\hat{p}^* < 0$ with $\hat{p} + |\hat{p}^*| = 10\%$.

These possibilities of internal and external price changes can be shown graphically in Figure 7.1. As will be shown later, if the US is a *small* country with respect to the world gold market and Germany *large*, we are more likely to get case (i), and vice versa for case (ii). When both countries have some *market power* (when they are able to change the foreign currency price of gold), case (iii) pertains.

We now turn to iron ore prices as another example. Australia produces about 12 per cent of the world's iron ore; and iron-ore exports from Australia represent almost 30 per cent of the total world trade in iron ore.

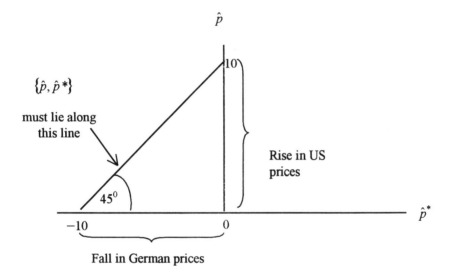

Figure 7.1 Internal and external prices

Thus, *prima facie* Australia can be considered as a *large* producer of iron ore in the world so that it can affect world prices. In other words, Australian iron-ore producers as a whole face a downward-sloping demand curve. Consider the effects of a 10 per cent depreciation of the $A. This increases returns to Australian iron ore producers in terms of $A, thereby increasing the profitability and production of iron ore as long as costs do not also increase equi-proportionally. Iron-ore exports now go up and this increase in export volumes decreases the world price of iron ore as Australia is a large producer. Hence, from equation (7.1), the $A price of iron ore, p, increases by less than 10 per cent; $\hat{p} < 10$ per cent as $\hat{s} = 10$ per cent by assumption, and $\hat{p}^* < 0$ by the large–country effect.

The above examples illustrate a general principle. Suppose the Europeans dominate the world gold market, so that an appreciation of the DM (= depreciation of the $US) by 10 per cent generates case (i) above. That is,

$$\hat{p}(\$US) = 10\%, \quad \hat{p}^*(DM) = 0.$$

Here gold producers as a whole gain from the increase in the $US price of gold. By a similar argument but now in reverse, iron ore producers as a whole are hurt by the depreciation of the $A as that depresses world iron ore prices (in terms of foreign currency). Thus, we obtain the general principle that *producers of a commodity dominated by a country whose currency appreciates will be better off, and producers of a commodity dominated by a country whose currency depreciates will be worse off.*

2.0 A FORMAL MODEL

For simplicity, consider a commodity (any internationally-traded commodity, not just gold or iron ore) produced only by one country and this country exports all of its production. For this commodity, the domestic supply function is an increasing function of the internal relative price:

$$q^s = q^s\left(\frac{p}{P}\right), \tag{7.2}$$

where p is the internal price of the commodity; P is the general price index internally; and p/P is the internal relative price. The corresponding foreign demand decreases with the external relative price:

$$q^d = q^d\left(\frac{p^*}{P^*}\right), \tag{7.3}$$

where p^*/P^* is the external relative price. Market clearing requires

$$q^s = q^d. \tag{7.4}$$

As before, let PPP hold for this commodity, so that

$$p = sp^*. \tag{7.5}$$

We now use this model to determine the effect of a change in the exchange rate on internal and external prices of the commodity. In change form, equations (7.2) and (7.3) are

$$\hat{q}^s = \varepsilon(\hat{p} - \hat{P})$$
$$\hat{q}^d = \eta(\hat{p}^* - \hat{P}^*),$$

where $\varepsilon > 0$ is the supply elasticity and $\eta < 0$ is the demand elasticity. Using equation (7.4) in percentage change form, $\hat{q}^s = \hat{q}^d$, and combining this with equation (7.5), we obtain $\hat{p}^* = -\alpha \hat{s} + \alpha \hat{P} + (1-\alpha)\hat{P}^*$, where $\alpha = \varepsilon/(\varepsilon - \eta)$ is a positive fraction, or

$$\hat{p}^* - \hat{P}^* = \alpha(\hat{P} - \hat{P}^* - \hat{s}). \tag{7.6}$$

equation (7.6) tells us the determinants of the relative price of the commodity in terms of the foreign currency. That is, the change in this price is a positive fraction, α, of the appreciation of the home country currency, adjusted for inflation. Note that the term in the bracket on the right-hand side of equation (7.6) is the change in the real exchange rate. When $(\hat{P} - \hat{P}^* - \hat{s}) > 0$, there is a real appreciation of the domestic currency, and vice versa for a real depreciation. It is obvious that if PPP holds for all goods, the real exchange rate is constant: $\hat{P} - \hat{P}^* = \hat{s}$.

Next, we consider the relative price in terms of the home currency, $(\hat{p} - \hat{P})$. From the PPP condition, this can be expressed as $\hat{p} - \hat{P} = \hat{p}^* + \hat{s} - \hat{P}$. From equation (7.6), this can be expressed as

$$\hat{p} - \hat{P} = [-\alpha \hat{s} + \alpha \hat{P} + (1-\alpha)\hat{P}^*] + \hat{s} - \hat{P}.$$

Collecting the terms, we have

$$\hat{p} - \hat{P} = (1-\alpha)(\hat{s} - \hat{P} + \hat{P}^*). \qquad (7.7)$$

Note that the second bracketed term on the right-hand side of equation (7.7) is the same as that in equation (7.6), except for the sign. We now consider equation (7.7) in conjunction with equation (7.6). These two equations reveal that a given change in the real exchange rate, $\hat{P} - \hat{P}^* - \hat{s}$, is divided up between a change in the external relative price, $\hat{p}^* - \hat{P}^*$, and the internal relative price, $\hat{p} - \hat{P}$. The fraction of the real exchange rate change that 'goes to' the external price is α, while the remainder, $1-\alpha$, goes to the internal price. If the currency depreciates, then the world price falls by α times the depreciation, and the domestic price rises by $1-\alpha$ times the depreciation. For example, suppose that the supply elasticity $\varepsilon = 1$, and demand elasticity $\eta = -1$ so that $\alpha = \varepsilon / (\varepsilon - \eta) = 1/2$. Then if the home–country's currency depreciates by 10 per cent in real terms, the world relative price of the commodity decreases by 5 per cent, while the internal price increases by 5 per cent.

It is to be emphasised that $\alpha = \varepsilon / (\varepsilon - \eta)$ is the key parameter in this framework. The value of α determines if a country is considered *large* or *small* in a given commodity market. A country is considered small if $\alpha \approx 0$, which occurs when $\varepsilon \approx 0$ or $|\eta| \approx \infty$. From our illustrations in the previous section, for example, the US is a small country in the world gold market with $\alpha \approx 0$, as it faces a close to horizontal demand curve at the world price for its gold output. On the other hand, a country is considered large if $\alpha \approx 1$ (when $\varepsilon \approx \infty$ or $\eta \approx 0$). When the supply of the commodity is highly elastic (relative to demand), a real depreciation stimulates exports to such an extent that the world price falls by the full amount of the depreciation. Similarly, when demand is completely inelastic, an increase in exports causes the world price to fall by a large amount.

Since the share α is expressed in terms of the two parameters, its role can be highlighted more elegantly in terms of equi–value contours. For this purpose, we rewrite $\alpha = \varepsilon / (\varepsilon - \eta)$ as $\varepsilon = [\alpha / (\alpha - 1)]\eta$ or, as $\eta < 0$,

$$\varepsilon = \left| \frac{\alpha}{\alpha - 1} \right| |\eta|.$$

The above expression can be used to plot ε against $|\eta|$ for a given value of α, as in Figure 7.2. As can be seen, for a fixed value of ε, α falls as $|\eta|$ rises. And as ε rises with $|\eta|$ fixed, α also rises. When a *large* country devalues, then from equation (7.6), it depresses the world price of the commodity in question by a large amount. In the limit when $\alpha = 1$,

$$\hat{p}^* - \hat{P}^* = \left(\hat{P} - \hat{P}^* - \hat{s} \right).$$

Similarly for small countries $\alpha = 0$ and $\left(\hat{p}^* - \hat{P}^* \right) = 0$. In this case, from equation (7.7), the entire real depreciation is translated into an equi-proportional increase in the domestic relative price of the commodity.

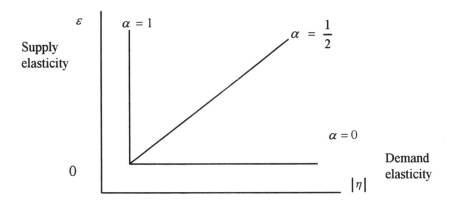

Figure 7.2 Equi-value contours

3.0 A GEOMETRIC ANALYSIS

In this section, we provide a geometric exposition of the above ideas. We first consider the relationship between relative prices at home (that is, in terms of domestic currency) and those abroad (in terms of foreign currency). From PPP, we have $p = sp^*$, or dividing through by the price level, P,

$$\frac{p}{P} = s\,\frac{P^*}{P}\cdot\frac{p^*}{P^*}.$$

This equation states that, under PPP, the relative price at home equals that abroad after adjusting for the real exchange rate, sP^*/P. We thus write the above equation as,

$$\frac{p}{P} = R\frac{p^*}{P^*} \qquad\qquad (7.8)$$

where R is the real exchange rate. From equation (7.8), if we hold the real exchange rate constant at R_o, we can graph the internal relative price against the external, as in Figure 7.3. In this figure, the ray from the origin, OX, is the real exchange rate schedule whose slope is the real exchange rate. A real depreciation causes the ray to get *steeper* and to shift from OX to OX' in Figure 7.3.

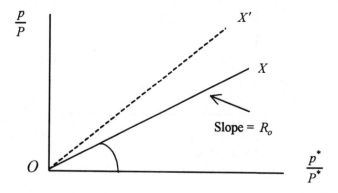

Figure 7.3 Internal and external relative prices

Next, we consider the world market for the commodity. Recall the supply and demand function for the commodity in question and the market clearing condition:

$$q^s = q^s\left(\frac{p}{P}\right), \quad q^s = q^s\left(\frac{p}{P}\right), \quad q^s = q^d .$$

If we increase the internal relative price p/P and hold p^*/P^* constant, then supply rises with demand unchanged, so that there is *excess supply*. That excess supply can be eliminated by decreasing the external relative price p^*/P^*, as this stimulates demand for the commodity. This can be seen from Figure 7.4. Here the downward-sloping schedule WW is the locus of relative prices for which the world market clears. Overall equilibrium requires that the prices be such that we are located on OX and the WW schedule simultaneously. The point E in Figure 7.5 is such an overall equilibrium, with $(p/P)_e$ and $(p^*/P^*)_e$ the associated relative prices. A real depreciation of the home currency causes

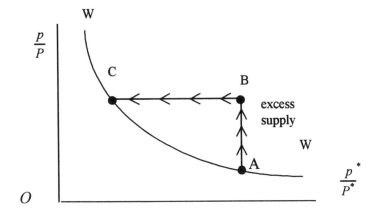

Figure 7.4 World-market clearing

the real exchange rate schedule to get steeper, which results in the new equilibrium point E' in Figure 7.5. The real depreciations thus causes external prices of the commodity to fall, and internal prices to rise.

As shown earlier, a *small country* ($\alpha = 0$) cannot affect world prices by a depreciation of its currency, and in this case the WW schedule is *vertical*, as in Figure 7.6. In this case, the internal relative price p/P rises by the full amount of the depreciation and the world price is unchanged.

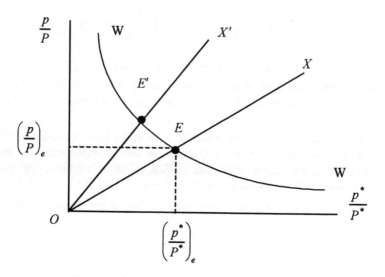

Figure 7.5 Overall equilibrium

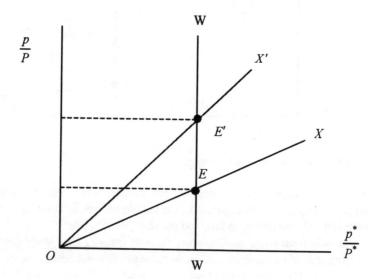

Figure 7.6 The small-country case

On the other hand, the WW schedule is *horizontal* for a *large country* ($\alpha = 1$), as in Figure 7.7. In this case, the world price falls by the full amount of the depreciation, while the internal price remains constant.

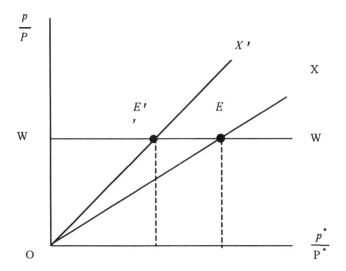

Figure 7.7 The large-country case

4.0 CONCLUSION

In this chapter we provided brief analytical notes on the interactions between exchange rates and commodity prices. Using PPP as the building block, we introduced a stylised model in which PPP holds for traded goods only. This model determines the impact of real exchange rate changes on the relative prices of commodities. The model illustrates the general principle that producers of a commodity dominated by a country whose currency appreciates will be better off, and producers of a commodity dominated by a country whose currency depreciates will be worse off. While the model is very simple and stylised (the commodity is produced in one country only and sales of this commodity are on the world market only), the above result holds in a more general setting, as is shown by Sjaastad (1985).

REFERENCES

Dornbusch, R. (1987), 'Exchange rates economics: 1986', *Economic Journal*, **97**, pp. 1–18.

Maizels, A. (1992), *Commodities in Crisis*, Oxford: Clarendon Press.

Ridler, D. and C.A. Yandle (1972), 'A simplified method for analysing the effects of exchange rate changes on exports of a primary commodity', *IMF Staff Papers*, 19.

Sjaastad, L.A. (1985), 'Exchange rate regimes and the real rate of interest', in M. Connolly and J. McDermott (eds), *The Economics of the Caribbean Basin*, New York: Praeger.

Sapsford, D. and W. Morgan (eds) (1994), *The Economics of Primary Commodities: Models, Analysis and Policy*, London: Edward Elgar.

8. The Price of Gold and the Exchange Rate

Larry A. Sjaastad and Fabio Scacciavillani

The main objective of this study is to identify the effect of major currency exchange rates on the prices of internationally traded commodities. For commodities that are traded continuously in organized markets such as the Chicago Board of Trade, a change in any exchange rate will result in an immediate adjustment in the prices of those commodities in at least one currency, and perhaps in both currencies if both countries are 'large'. For example, when the dollar depreciates against the deutsche mark, dollar prices of commodities tend to rise (and DM prices fall) even though the fundamentals of the market – all relevant factors other than exchange rates and price levels – remain unchanged. The power of this effect is suggested by the events surrounding the intense appreciation of the dollar from early 1980 until early 1985 during which the US price level rose by 30 per cent but the IMF dollar-based commodity price index *fell* by 30 per cent, and dollar-based unit-value indices for both imports and exports of commodity-exporting countries as a group *declined* by 14 per cent. The explanation for this anomaly may lie in the exchange rate: with respect to the DM, for example, the dollar appreciated by more than 90 per cent in nominal terms, and by 45 per cent in real terms.

The potential importance of this phenomenon is not limited to the major currency countries. With more than two-thirds of the minor currencies of the world being directly or indirectly tied to one of the three major currencies (the dollar, the deutsche mark and the yen) or to a currency basket, shocks to the major currency exchange rates may be felt not only by producers and consumers of internationally-traded commodities in the major currency countries but also by many of the smaller, commodity-exporting countries in the form of inflationary (or deflationary) shocks transmitted by fluctuations in the international prices of commodities.[1]

In the first of the five sections to foliow, an international pricing model is developed, which predicts that changes in major currency exchange rates will impact on the prices of many commodities in all currencies – major and minor alike. Section 2 is concerned with preliminary test of the data and Section 3 – the core of the chapter – reports the findings of a pilot study of the international market for gold. In Section 4 we quantify the contribution of floating exchange rates to the coefficient of variation of the international price of gold since the dissolution of the Bretton Woods system in 1973. A short summary section concludes the chapter.

Gold is a prime candidate for a pilot study of the effects on commodity prices of fluctuations in major currency exchange rates. A highly homogeneous commodity, gold is traded almost continuously in well organised spot and future markets. Moreover, as annual production (and consumption) of gold is minuscule compared with the global stock, the gold producing countries, whose currencies typically are not traded in organised markets, are unlikely to dominate the world gold market.

1.0 EXCHANGE RATES AND COMMODITY PRICES: THE MODEL

The model developed in this section focuses on the effect of movements in the exchange rates on the international price of a homogeneous commodity that is traded in an organised market; it is not the usual asset pricing model as it is not concerned with the rate of return on holding the commodity in question.[2] The model has two basic elements: the law of one price and global market clearing in a world of M countries or currency blocs. Ignoring all barriers to trade and with all variables expressed in natural logarithms, the law of one price for an internationally-traded commodity is simply:

$$P_1 = P_j + E_{1j}, \; j = 1,...,M, \tag{8.1}$$

P_j being the commodity price in currency j and E_{1j} price of currency j in terms of the reference currency 1. Feedback from the commodity market to exchange rates is assumed to be negligible.

The excess demand (that is, net imports), Q_j, for that commodity in currency bloc j is a function of its *real* price, $P_j^R \equiv P_j - P_j^*$, where P_j^* is the price level in that bloc, and a 1 by N vector $X_j = (X_{j1}, X_{j2},...,X_{jN})$ of (yet to be specified) market 'fundamentals' specific to the commodity in question and currency bloc j:

$$Q_j = Q_j(P_j^R, X_j), \partial Q_j / \partial P_j^R \leq 0, \ j = 1,..., M.$$

Global market clearing requires:

$$\sum_{j=1}^{M} Q_j(P_j^R, X_j) = 0,$$

and hence a local log-linear approximation can be written as:

$$\sum_{j=1}^{M} \left(\partial Q_j / \partial P_j^R \right) \cdot \left(P_j^R - \bar{P}_j^R \right) + \sum_{j=1}^{M} \left(\sum_{i=1}^{N} \left(\partial Q_j / \partial X_{ji} \right) \cdot \left(X_{ji} - \bar{X}_{ji} \right) \right) = 0, \quad (8.2)$$

where $\bar{P}_j^R$ and $\bar{X}_{ji}$ are means of the distributions of P_j^R and X_{ji}, respectively.

From equation (8.1), $P_j^R = P_1 - E_{1j} - P_j^*$, so equation (8.2) can be rearranged into a fairly simple expression for P_1:

$$P_1 = \text{constant} + \sum_{j=1}^{M} \theta_j (E_{1j} + P_j^*) + K(X), \quad (8.3)$$

where $\theta_j = (\partial Q_j / \partial P_j^R) / \Sigma_j^M (\partial Q_j / \partial P_j^R)$; while Q_j may be positive or negative, $\partial Q_j / \partial P_j^R$ is non-positive so the θ_j are non-negative fractions that sum to unity. The global fundamentals are captured by $K(X) = -\Sigma_j^M \Sigma_i^N [(\partial Q_j / \partial X_{ji}) \cdot X_{ji}] / \Sigma_j^M (\partial Q_j / \partial P_j^R)$; that is X is a vector containing all elements of the country-specific X_j vectors.[3] Since $P_k = P_1 - E_{1K}$ and $E_{kj} = E_{1j} - E_{1k}$, equation (8.3) can be specified in any currency k: $P_k = \text{constant} + \Sigma_{j=1}^M \theta_j \cdot (E_{kj} + P_j^*) + K(X)$. Changes in the global fundamentals have identical effects on the price of the commodity in question regardless of currency of denomination.

By subtracting P_1^* from both sides of equation (8.3) we obtain:

$$P_1^R = \sum_{j=1}^{M} \theta_j \cdot E_{1j}^R + K(X), \quad (8.3R)$$

where $E_{1j}^{R} \equiv E_{1j} + P_{j}^{*} - P_{1}^{*}$ is the common PPP *real* exchange rate between currency blocs 1 and j. For the commodity in question, then, θ_j is simultaneously the elasticity of its *nominal* price in currency bloc 1 with respect to the *nominal* exchange rate (or price level) of bloc j, and the elasticity of its *real* price in currency bloc 1 with respect to the PPP *real* exchange rate between blocs 1 and j, holding all other variables constant in both cases. While the θ_j can be estimated with either nominal or real variables, the actual estimation will use forecast errors.

1.1   An Interpretation of the 'thetas'

The 'thetas' in equation (8.3) are key to the analysis as they measure the *relative market power* possessed by each participant in the world market for the commodity in question. Consider a small depreciation of currency 1 against all other currencies (holding all P_j^* constant); the effect of that depreciation on P_1 is $\sum_{j=2}^{M}\theta_j = 1-\theta_1$. If currency bloc 1 is a price-*taker* in, say, the world gold market, that depreciation will have no effect on the price of gold in other currencies so the entire impact falls on the price of gold in currency 1 and hence $\theta_1 = 0$. In other words, currency bloc 1 is the classic 'small' economy in the world gold market. On the other hand, if bloc 1 is an absolute price-*maker*, that depreciation will have no effect on the price of gold in currency 1 as that bloc totally dominates the world gold market, so $\theta_1 = 1$; all of the effect of the depreciation will appear in the price of gold in other currencies.

To dominate the world market for any commodity, a country must have an extremely elastic excess demand for that commodity. When stocks are small compared with annual production and consumption (as in the case of wheat or copper), a country must be a major producer and/or consumer in order to dominate the price of a commodity. Precious metals are unusual in that *stocks* are very large compared with annual production or consumption and hence a country with a high propensity to hoard gold might dominate the world gold market without being a major producer.

Given the high variability of major currency exchange rates since 1973, the term $\sum_{j=1}^{M}\theta_j(E_{ij} + P_j^*)$ of equation (8.3) is a potentially important source of shocks to the price of a commodity such as gold, and hence estimates of the θ_j can be useful.[4] That information can help identify the sources (exchange rates vs the fundamentals) of the price shocks experienced by consumers and producers of gold, to the extent that exchange rates can be predicted, one can forecast the effects of movements in those rates on the price of gold. Finally, information about the θ_j can be exploited for portfolio management; by denominating their assets and liabilities in foreign currency in accordance with the θ_j, firms involved with gold can reduce the financial impact of exchange rate shocks.

1.2 The Forecast Error Approach

With appropriate time series data, the θ_j coefficients in equation (8.3) can be estimated, but that procedure confronts longstanding issues such as the stationarity of the exchange rates. However, when the currencies and commodities are traded in both spot and *forward* markets, those issues can be finessed by using forecast errors, which involves writing equation (8.3) in terms of those errors extracted from spot and forward price and exchange rate data rather than with actual prices and exchange rates. As forecast error data are usually stationary and, if the relevant markets are 'efficient', serially uncorrelated as well, the econometric analysis is considerably simplified.

To develop this approach, we begin with spot and forward versions of equation (8.3); apart from notation, the former is identical with equation (8.3):

$$P_{1,t}^S = \text{constant} + \sum_{j=1}^{M} \theta_j \cdot \left(E_{1j,t}^S + P_{j,t}^* \right) + K^S(X_t), \qquad (8.3\text{S})$$

and the forward version is written as:

$$P_{1,t,n}^F = \text{constant} + \sum_{j=1}^{M} \theta_j \cdot \left(E_{1j,t,n}^F + P_{j,t,n}^{*F} \right) + K^F(X_t), \qquad (8.3\text{F})$$

where S and F superscripts denote spot and forward, P_j^{*F} and $K^F(X)$ are unobserved market forecasts of P_j^* and $K^S(X)$, and n is the length of the forward contract. The θ_j are set equal in equations (8.3S) and (8.3F) as there is no reason to expect them to differ for short-term (such as 90-day) contracts.

The forecast error for the price of the commodity in question, $Z_{1,t,n}$, is the difference between realised and forward prices:

$$Z_{1,t,n} \equiv P_{1,t}^S - P_{1,t-n,n}^F ,$$

and for exchange rates, the forecast error is:

$$Z_{E1j,t,n} \equiv E_{1j,t}^S - E_{1j,t-n,n}^F ,$$

Neglecting the constant term, the forecast error version of equation (8.3) is just the difference between equations (8.3F) and (8.3S), with an n period lag:

$$Z_{1,t,n} = \sum_{j=1}^{M} \theta_j \cdot \left(Z_{E1j,t,n} + \left[P_{j,t}^* - P_{j,t-n,n}^{*F}\right]\right) + \left[K^S(X_t) - K^F(X_{t-n})\right]$$

$$= \sum_{j=1}^{M} \theta_j \cdot Z_{E1j,t,n} \left[P_{W,t}^* - P_{W,t-n}^{*F}\right] + \left[K^S(X_t) - K^F(X_{t-n})\right] ,$$

where $P_{W,t}^* = \sum_{j=1}^{M} \theta_j \cdot P_{j,t}^*$ is the 'world' price level and, as $P_{W,t-n}^{*F}$ is the forecast of $P_{W,t}^*$, the terms $P_{W,t}^* - P_{W,t-n}^{*F} \equiv Z_{p,t,n}$ and $K^S(X_t) - K^F(X_{t-n}) \equiv Z_{K,t,n}$ also are forecast errors. Since neither $Z_{p,t,n}$ nor $Z_{k,t,n}$ are observable, the forecast error of equation (8.3) is written as:

$$Z_{1,t,n} = \text{constant} + \sum_{j=1}^{M} \theta_j \cdot Z_{E1j,t,n} + \upsilon_{1t} , \qquad (8.4)$$

where $\upsilon_{1t} \equiv Z_{p,t,n} + Z_{k,t,n}$ also is a forecast error.

If markets are weakly efficient, $K^F(X_{t-n}) = E\left[K^S(X_t)|I_{t-n}\right]$ and $P_{W,t-n}^{*F} = E(P_{W,t}^*,I_{t-n})$, where $E(\cdot)$ is the conditional expectation operator and I_{t-n} the information set at time $t - n$, and hence $Z_{p,t,n}$, $Z_{k,t,n}$ and υ_{1t} are serially uncorrelated. Weak market efficiency implies, then, that all variables in equation (8.4) are serially uncorrelated.[5] Given the potentially superior characteristics of forecast error data, equation (8.4) will be the centerpiece for the empirical implementation of the pricing model.

2.0 PRELIMINARY TESTS ON THE DATA

The spot gold price data consist of daily observations from January 1982 through December 1990 and the forward price data refer to 108 90-day contracts let at the beginning of each month during the same period, both in US dollars. The daily spot gold prices are from the London Gold Market (Reuters), and forward gold prices were computed using closing quotations on 3-month COMEX contracts. Spot and 90-day forward exchange rates between the US dollar and the deutsche mark, the UK pound sterling, and the Japanese yen were obtained from the International Monetary Fund Data Bank and cover the same period. Because the forecast errors require a 3-month lag on the forward series, the useful data set is reduced to 105 overlapping (and hence serially correlated) observations. Alternatively, the data can be divided into three subsets of 35 non-overlapping observations for the same period. Finally, preliminary tests indicated that UK 'theta' is approximately zero, so the pound starling was designated currency 1 and the price of gold and all exchange rates were denominated in pounds.

As the empirical analysis focuses on the relation between exchange rates and the price of gold, and since the fundamentals are difficult to specify in advance (apart from world inflation, which may influence the appeal of gold as a store of value), we made no attempt to do so; accordingly, in estimating equation (8.4), we assume that the exchange-rate forecast errors, $Z_{E1j,t,n}$, and those concerning gold-market fundamentals, υ_{lt}, are orthogonal. The period of analysis, 1982–1990, however, was deliberately chosen to exclude the price explosion of 1979–1980 due to international political instability; moreover, as the IMF *International Financial Statistics* indicate that central bank gold reserves remained quite constant at just under one billion fine troy ounces throughout the 1982–1990 period, the world gold market was not influenced by large net sales of gold on the part of central banks during that period.

2.1 Stationarity Tests

Two distinct stationarity tests based on all 108 overlapping observations on spot and forward gold prices and the original US dollar exchange rate data indicate that all spot and forward series are non-stationary; these results are reported in the Appendix. This finding suggests that those variables may be cointegrated, and hence the relationship described by equation (8.3) might be represented by the Engle–Granger (1987) error correction mechanism. Tests of the no-cointegration null hypothesis were based on a technique proposed by Hamilton (1994, Chapter 19), which consists of estimating the cointegration vector via a regression in which the regressors are exchange rates and the dependent variable is the price of gold, and then test the residuals for unit roots using the augmented Dickey–Fuller (1981) (ADF) test. The results of the unit-root tests on both spot and forward data are reported in Table 8.1; as the no-cointegration null hypothesis is not rejected in either case, the error correction approach is not appropriate.[6]

As estimation of equation (8.4) requires stationarity of forecast errors rather than prices and exchange rates, the non-overlapping forecast error data were tested for stationarity by ADF unit-root tests with up to five lags. The usual procedure involves testing the ADF statistic corresponding to highest lag with a significant t-lag statistic but, as is indicated in Table 8.1, none of the t-lag statistics were significant at even the 10 per cent level.[7] While this inclusive result may be due to sample size, augmented Dickey–Fuller tests often fail to provide solid evidence.

Table 8.1 Augmented Dickey–Fuller unit root tests on residuals of cointegration equations: gold prices and exchange rates, 1982(07)– 1990(12)

| | Spot | | | Forward | | |
| | | t-lag statistic | | | t-lag statistic | |
LAG	t-ADF stat	Value	P-value	t-ADF stat	Value	P-value
1	−2.7826	−0.7844	0.4346	−2.7203	−2.1173	0.0369
2	−2.5501	−0.5546	0.5804	−2.1900	−1.7289	0.0872
3	−2.4526	−0.2514	0.8021	−2.0284	−0.3696	0.7125
4	−2.7099	−1.4279	0.1565	−1.5853	−1.4108	0.1617
5	−2.5899	−0.0312	0.9751	−1.5125	−0.0346	0.9725

Notes: Critical values are for non-zero drift in the explanatory variables. Critical values for t-ADF statistic: 5 per cent = −3.66, 1 per cent = −4.65

More conclusive stationarity tests were obtained by using the fractional differencing approach, which involves a non-integer 'order of differentiation', d. For any series, X_t, the Wald representation is:

$$(1 - L)^d X_t = A(L)\varepsilon_t,$$

where ε_t is white noise, L is the usual lag operator, and stationarity is determined by the value of d (see the Appendix for further details). We used the Sowell (1991) maximum likelihood estimate, which gives more reliable results, particularly with small samples. The parameter d was estimated for each of the three subsets of 35 forecast error observations (based on the original data set), and the results appear in Panel A, Table 8.2.[8] As none of the estimates of d are significantly different from zero, the forecast error for all four series appear to be stationary.[9]

Table 8.2 Stationarity and market efficiency tests on forecast error data 1982(02)–1990(04)

	Panel A: Stationarity tests on forecast error data			
	Maximum likelihood estimates of d (with t-statistics)			
Subset	Gold	Mark	Yen	Pound
First	−0.07	0.19	0.03	0.10
	(−0.32)	(0.93)	(0.22)	(1.12)
Second	−0.15	0.15	0.11	0.05
	(−0.30)	(0.88)	(1.53)	(0.18)
Third	−0.08	0.20	0.03	0.18
	(−0.47)	(1.07)	(0.70)	(1.44)

	Panel B: Market Efficiency Tests							
	Weak (equation (8.5))				Semi-strong (equation (8.6))			
	Forecast error for:				Forecast error for:			
Statistic	Gold	DM	Dollar	Yen	Gold	DM	Dollar	Yen
$\chi^2(1)^a$	0.03	0.00	1.13	1.05	2.58	17.22	15.02	10.46
P-Value	0.87	1.00	0.29	0.31	0.63	0.00	0.00	0.03
$F(1,100)^b$	0.06	0.00	1.50	1.06	0.48	15.25	4.41	8.74
P-Value	0.81	1.00	0.22	0.30	0.75	0.00	0.00	0.00

Notes:
a OLS estimates using White's (1980) Robust Error routine with 2 lags.
b Standard errors estimated by the Hansen–Hodrick (1980) method.

2.2 Market Efficiency Test

As argued earlier, if the gold and foreign exchange markets are efficient, estimation of equation (8.4) is simplified as both the forecast errors and the residuals of equation (8.4) will be serially uncorrelated. Tests of both weak and semi-strong market efficiency were conducted.

2.2.1 Weak market efficiency
The classic test for weak market efficiency is based on estimating the equation $P_{i,t}^s = \alpha + \beta \cdot P_{i,t-3,3}^F$ and testing the joint restriction $\alpha = 0$ and $\beta = 1$. But as market efficiency also requires serially uncorrelated forecast errors, the

test for market efficiency was based on equation (8.5):

$$Z_{.,t,3} = \gamma + \delta \cdot Z_{.,t-3,3} ,$$ (8.5)

in which estimates of δ should not differ significantly from zero. Four χ^2 statistics on the restriction $\delta = 0$ based on OLS estimates of equation (8.5) for the 105 overlapping observations using White's (1980) robust standard error routine appear in Panel B of Table 8.2; the restriction is not rejected.[10] The standard errors were re-estimated by the Hansen–Hodrick (H–H) (1980) method and since the significance of F statistics on the $\delta = 0$ restriction, also reported in Panel B of Table 8.2, are similar to the χ^2 statistics, weak market efficiency cannot be rejected.

2.2.2 Semi-strong market efficiency

In the context of the model developed in Section 1, semi-strong market efficiency requires past gold price and exchange-rate forecast errors to be orthogonal with both the current gold price and exchange-rate forecast errors. The test for the gold market involves estimating the following equation:

$$Z_{1,t+3,3} = \mu + \vartheta_1 \cdot Z_{1,t,3} + \sum_{i=2}^{4} \vartheta_i \cdot Z_{Eli,t,3}$$ (8.6)

and, for the jth exchange rate, Z_1 is replaced with Z_{E1j} . Semi-strong market efficiency is tested by the joint restriction that estimates of all four ϑ_i are zero. Panel B of Table 8.2 presents the four χ^2 statistics on that joint restriction based on OLS robust-error estimates of equation (8.6) using the 105 overlapping observations, and the four F statistics based on H–H estimates of standard errors; semi-strong market efficiency is not rejected for gold, but is decisively rejected for all exchange rates. In summary, all forecast error series are stationary and hence no filtering is required; in addition, weak market efficiency cannot be rejected for any case, but semi-strong efficiency can be rejected for all exchange rates.

3.0 ESTIMATES OF THE 'THETAS' FOR THE WORLD GOLD MARKET

As the pound sterling was designated currency *1* (the reference currency) and the price of gold and all exchange rates were denominated in that currency, there are but three parameters to estimate: $\theta_{DM}, \theta_{US\$}$ and θ_{Yen}. Equation (8.4) was estimated using all 105 overlapping observations with the standard errors estimated by the H–H method.[11] As a *t*-test on the estimates of the θ_j parameters, reported in Panel A of Table 8.3, indicates that the unit–sum restriction cannot be rejected, that restriction was imposed and the results (again with standard errors estimated by the H–H method) are summarised in Panel B of Table 8.3. As that restriction was not binding, the restricted and unrestricted regressions are nearly identical – apart from an increase in the *t* statistics. Apparently the major gold producers, which includes Australia, South Africa, and the former USSR, have little power in the world gold market. Rather, that market is dominated by the ECU and dollar blocs (with the ECU having by far the larger weight), and to a lesser extent by the yen bloc.

Table 8.3 OLS estimate of equation (8.4): gold, 1983(01)–1990(12) (Hansen–Hodrick standard errors)

Panel A Unrestricted			
Sum of θ_j coefficients:		0.9756	
Standard error of sum		0.0852	
t-statistic (against unity):		–0.2862	
P-Value:		0.7754	
Panel B Restricted			
Parameter	Estimate	*t*-Statistics	*P*-Value
θ_{DM}	0.5339	4.0913	0.0001
$\theta_{US\$}$	0.2759	3.4978	0.0007
θ_{Yen}	0.1902	1.8940	0.0614

Notes: $\bar{R}^2 = 0.3904$; SEE=0.0596; D–W=1.1824; Q(24)=41.7801; P-Value=0.0137

Note further that, while the estimates of θ_{DM} and $\theta_{US\$}$ are significant at the 0.001 per cent level, that of θ_{Yen} is not significant at the 5 per cent level.[12]

To test whether the θ estimates vary over time, equation (8.4) was re-estimated using two subsamples of equal length, which resulted in the following estimates: 0.5455 and 0.4995 for θ_{DM}, 0.2472 and 0.3045 for $\theta_{US\$}$ and 0.2073 and 0.1960 for θ_{Yen}, respectively, for the subperiods 1983(01)–1986(12) and 1987(01)–1990(12). While the importance of the dollar bloc may have increased over time (and that of Europe declined), in no case did the difference between the two estimates exceed the smaller of the two standard errors.

3.1   World Inflation and the Price of Gold

The estimate of equation (8.4) reported in Table 8.3 does not include any variables for the fundamentals, which are captured in equations (8.3S) and (8.3F) by $K^S(X_t)$ and $K^F(X_{t-3})$. A likely candidate is world inflation, changes in which may affect the price of gold (but not exchange rates). The 'world' price level, P_w^*, was defined as the natural logarithm of a weighted average of the European, US, and Japanese price levels, the weights being the theta estimates reported in Table 8.3.[13] The quarterly world inflation rate, defined as $\Pi_t P_{w,t}^* - P_{w,t-3}^*$, was converted to an annual rate Π_t and, as inflation may have lagged effects, the inflation components of $K^S(X_t)$ and $K^F(X_{t-3})$ were defined as $\gamma(L) \cdot \Pi_t$ and $\gamma(L) \cdot \Pi_{t-3}$. The inflation component of v_{1t} is $\gamma(L) \cdot (\Pi_t - \Pi_{t-3})$, and was parameterised as $\gamma_0(\Pi_{t,3} - \Pi_{t-3,3}) + \gamma_1 \cdot (\Pi_{t-1,3} - \Pi_{t-4,3}) + \gamma_2 \cdot (\Pi_{t-2,3} - \Pi_{t-5,3})$. Moreover, using the property of any polynomial $A(L) = \sum_{i=0}^{N} a_i \cdot L^i$ and any time series Y_t, that $A(L) \cdot Y_t$ can be parameterised in error correction form as:

$$A(L) \cdot Y_t = \sum_{i=0}^{N-1} \left(\sum_{j=0}^{i} a_j \right) \cdot \Delta Y_{t-i} + A(1) \cdot Y_{t-N},$$

the inflation term $\gamma(L) \cdot (\Pi_t - \Pi_{t-3})$ is expressed, in the case of two lags, as $\gamma_0 \cdot \Delta(\Pi_t - \Pi_{t-3}) + \gamma_1 \cdot \Delta(\Pi_{t-1} - \Pi_{t-4}) + \gamma(1) \cdot (\Pi_{t-2} - \Pi_{t-5})$ which permits a direct estimate of $\gamma(1)$, the long run impact on the spot price of gold of a permanent change in the rate of world inflation.

When the inflation variable was included, the no-cointegration null hypothesis was not rejected, nor was stationarity of the inflation variable rejected: the estimate of d for $\Pi_{t,3} - \Pi_{t-3,3}$ was 0.082. The results of an OLS estimate of equation (8.4) augmented by the inflation variable with two lags are summarised in Table 8.4; the estimate of θ_j are similar to those reported in Table 8.3, although the standard errors are smaller. The results show that world inflation, as a fundamental, is an anemic one: a (permanent) rise in the (annual) rate of world inflation by one percentage point leads to a mere 0.78 per cent rise in the price of gold.

Table 8.4 OLS estimate of equation (8.4) with inflation variables: gold, 1983(01)–1990(12) (Hansen–Hodrick standard errors)

Panel A. Unrestricted	
Sum of θ_j coefficients:	0.9718
Standard error of sum:	0.0837
t-statistic (against unity):	–0.3365
P-value:	0.7373

Panel B. Restricted				
Parameter	Lag	Estimate	t-statistic	P-value
θ_{Dm}	–	0.5478	4.3817	0.0000
$\theta_{US\$}$	–	0.2521	3.5118	0.0007
θ_{Yen}	–	0.2001	2.2683	0.0257
$\gamma(1)$	2	0.7777	3.2081	0.0019

Notes: $\overline{R}^2 = 0.4074$; SEE=0.0587; D–W=1.2521; Q(24) = 40.8280; P-Value = 0.0174

3.2 A More General Formulation

The *overlapping* nature of the forecast error data results in strong serial correlation in the data and in the residuals of OLS estimates based on those data; indeed, the partial auto-correlations for the forecast error data are high for up to seven or eight lags and the Q statistics reported in Table 8.3 and 8.4 are highly significant. This serial correlation suggests that lags may be useful even though weak market efficiency was not rejected. A more general specification of equation (8.4), which incorporate lags, is the following:

$$\alpha(L) \cdot Z_{1,t,n} = \text{constant} + \sum_{j=2}^{M} \Theta_j(L) \cdot Z_{E1j,t,n} + \gamma(L)(\Pi_t - \Pi_{t-3}) + \upsilon_{1t} \quad (8.4')$$

Experimentation indicated that lags on the independent variables became redundant (that is, $\Theta_j(L) \equiv \Theta_j$) once lags on the dependent variable were introduced; accordingly, the final effect on the spot price of gold of a permanent shock to the jth exchange rate is $\theta_j \equiv \Theta_j / \alpha(1)$, where $\alpha(1) = \Sigma_{i=0}^{l} \alpha_i$ and $\alpha_0 = 1$, and the long-run reaction of the real spot price of gold to a permanent shock to world inflation is captured by the parameter $\Gamma \equiv \gamma(1) / \alpha(1)$.

With this modification equation (8.4') was estimated by OLS with lags being added until the estimate of $\alpha(1)$ stabilised (which occurred after the eight lags) and the standard errors were estimated by the H–H technique; the results appear in Panel A in Table 8.5.[14] Since the unit-sum restriction on the θ_j was not rejected at the 70 per cent level of significance, equation (8.4′) was re-estimated with that restriction imposed; the results for both the Θ_j and θ_j are reported in Panel B in Table 8.5.

Table 8.5 OLS estimate of equation (8.4′) with inflation variables and nine lags on dependent variable: gold, 1983(01)–1990(12) (Hansen–Hodrick standard errors)

Panel A Unrestricted				
Sum of θ_j coefficients			0.9654	
Standard error of Sum			0.0933	
t-Statistic (against unity)			−0.3705	
P-Value:			0.7120	
Panel B Restricted				
Parameter	Lag	Estimate	t-Statistic	P-Value
Θ_{DM}	0	0.4919	5.4858	0.0000
$\Theta_{US\,\$}$	0	0.1284	2.7900	0.0053
Θ_{Yen}	0	0.1327	2.3992	0.0164
$\alpha(1)$	9	−0.7531	−12.6609	0.0000
θ_{DM}	0	0.6532	5.2959	0.0000
$\theta_{US\,\$}$	0	0.1705	2.9334	0.0044
θ_{Yen}	0	0.1763	2.3580	0.0208
Γ	2	0.6446	2.8119	0.0062

Notes: $\overline{R}^2 = 0.5105$; SEE = 0.0507

Despite first differencing of the dependent variable, the new estimate of equation (8.4′) dominates those reported in Tables 8.3 and 8.4. The $\overline{R}^2$ has increased by one quarter to 0.51 and the standard error of estimate has declined to 0.051 from 0.059. The estimate of all thetas, both short- and long-run, are significant at the 2 per cent level, and the point estimate of θ_{DM}, which increased from 0.55 to 0.65, is nearly four times that of both $\theta_{US\,\$}$ and of θ_{Yen}. The estimate of Γ also is highly significant but declined from 0.78 to 0.64: a (permanent) rise by one point in the annual rate of world inflation rate leads to an increase in the real spot price of gold of only two-thirds of 1 per cent.

It is clear from Table 8.5 that the European countries heavily dominate the international market for gold and hence movements in European exchange rates against the US dollar impact heavily on the dollar price of gold. While a 10 per cent appreciation of the deutsche mark (against all other currencies) increases the dollar price of gold by 6.5 per cent (and vice versa), the same appreciation of the yen increases the dollar price of gold by only 1.7 per cent. A 10 per cent appreciation of the dollar against both currencies depresses the dollar price of gold by about 8 per cent, and vice versa.

Three simulations based on the restricted estimate of equation (8.4′), depicting the response of the US dollar price of gold to transitory and permanent depreciations of the US dollar vis a vis the DM, the yen, and both currencies are reported in Figure 8.1. The striking effect of the dollar/DM (that is, US dollar/ECU) exchange rate on the dollar price of gold is readily evident.

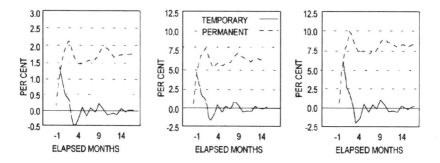

Figure 8.1 Simulated response of US dollar price of gold to a 10 per cent depreciation of the dollar against: the yen, the DM, both.

4.0 FLOATING EXCHANGE RATES AND THE STABILITY OF THE GOLD MARKET

There can be little doubt that floating exchange rates among the major currencies have contributed substantially to the variability of the price of gold during the 1980s. There is, of course, no way of divining the behavior of the free market price of gold had the Bretton Woods fixed exchange rate system endured (but without the link between the dollar and gold), but to gain an idea of the degree to which the world gold market has been influenced by floating exchange rates, an experiment was conducted. Equation (8.4′) was parameterised in level form as:

$$Z_{1,t,n} = \text{constant} + \sum_{k=1}^{9} \alpha_k \cdot Z_{1,t-j,n} + \sum_{j=2}^{4} \theta_j \cdot Z_{E1j,t,n} + \upsilon_{1t},$$

and OLS estimates of the α_k and θ_j, with the unit-sum restriction (that is, $\sum_{j=1}^{3} \hat{\theta}_j - \sum_{k=1}^{9} \hat{\alpha}_k = \hat{\alpha}_0 = \alpha_0 = 1$) imposed on the long run thetas, were used to calculate the residuals of a reparameterised version of equation (8.3S):

$$\hat{u}_{1t} = P_{1t}^S - \sum_{k=1}^{9} \alpha_k \cdot P_{1,t-j}^S \sum_{j=2}^{4} \hat{\theta}_j \cdot E_{1j,t}^S \qquad (8.3S')$$

Those residuals, which reflect all influences on the real spot price of gold *other than major currency exchange rates*, were taken as estimates of the fundamentals (the $K(X)$ term in equation (8.3)).

As all variables in equation (8.3S′) are in natural logs, the calculated residuals, $\hat{u}_{1t}$, were transformed into arithmetic values to be dimensionally identical with the spot price of gold and then converted into both nominal and real 'prices' in all four currencies. The coefficients of variation of the spot gold price and the transformed residuals appear in Panel A, Table 8.6. For the 1982(11)–1990(12) period, the coefficient of variation of the actual spot prices of gold – both nominal and real – are roughly 80 per cent larger than those of the transformed residuals and, apart from the case of the pound sterling, the differences according to currency of denomination are very small.[15] Fluctuation in real exchange rates appear to account for nearly half of the variance in gold prices during the sample period.

It cannot be assumed that real exchange rates would have been constant had the Bretton Woods regime been preserved (again without the link between the dollar and gold), nor is it possible to know how they would have behaved under that system since 1973. Mussa (1986) and others have shown that there is ample evidence that real exchange rates have been far less stable with floating exchange rates than under the Bretton Woods regime. To quantify the effect of the regime change, we calculated the standard deviations of quarterly first differences of the natural logarithms of the real exchange rates between the UK and the US, Germany and Japan for 1960–1970 and 1973–1990 periods; price levels and exchange rates were defined as the natural logarithms of quarterly averages. The results, presented in Panel B of Table 8.6, show that the variability in the UK real exchange rates with the US and Japan have nearly tripled since 1973. Moreover, despite the growing monetary integration between the UK and

Germany, that variability of that real exchange rate has more than doubled. While not definitive, these results support the proposition that floating exchange rates among the major currencies have exacerbated the instability of the free market price of gold since 1973.

Table 8.6 The stability of the gold market and real exchange rates

Panel A. Sources of variation in gold prices: 1982(11)–1990(12)

Currency of Denomination	Coefficient of variation of the					
	Nominal price of gold			Real price of gold		
	Actual Prices	$\hat{u}_{lt}$	Ratio	Actual Prices	$\hat{u}_{lt}$	Ratio
Pound:	5.11	2.43	2.10	5.40	2.53	2.14
Mark:	5.28	2.88	1.83	5.33	2.91	1.83
Dollar:	4.92	2.78	1.77	5.04	2.83	1.78
Yen:	5.68	3.15	1.80	5.63	3.10	1.82

Panel B. Standard deviations of quarterly first differences of logarithms of the UK real exchange rates with Germany, the US and Japan: 1960–1970 and 1973–1990, in per cent

Real Exchange Rate defined on:	Years	Germany	Us	Japan
Consumer prices:	1960–1970	2.1067	1.7755	2.1934
	1973–1990	4.8402	5.4086	5.6491
Ratio:		2.30	3.05	2.58
Producer prices:	1960–1970	2.0059	1.6974	2.1153
	1973–1990	4.6049	5.3005	5.7939
Ratio:		2.30	3.12	2.74

5.0 SUMMARY OF THE MAIN RESULTS.

While we cannot claim that the empirical results for the case of gold can be generalised to other commodities, the main findings, based on an analysis of the gold and foreign exchange markets for the 1982–1990 period, are:

- The world gold market is dominated by the European currency bloc which possesses about two-thirds of the 'market power' enjoyed by all participants in that market. Accordingly, real appreciations or depreciations of the European currencies have profound effects on the price of gold in all other currencies.
- Although gold is usually denominated in US dollars, the dollar bloc has but a small influence on the dollar price of gold. Moreover, the major

gold producers of the world (Australia, South Africa and the former USSR) appear to have no significant influence on the world price of gold.

- Gold continues to be a store of value as 'world' inflation increases the demand for gold; it is estimated that the real price of gold rises by between two-thirds and three-quarters of 1 per cent in response to a one point increase on the world inflation rate.
- The evidence strongly supports the market efficiency hypothesis for the international gold market for the 1982–1990 period.
- During the 1982–1990 period, floating exchange rates among the major currencies contributed substantially to the instability of the world price of gold; indeed, fluctuations in the real exchange rates among the major currencies account for nearly half of the observed variance in the spot price of gold during that period.

APPENDIX

Fractional Differencing

In Box–Jenkins (1976) terminology, time-series data usually are assumed to be integrated of either degree zero or one (and occasionally of degree two); when a variable X_t is integrated of degree zero [that is, $X_t \sim I(0)$], its variance is finite and innovations have no lasting effect as the auto-correlation decays at an exponential rate for distant lags. However, if $X_t \sim I(1)$, the variance of X_t is not finite and, as X_t is the sum of all previous innovations, those innovations have a permanent effect.

A limitation of the conventional approach is that it allows only for discrete values for the degree of integration whereas there may exist a range of intermediate values that involve the so-called long memory models. These models stem from Granger (1966) who demonstrated that economic variables have a 'typical spectral shape', concluding that 'long term fluctuations in economic variables, if decomposed into frequency components, are such that the amplitudes of the components decrease smoothly with decreasing period'. In other words, the spectral density of economic time series is bounded at the origin and the auto-correlation function declines smoothly as the lag between observations increases. This means that variables tend to display long, irregular cycles or, stated differently, shocks are persistent.

The correct method for analysing economic time series, developed in the early 1980s, is known as fractional differencing. The intuition is rather straightforward. Standard time-series methodology considers only processes such as ARIMA (p,d,q) where d, the order of differentiation, is assumed to be an integer. Granger and Joyeaux (1980) and Hosking (1981) argue, however, that d is not necessarily an integer; rather, it is a real number. They suggested a procedure by which d is estimated (which is closely related to unit-root tests) and then a filter based on the estimate of d is applied to preserve the information on persistence. The transformed series then can be analysed as an ARMA (p,q) process or by traditional time series methods.

The simplest long memory process – the basic building block – is the fractional noise defined as:

$$(1-L)^d X_t = \sum_{j=0}^{\infty} a_j \cdot \varepsilon_{t-j} = A(L)\varepsilon_t ,$$

where d is a real number and ε_t is white noise. The process is stationary and invertible if $-0.5 < d < 0.5$ and the binomial expansion of $(1-L)^d$ allows one to express a_j, as:

$$a_j = \frac{\Gamma_{(j-d)}}{\Gamma_{(j+1)} \cdot \Gamma_{(-d)}} ,$$

which converges in mean square for $-0.5 < d < 0.5$. The fractional noise for $-0.5 < d < 0.5$ has an auto-regressive representative:

$$\sum_{j=1}^{\infty} \left(\frac{\Gamma_{(j-d)}}{\Gamma_{(j+1)} \cdot \Gamma_{(-d)}} \right) L^j X_t = \varepsilon_t ,$$

and a moving average representation:

$$X_t = \sum_{j=1}^{\infty} \left(\frac{\Gamma_{(j-d)}}{\Gamma_{(j+1)} \cdot \Gamma_{(d)}} \right) L^j \varepsilon_t ,$$

More general processes can be obtained from fractional noise; these are usually referred to as Auto-Regressive Fractionally Integrated Moving Average (ARFIMA) and, in addition to the long memory component, they contain an ARMA component that determines the short-term movements:

$$(1-L)^d B(L)X_t = C(L)\varepsilon_t$$

If d is in the open interval (0, 0.05), the series X_t is stationary but displays non-periodic, irregular cycles. The auto-covariance of the series is positive and decays at a geometric rate (compared to the standard ARIMA models). Alternatively, if $d \in (0.5,1)$ the series is non-stationary; in either case, if d is significantly different from zero, a filter $(1-L)^d$ is required to obtain a series integrated of degree zero.

Stationarity Tests on Basic Data

The first test to determine if the gold price and exchange rate data are random walks or (possibly non-stationary) long memory processes utilises a procedure designed by Diebold (1989) and based on the variance time function. With sample of size T and mean μ, the variance of the kth difference is:

$$\sigma_X^2(k) = \sum_{t=k}^{T}(X_t - X_{t-k} - k \cdot \mu)^2 /(T-k+1),$$

and if X_t follows a random walk, $\sigma_X^2(k)$ is proportional to k:

$$\sigma_X^2(k) = k \cdot \sigma_X^2(1),$$

Under the null hypothesis that the series follows a random walk with drift, a sample scalar asymptotic test statistic, $R2(k)$, is calculated as:

$$R2(k) = k \cdot \sigma_X^2(1)/\sigma_X^2(k),$$

The fractiles of the $R2(k)$ statistic for k = 1, 2, 4, 8, 16, 32 corresponding to the (random-walk) null hypothesis that $R(k)$ = 1 and the fractiles of a joint test statistic, $J2$, under the null hypothesis that all $R2(k)$ are equal unity have been calculated by Diabold (1989). The $R2$ and $J2$ tests statistics computed for all 108 overlapping observations on gold prices and exchange rates are reported in Panel A of Table 8.7. The null hypothesis of random walk with drift is rejected only in the case of the deutsche mark, where the $J2$ joint test statistics rejects it.

Table 8.7 Stationarity tests on gold price and exchange rate data

	Panel A. Diebold random walk test on gold prices and exchange rates							
	Gold		Mark		Yen		Pound	
Test	Spot	Forward	Spot	Forward	Spot	Forward	Spot	Forward
R2(2)	0.98	0.91	1.17	1.19	1.10	1.11	0.90	0.80
R2(4)	0.86	0.76	0.93	0.95	0.87	0.90	0.96	0.93
R2(8)	1.84	2.30	0.65	0.65	0.58	0.61	1.11	1.14
R2(16)	1.42	1.85	0.47	0.45	0.81	0.82	0.81	0.85
R2(32)	1.95	2.06	0.20	0.20	0.34	0.34	0.33	0.34
J2	0.94	1.77	4.96	5.27	2.08	1.97	1.60	1.48
	Panel B. Maximum likelihood estimates of d: gold and the exchange rates							
Prices			Gold		Mark	Yen		Pound
Spot			0.83		1.02	1.07		1.05
Forward			0.86		1.08	1.07		1.06

The results of stationarity tests using maximum likelihood estimates of the order of differentiation, d, based on all 108 overlapping observations on spot and forward gold prices and the original US dollar exchange rate data are reported in Panel B of Table 8.7. As none of the estimates of d differ significantly from unity, all series, both spot and forward, appear to be non-stationary; moreover, a model selection procedure based on the Akaike and the Schwarz information criteria indicates that the series have no ARMA component hence can be treated as random walks.

ACKNOWLEDGEMENTS

The authors are grateful for comments by participants in seminars at the Australian National University, Curtin University of Technology, the universities of Chicago and Western Australia and particularly for comments by Kenneth Clements and Michael McAleer; the usual disclaimer holds.

REFERENCES

Box, G.E. and G.M. Jenkins (1976), *Time Series Analysis Forecasting and Control*, 2nd edn, San Francisco: Holden Day.

Dickey, D.A. and W.A. Fuller (1981), 'Likelihood ratio statistics for auto-regressive time series with a unit root', *Econometrica*, **49**, pp. 1057–1072.

Diebold, F.X. (1989), 'Random walks versus fractional integration', in B. Raj (ed.), *Advances in Econometrics and Modeling*, Kluwer Academic Publishers.

Dornbusch, R. (1987), 'Exchange rates economics', *Economic Journal*, **97**, pp. 1–18.

Edwards, S. (1989*), Real Exchange Rates, Devaluation, and Adjustment: Exchange Rate Policy in Developing Countries*, Cambridge: The MIT Press.

Engle, R.F. and C.W.J. Granger (1987), 'Co-integration and error correction: representation, estimation and testing', *Econometrica*, **55**, pp. 251–276.

Frenkel, J. (1981), 'The collapse of purchasing power parity during the 1970s', *European Economic Review*, **16**, pp. 145–165.

Granger, C.W.J. (1966), 'The typical spectral shape of an economic variable', *Econometrica*, **34**, pp. 151–161.

Granger, C.W.J. and R. Joyeaux (1980), 'An introduction of long memory time series models', *The Journal of Time Series Analysis*, **4**, pp. 221–228.

Hamilton J.D. (1994), *Time Series Analysis*, Princeton: Princeton University Press.

Hansen L.P. and R.J. Hodrick (1980), 'Forward exchange rates as optimal predictors of future spot rates: an econometric analysis', *The Journal of Political Economy*, **88**, pp. 829–853.

Hosking, J.R.M. (1981), 'Fractional differencing', *Biometrika*, **68**, pp. 165–176.

Mussa, M. (1986), 'National exchange rate regimes and the behavior of real exchange rates: evidence and implications', *Carnegie–Rochester Conference Series on Public Policy*, Amsterdam: North-Holland Publishing Company, **25**, pp. 117–213.

Ridler, D. and C.A. Yandle (1972), 'A simplified method for analysing the effects of exchange rate changes on exports of a primary commodity', *International Monetary Fund Staff Papers*, **19**.

Sjaastad, L.A. (1985), 'Exchange rate regimes and the real rate of interest', in M. Connolly and J. McDermott (eds), *The Economics of the Caribbean Basin*, New York: Praeger.

Sowell, F. (1991), *Maximum Likelihood Estimation of Stationary Univariate Fractionally Integrated Time Series Models*, (mimeo), Graduate School of Industrial Administration, Pittsburgh: Carnegie Mellon University..

White, H. (1980), 'A heteroscedasticity-consistent covariance matrix estimator and a direct test for heteroscedasticity', *Econometrica*, **48**, pp. 817–838.

NOTES

1   Of the currencies corresponding to the 150 members of the International Monetary Fund as of mid-1990, 12 were major currencies (10 of which comprised the European Monetary System (the EMS)), leaving 138 minor currencies. Fifty-five minor currencies were tied to a single currency, 42 to a currency basket, and 41 were floating.

2   To the best of the authors' knowledge, Ridler and Yandle (1972) were the first to use this approach to analyse the effect of exchange rate adjustments on commodity prices. The

model presented here first appeared in Sjaastad (1985); a similar approach was developed by Dornbusch (1987)

3   Global fundamentals are defined as all factors other than exchange rates and price levels that influence the global demand for the supply of the commodity in question, including expectations.

4   See Frehkle (1981) concerning the large fluctuations in PPP, and hence in real exchange rates, experienced by the major currencies during the 1970s and Edwards (1989) for a massive compilation of real exchange rate data for smaller countries.

5   Lack of serial correlation in forecast errors also requires the absence of time-dependent risk premia; in what follows, that property is assumed to hold – and is subsequently tested – on forecast errors for exchange rates and the price of gold.

6   For the case at hand, the critical values for the t-statistic (two of which are reported in Table 8.1) are not the standard one; for the correct critical values, see Hamilton (1994, p. 592 and his Appendix tables).

7   While some t-lag statistics were significant for the pound/US dollar exchange rate, those forecast errors were never used in the actual estimation of the equation (8.4). The rather voluminous details of these stationary tests are available from the authors upon request.

8   The first subsets contains all observations for the first month of each quarter, the second subset contains those on the second month.

9   The cointegration tests were made using PCGIVE, version 8.0. The maximum likelihood estimates were made with a program kindly supplied by F. Sowell. Remaining estimation was by ESTIMA RATS 386 version 4.10c.

10 If equation (8.5) were estimated with a single lag on the independent variable, the expected value of the estimate of δ would be roughly 0.67 since two-thirds of the innovations in any observation on forecast errors tend to be common to adjoining observations. To avoid that bias, the independent variable was lagged three periods (that is one prediction period).

11 Since subsequent estimates of equation (8.5) using lags on the dependent variable reduces the regressions to the period 1983(01)–1990(12), all estimates were made with data over this range to facilitate comparisons.

12 Because the observations are overlapping, the residuals are serially correlated and hence it is not possible to conduct the usual LM tests for ARCH or normality tests, as those tests assume the residuals to be i.i.d.

13 The European price level was computed as a weighted average of German, UK and Italian producer prices, and French consumer prices (producer prices are unavailable for France). The weights, 0.3142, 0.2594, 0.2109 and 0.2125, respectively, were based on relative real GDPs for the 1982–1990 period.

14 An alternative procedure was used to set the weights in the world price level equal to the estimates of thetas. Equation (8.4′) was not parameterised to provide direct estimates of $\theta_j \equiv \Theta / \alpha(1)$ and $\Gamma \equiv \gamma(1) / \alpha(1)$ since the resulting non-linear equation would preclude using the Hansen–Hodrick (1980) method to estimate standard errors; instead, estimation was by OLS and the standard errors of θ_j and Γ were obtained by Taylor expansions.

15 Prior to calculating the standard deviations, the transformed residuals and spot prices were first differenced to remove negative trends, which are quite pronounced in the deutsche mark and yen series. The sample average spot price of gold was used to compute coefficients of variation.

9. Is the $A a Commodity Currency?

John Freebairn

At various times in its history Australia has been described as riding on the sheep's back or on the coal train. There is no doubt that Australia has a comparative advantage in the production and international trade of natural resource-based commodities. Further, I am confident that commodity exports will earn more than a half of Australian export receipts over the next few decades. It also is a fact of life that world commodity prices are both very volatile and difficult to predict. Those in the commodity and financial markets, and others, are aware that world commodity price fluctuations often set in train changes to the value of the $A relative to foreign currencies, changes to domestic inflation and wages, and changes in other variables which influence the short-term and longer-term profitability of business activities and the general economic performance of the economy.

The objective of this chapter is to investigate some of the direct and indirect effects of world commodity price fluctuations on the profitability of Australian commodity export industries, other export industries, manufacturing import substitute industries, and the non-traded service industries. The analysis takes into consideration the direct effects of the world commodity price fluctuations and the indirect effects of world commodity price fluctuations on the nominal exchange rate and on the growth rate of Australian inflation and labour costs. It is argued that these indirect effects of fluctuating world commodity prices cushion the direct effects of world price changes on profitability of the export industries, and that at the same time they influence the profitability of other sectors of the economy.

The chapter is in three parts. Section 1 describes the underlying structure of a commodity currency. It indicates the way in which world commodity price changes can induce changes in the nominal exchange rate and in domestic inflation rates. Section 2 considers the supporting evidence for the $A being a commodity currency. The final section then evaluates the combined implications of fluctuating world commodity prices and a $A commodity currency for the profitability over time of Australian export, import competing and non-traded industries.

1.0 THE MEANING OF A COMMODITY CURRENCY

In its simplest form a commodity currency means that the real exchange rate moves in sympathy with world commodity prices.[1] When commodity prices boom, the real exchange rate appreciates by a combination of appreciation of the nominal exchange rate (that is, an increase in the number of units of foreign currency that can be exchanged for one $A) and faster growth of domestic inflation relative to inflation of other countries. Conversely, when commodity prices fall the real exchange rate depreciates. This section explains the causal forces driving such a relationship and highlights the key assumptions behind such a mechanism. We begin with a very simple model and progressively add complications that bring us closer to the workings of the Australian economy. The conceptual analysis is designed to pinpoint key pieces of data to be assessed in the following section for determining whether the $A is a commodity currency or not.

We begin with a very simple model, but one which is especially favourable to the commodity currency idea. Suppose a country (Australia) depends on one commodity for all its exports (say, wool), and the world price of the commodity exhibits considerable volatility and is little influenced by Australian activities (including wool production); the country imports goods and services (say, manufactured goods) with relatively stable world prices; international capital flows are relatively small so that the balance of trade has to be close to zero (that is, wool export income roughly equals import outlays on manufactures); and we start from a state of equilibrium.

Now, consider the effects of a significant boost in the world commodity price (say, as the result of the Korean War commodity boom, the outbreak of a disease which reduces wool production in other producer countries, or a fashion change especially favourable to wool). This increase in the Australian foreign terms of trade, that is, increase in the ratio of world prices received for our exports relative to world prices paid for our imports has two sets of effects. First, the boost to export income generates a trade balance surplus and a net demand increase by foreigners for Australian dollars. These forces work to increase the nominal value of the Australian dollar relative to other currencies, and in a flexible exchange rate world the nominal value of the Australian currency will appreciate. The appreciating currency will directly reduce the magnitude of the $A price increase of the export commodity as seen by Australian export producers relative to the world price increase of the commodity, and the currency appreciation will reduce the $A price of imports. These price changes encourage quantity adjustments for more imports and less exports. Assuming satisfaction of the Marshall–Lerner elasticities conditions, these quantity adjustments, probably after an extended period of time to enable changes in expectations, investment and production, will bring the trade account back to balance at a higher nominal exchange rate following the world commodity price boom.

A second set of effects of the significant boost in the world commodity price is the increased income and wealth of the Australian exporters. Much of this real gain will be spent on non-traded goods and services, but some will be spent on extra imports and perhaps some on previously exported products. The extra domestic outlays on the traded goods will help to reduce the traded account surplus, but in most cases by relatively little compared to the first round increase effect of the higher world commodity price on the trade account. The more important income and wealth effect of the commodity price boom comes from the increased demand for non-traded goods and services. So long as there is some elasticity of supply of non-traded products,[2] an increase in the output and a rise in prices of these products will follow. The price effect flows into a faster growth rate than otherwise of general prices or inflation. This inflationary impetus flowing from the world commodity price boom works to achieve a real exchange rate appreciation by increasing the growth rate of Australian prices relative to other country prices. It will be the dominant force of real exchange rate adjustment in a world of fixed nominal exchange rates. The resulting induced fall in relative prices of traded goods and services to the prices of non-traded goods and services helps to bring the trade account back to balance by squeezing the profitability of the export and import competing sectors. It also means that for the exporting industries some of the initial boost to profitability of the export commodity from the world commodity price surge is offset by the increase in input costs of items purchased from the non-traded sector and an increase in the cost of nationally mobile inputs, including labour.

Then, in our simple model, a world commodity price boom sets in motion forces to cause the nominal value of the Australian dollar relative to other currencies to rise and for Australian inflation and production costs to rise relative to overseas inflation and production costs. Both sets of changes result in a real appreciation of the Australian dollar. Also, these very same adjustments work to restore a new balance of trade equilibrium at a higher real exchange rate.

For the case of a world commodity price fall (due to, say, a downturn in world economic growth, new protectionist trade policies, and a fashion swing against wool), the effects of the nominal exchange rates and on domestic inflation are a mirror image of the price boom story. Pressures from the resulting trade account deficit work for depreciation of the nominal exchange rate, and pressures and reactions from the fall in real income, wealth and expenditure work to reduce the rate of inflation. Together, they promote a real depreciation of the Australian currency. This real currency depreciation cushions the impact of the world commodity price fall on Australian exporters, and it increases the international competitiveness of import competitors.

This simple process of effects of world commodity price fluctuations on the trade account and on the wealth of exporters underlie changes in nominal exchange rates and changes in relative rates of domestic and overseas inflation which determine the real exchange rate adjustments of a commodity currency. The analysis also highlights some key assumptions.

The role of expectations and international capital flows are critical to the commodity currency outcome. The simple model made the extreme assumption of naïve expectations about the paths of future commodity prices and real income, and the model assumed no international capital flows. Quite reasonable alternative assumptions of perfect foresight expectations and of international capital flows are sufficient to eliminate the commodity currency outcome. Suppose it is well known that commodity prices wildly fluctuate about a long-term trend whose value is known and whose long-term value is used in planning production and consumption, and that expectations about permanent wealth and income used in determining production and consumption decisions are based not on today's income but on the long-term trend values of these variables. Then, world commodity price fluctuations, up or down, have no effect on these expectations, and thus there are no production or expenditure changes as assumed in our simple model described above. During the temporary world commodity price boom, the wealth windfall is saved, with most of this windfall going to the purchase of overseas assets,[3] and this capital outflow matches the trade account surplus. Conversely, during the world commodity price slump, expenditure is maintained by drawing on accumulated wealth or borrowing against future income, with the associated capital inflow balancing the trade account deficit.

Perhaps the real world is not as rational as assumed in this extreme model and world capital markets are not so perfect, but neither does the naïve expectations and zero capital flow model seem realistic. That is, reality likely is somewhere between. In this case where expectations are partly driven by current events and partly by long-run trends, and where international capital flows are important, we would still obtain a commodity currency. The real exchange rate would be much less sensitive to world commodity price fluctuations than under the naïve expectations model, but it would be more sensitive to world commodity price fluctuations than under the perfect foresight model. That is, the direction of causation from commodity price movements to changes in the real exchange rate remains, but the magnitude of change is greatly diminished. We might call this intermediate situation a modified commodity currency model.

A number of alternative assumptions about the operation of the Australian economy will influence the details of and the magnitudes of the real exchange rate response to world commodity price fluctuations. Assumptions about exchange rate flexibility and about flexibility of nominal and real prices and wages clearly affect the mix of the real exchange rate change as between nominal exchange rate changes and changes in Australia's inflation rate relative to that of other countries. Other important parameters include elasticities of sector supply, intersectoral input–output linkages, relative factor intensities in the different production sectors, and income and price elasticity of demand. Cook and Porter (1984) provide a detailed qualitative and quantitative assessment of many of the optional assumption sets in analysing the related issue of a mineral commodity boom; in fact, their demand boost story is akin to a commodity price boom discussed here. Except for some extreme and unlikely assumption sets, the more detailed and carefully developed analysis by Cook and Sieper indicate that the general pattern of real exchange rate adjustments in response to world commodity price fluctuations generated by our simple model are robust to a variety of assumptions about inter-industry linkages, nominal and real wage fixity/flexibility, and of supply and demand elasticities.

Government macroeconomic and other policies can influence the response of the economy to fluctuations in world commodity price fluctuations. Much of the temporary fluctuations in national income and wealth associated with commodity booms and slumps might be absorbed or largely neutralised by variations in fiscal policy – a large surplus in times of booms and a large deficit in times of slumps – if governments could correctly ascertain world commodity price booms and slumps and effect necessary changes in taxation and public expenditure. Monetary policy might be manipulated to influence levels of aggregate demand and in turn inflation rates, and it might be used to modify the volume of international capital flows and in turn the nominal exchange rate.

In practice a large number of factors influence real exchange rates as well as the world commodity price fluctuations of our simple model. Nominal exchange rate movements are influenced by such factors as: relative general price movements at home and abroad (purchasing power parity)[4]; real changes affecting the economy such as resource discoveries, new technology, changes in industry and trade policy and real income growth; monetary policy and interest rate differentials; and expectations and sentiment. Inflation too is influenced by a number of forces, including: wages and other elements of labour costs; aggregate demand relative to capacity; competitive pressures; fiscal and monetary policy. These potential influences on the real exchange rate are not denied. Clearly they are important factors, as well as world commodity price fluctuations, driving Australia's real exchange rate. Such a number of important causal forces make it difficult to disentangle from observed data that component of influence due to world commodity price fluctuations. The focus of this chapter is to assess the incremental effect of world commodity price fluctuations on the real exchange rate.

Clearly, the empirical details of the Australian situation have a major bearing on the commodity exchange rate story. These details relate to the commodity composition of exports and also imports, trends in commodity prices, variability of commodity prices, particularly as the world prices of the different commodities are correlated with one another, and information about the formation of commodity price expectations. Such details provide a background of the underlying structural relationships that generate the observed reduced form relationship between fluctuations in world commodity prices and changes in the real exchange rate.

2.0 SOME FACTS

This section considers empirical data bearing on the question of whether the Australian dollar is a commodity currency. The evidence comes in two steps. Initially we look at background evidence on validity of the assumptions that provide necessary conditions for a commodity currency. More specifically, our objective here is to consider the role of commodities in the Australian economy, and especially in the trade picture, and we consider trend and cyclical movements in Australia's terms of trade and world commodity price movements. These observations generally support the preconditions for a commodity currency.

The section then considers evidence on behavioural responses of the Australian economy to fluctuations in world commodity prices. The focus is on observed correlations between world commodity prices and Australia's terms of trade on the one side and of changes in the nominal exchange rate, domestic real economic activity and inflation, and the real exchange rate on the other side. Consideration also is given to some econometric modelling of the determination of the real exchange rate. There is considerable evidence that large and sustained world commodity price fluctuations significantly influence the Australian real exchange rate, but that other factors are important determinants, and hence the commodity currency fit is imperfect. That is, we conclude that we have a modified commodity currency.

2.1 Commodities in the Australian Economy

Agricultural, energy and mineral products are an important component of the Australian economy. Around the turn of the century they accounted for over 30 per cent of national income (20 per cent for agricultural and 10 per cent for mining), and today commodities account for just over 10 per cent of national income (just under 5 per cent for agricultural and over 5 per cent for mining).

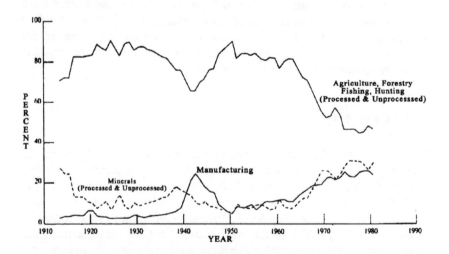

Source: Year Book Australia, Various Years. Cook and Porter (1984, p. 6).

Figure 9.1 Estimates of the sectoral composition of exports 1913–1914 to 1981–1982

While the relative importance of agriculture as a share of national income was relatively constant from the turn of the century to the 1950s and then has declined, the importance of mining declined rapidly in the first two decades of the century and only since the late 1960s has its importance increased.

It is in the area of international trade that commodities loom especially large in the Australian economy. Commodities, and simply processed commodities, have supplied over 80 per cent of our export income throughout this century (see Figure 9.1), but the composition of these commodity exports has undergone considerable change.

Table 9.1 provides a more detailed picture of changes in the commodity composition of Australian exports over a period of forty years. In the 1950s rural products, and especially wool, dominated Australian exports, with wool alone providing over 60 per cent of exports and rural in total just over 80 per cent.

Table 9.1 Changes in the composition of commodities in Australia's exports of goods, 1950–1951 to 1988–1989 (percentage share of total exports)

Five year average for years	Rural				Mining					
	Meat	Cereal fibres	Textile	Total rural	Core	Iron Ore	Alum–ina	Other Ore	Metals	Total mining
1950/51– 1953/54	5.8	13.3	52.1	82.3	0.1	–	na	2.1	5.3	7.5
1954/55– 1958/59	7.9	9.9	44.1	76.3	0.4	–	na	2.5	6.8	9.7
1959/60– 1963/64	8.9	14.8	36.0	72.8	0.1	–	na	2.5	7.0	10.5
1964/65– 1968/69	9.7	13.3	26.7	62.3	2.6	3.4	na	4.0	9.0	19.0
1969/70– 1973/74	11.3	10.9	15.8	48.4	4.7	7.4	2.5	5.1	10.0	29.7
1974/75– 1978/79	8.1	12.4	10.3	41.4	10.7	7.6	4.7	5.9	9.9	38.8
1979/80– 1983/84	7.6	11.9	9.0	38.2	11.7	6.2	5.2	5.7	9.1	37.9
1984/85– 1988/89	5.5	9.1	11.5	34.2	13.98	5.1	4.5	4.7	9.4	37.6

Sources:
W.E. Norton and C.P. Aylmer (1988), Australian Economic Statistics, 1949–50 to 1986–87, Occasional Paper 8a, Reserve Bank of Australia, Sydney.
ABS Cat. No. 5434.0, Exports, Australia, June Quarter 1989.
ABS Cat. No. 5424.0, Exports, Australia 1987–88.

Since then, the relative importance of wool in particular and rural products in general as a share of total exports has declined – although their absolute real value has continued to increase – to the extent that in the late 1980s wool and rural exports provide 10 per cent and 35 per cent, respectively, of Australian exports of goods.

The relative importance of each of meat and cereal products has fluctuated from lows of 5 per cent up to highs of 15 per cent of total exports. The importance of mining exports has increased substantially from 10 per cent in the early 1950s to 38 per cent in the late 1980s. The expansion reflects primarily the rapid expansion of iron ore and bauxite/alumina exports beginning in the late 1960s, and of coal from the mid 1970s and again in the 1980s. Base metals have made a steady contribution, and the relative importance of petroleum products, gold, uranium, diamonds and mineral sands has changed over the years.

Commodities are not unimportant components of Australian imports. Up to 30 per cent of imports represent raw materials, with oil, phosphate rock and chemicals having world price experiences not too dissimilar to those of our commodity exports. Still, the majority of Australian imports can be characterised as manufactured goods. Relative to the commodities, price series for manufactured goods are smooth.

There are other important interrelationships between the commodity sector of the economy and the rest of the economy which should not be ignored in assessing the effects of world commodity price fluctuations on the Australian economy. Over 50 per cent of mining output and over 40 per cent of rural output are used as inputs in other Australian industries or for final domestic consumption. These interrelationships ensure that world commodity price fluctuations directly affect prices and costs in other parts of the economy as well as the commodity sector. Also, the rural and mining sectors use as inputs materials and services from other sectors of the economy and they use nationally mobile labour and capital factors.

For the most part the Australian natural resource industries are capital- and skill-intensive, labour-extensive, and they are internationally competitive and receive little industry-specific direct government assistance.

Overall, the industry structure of the Australian economy is compatible with the assumptions of our commodity currency model, but in a more complex way than described in the simple model of the previous section. Commodities dominate exports, but there are many important commodities with quite different production and consumption determinants. It therefore becomes important to assess the extent to which fluctuations in world prices of the different commodities are correlated with each other; if they move together then we have a similar story as a single commodity, but if they move in offsetting directions much of the instability implications disappear. Also, just as the commodity composition of Australian exports has changed over our history, it is reasonable to anticipate further changes in composition in the future.

2.2 World Commodity Prices

A key building block of the commodity currency model is that there be significant volatility of world prices for the key Australian export commodities. We look at two sets of data on this issue. First, we consider a terms of trade index based on the ratio of an index of prices received for Australian exports (which mostly represent commodities) and the index of prices paid for Australian imports (which mostly represent manufacturers). The terms of trade index provides an aggregate picture of relative external price shocks facing the Australian economy. Second, we consider data on world prices for individual commodities which are important to Australia. In particular, we assess the degree of correlation of movements of real prices for the different export commodities.

Consider first the terms of trade. Figure 9.2 shows the terms of trade over the long-term period 1860–1988. The figure illustrates two key features of the evolution of relative world prices for Australian exports and imports. First, there has been a general long-term trend for export prices to rise more slowly than import prices, although the precise magnitude is very sensitive to the chosen data period. Over the 1860–1988 period the trend decline in the terms of trade is about 0.3 per cent per year and over the post-war period this trend decline in the terms of trade is estimated to be greater at about 0.6 per cent per year.

A second key characteristic of the history of Australia's external terms of trade is the volatility. Most of this volatility is due to sharp swings in export commodity prices. There are examples of the terms of trade ratio jumping by at least 50 per cent over a one or two year period (including the early 1900s, the early 1920s, the late 1930s, the late 1940s, and the mid 1970s) and of the ratio falling by at least 50 per cent (including the 1890s, after World War I, the early 1930s, the early 1950s, the late 1970s and 1985–1986). There is no smooth pattern of regular cycles to make forecasting a simple and error free task, although periods of dramatic boom or slump tend to be reversed in due course with a return to the trend path.

A more detailed picture of individual commodity price movements on the world market over the post-World War II period is based on International

Monetary Fund data for selected commodity prices.

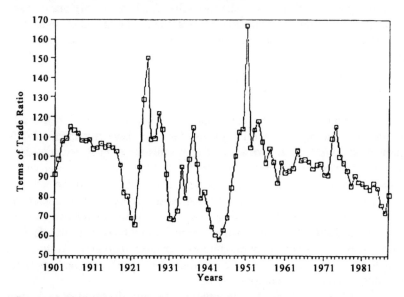

Source: *Maddock and McLean (1988), and ABS Cat. No. 5204.0.*

Figure 9.2 Terms of trade index (ratio of the implicit price deflator for exports and the implicit price deflator for imports; index base 1975 = 100)

All raw prices, which are recorded in US currency, have been deflated by the US wholesale price index to give real price series. Table 9.2 provides measures of trend movements of the real prices shown as average annual percentage rates of change.

Most, but by no means all, commodity prices exhibit significant downward trends, and in this sense they are consistent with the terms of trade trend picture. In Table 9.2, measures of the variability of real commodity prices are given by the percentage coefficient of variation about the trend. (About two-thirds of annual price changes are within plus or minus the number shown in Table 9.2, and 95 per cent are within plus or minus twice the number reported.)

Table 9.2 indicates that real world commodity prices exhibit considerable volatility. As one would expect, individual commodity prices show greater volatility than the indexes for groups of commodity prices and, in turn, these are more variable than the larger aggregate terms of trade index.

Measures of the similarity or otherwise of commodity price movements are given by the matrix of correlation coefficients shown in Table 9.3, and Figure 9.3 graphs the (nominal) price indices for the three commodity groupings, food, agricultural raw materials and metals.

Table 9.2 Measures of trend movements and the volatility of real prices for selected commodities over the period 1950–1988

	Average Annual Trend Change of Real Price (per cent per year)	Coefficient of Variation of Real Price Around Trend (per cent)
Commodities		
Bauxite	1.27	16.5
Iron Ore	−1.30	15.8
Lead	−0.49	31.5
Nickel	0.45	28.4
Zinc	0.17	37.4
Copper	−0.26	34.2
Coal	0.44	22.0
Gold	3.20	32.7
Beef	−0.56	18.0
Butter	0.16	17.4
Rice	−0.55	30.6
Wheat	−0.36	26.1
Sugar	−0.28	71.0
Wool	−0.69	31.3
Cotton	−0.80	16.1
Price Indices		
Food Price	−0.05	20.5
Agricultural raw materials	−0.33	16.6
Metals	−0.37	16.3
Australian Terms of Trade	−0.60	12.6

Notes:
IMF data for commodities and price indices. All prices deflated by US wholesale price index. Not all prices cover the full sample period. Average annual trend change is derived from the regression: $\log P = a + bT$, where P is real commodity price and T is an index of time. Coefficient of variation is calculated from the ratio of the standard error of the regression $P = c + dT$ to the sample mean. Terms of trade data from implicit price deflators of ABS, Australian National Accounts.

For many commodities we find a high positive correlation between the different price series, particularly within the agricultural commodities (except butter), within some of the mining commodities and between some of the agricultural and mining commodities (such as the grains and base metals). These positive correlations indicate that boom and slump periods for one commodity correspond with boom and slump periods for other commodities. But also, there are important examples of large negative correlations, such as between iron ore and bauxite.

Figure 9.3 illustrates the general pattern of sympathetic movements of price indices for food, agricultural raw materials and metal prices, but there are important examples of particular years of countervailing fluctuations. Martin (1989), using a shorter time period of data, 1970–1986, finds more important negative correlations between indices of mineral prices and indices of agricultural product prices than reported in Table 9.3 and Figure 9.3. Overall, within our longer and more detailed data series the positive correlations tend to dominate, and it is this dominance which generates the fluctuations in the terms of trade which measures the net disturbances in world commodity prices on the Australian economy.

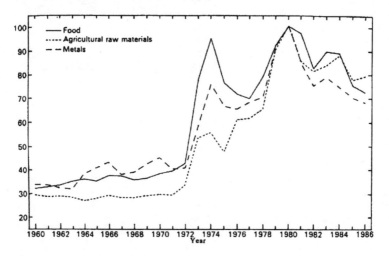

Source: Fitzgerald and Urban (1989, p. 249).

Figure 9.3 Commodity price index 1960–1986 (1980 =100)

Underlying reasons for the extreme volatility of world commodity prices, both in the past and likely to continue in the future, include the inelasticity of demand and supply, especially in the short run, the flex-price characteristic of commodity markets, and important and frequently unanticipated shifts to demand and supply.

Table 9.3 Correlation matrix for real commodity prices, 1952–1988

| | Mining Commodities | | | | | | | | Agricultural Commodities | | | | | | |
	Bauxite	Iron	Lead	Nickel	Zinc	Copper	Coal	Gold	Beef	Butter	Rice	Wheat	Sugar	Wool	Cotton
Bauxite	1.0														
Iron ore	-0.65	1.0													
Lead	0.02	0.36	1.0												
Nickel	0.12	-0.40	0.08	1.0											
Zinc	-0.16	-0.06	0.47	0.29	1.0										
Copper	-0.37	0.09	0.33	0.28	0.33	1.0									
Coal	0.71	0.17	0.17	0.19	0.15	-0.51	1.0								
Gold	0.82	-0.73	-0.02	0.14	0.06	-0.57	-0.36	1.0							
Beef	-0.43	0.33	0.53	0.30	0.23	0.64	-0.36	-0.34	1.0						
Butter	0.67	-0.22	0.42	0.29	-0.12	-0.26	0.41	-0.47	-0.03	1.0					
Rice	-0.25	0.28	0.46	0.13	0.57	0.51	0.11	-0.24	0.41	-0.15	1.0				
Wheat	-0.15	0.30	0.47	0.19	0.74	0.39	0.85	-0.17	0.38	-0.07	0.89	1.0			
Sugar	0.16	0.01	0.34	0.29	0.69	0.11	0.46	0.14	0.11	0.15	0.66	0.77	1.0		
Wool	-0.22	0.51	0.54	-0.08	0.50	0.10	-0.19	-0.01	0.42	-0.04	0.39	0.58	0.23	1.0	
Cotton	-0.09	0.79	0.53	-0.24	0.29	0.11	0.29	-0.30	0.41	-0.03	0.50	0.67	0.33	0.67	1.0

Notes: Raw data on wholesale prices in US$ from International Monetary Fund, International Financial Statistics, Washington DC. All prices deflated by the US wholesale price index. Some price series do not cover the complete 1952–1988 period

The supply of agricultural and mineral products is characterised by long investment lags, long gestation lags, and by large capital costs which once incurred become sunk or fixed costs. This means that in the face of quite sharp price falls, production is reduced little in the short run, which extends beyond a year and up to five years, and similarly it takes time to increase production in response to price rises.

In most cases demand also is inelastic. Minerals and some agricultural raw materials, such as wool, are inputs for further processing and they have limited substitution possibilities with other inputs. In the case of most countries and products, food demand is price inelastic. Protectionist trade and domestic industry policies, particularly affecting agricultural, but also some mineral commodities, effectively increase the inelasticity of commodity supply and demand on the residual world commodity market.

The demand and supply of mineral and agricultural products are subject to random shifts, including from changes in seasonal conditions, discoveries, extended strikes and policy flips, and to more systematic influences. Of the systematic influences, changes in rates of growth of national income have important influences on world commodity demand. In the case of minerals, changes in real income and manufacturing activity of the developed countries generate accelerated changes in demand and account for most of the short run price volatility. OECD estimates indicate a 1 per cent drop in the real income growth rate of developed countries reduces mineral prices by 6 per cent. In the case of food products, changes in the growth rate of real income of developing countries and of the centrally planned economies are the more important sources of demand fluctuations. Sjaastad, in his chapter in this volume, demonstrates a significant influence of changes in exchange rates of the major currency blocks (the US, Europe and Japan) on world commodity prices.

A large part of shifts in the supply of and demand for mineral and agricultural commodities is absorbed as price changes. Certainly, stock holding, both by the private sector and often also by the public sector, provides some cushion to market shocks. However, relative to the behaviour of markets for manufacturers and services, commodities appear to reflect market disturbances primarily as significant price disturbances. The real income link provides much of the positive correlation between price movements of the various commodities. However, other disturbances which tend to be more commodity specific explain the less than perfect correlation.

While the reality is that Australia exports a wide variety of different agricultural and mineral commodities, and that the prices of different commodities sometimes move in different directions, and overall assessment of price movements, together with a high degree of commonality of key factors causing commodity price fluctuations, results in a high level of volatility of the terms of trade facing Australia which is consistent with our simplified commodity currency model. Further, on the basis of history and the discussion of the underlying causal forces behind the commodity price fluctuations, it seems reasonable to extrapolate that such volatility will continue in the future decades. It is worth reiterating that the fluctuations are not regular cycles, although there is a tendency for large positive and negative deviations from trend to be reversed in due course.

A key assumption of the commodity currency model is that short-run changes in world commodity prices have a significant influence on the expectations of currency traders about the short- , medium- and long-term terms of trade and the trade balance, and also on expectations of consumers and investors about short- , medium- and long-term Australian real income levels. The expectations assumption is extremely difficult to evaluate because of the absence of data on expectations held by the key players. However, some indirect evidence is available.

Published studies and public conferences on future commodity price movements, for example, work by the Commonwealth Australian Bureau of Agricultural and Resource Economics, make use of structural models of commodity markets in forming forecasts and projections of commodity prices (see also Trewin and O'Mara, 1990). And it is clear that business investors also take into account longer-term structural forces influencing commodity prices in their investment and production planning exercises. That is, longer-term structural forces influencing commodity market outcomes, and not just current prices, are used to forecast prices.

Yet, most econometric studies of the supply of and demand for mineral, agricultural and energy commodities contain proxy measures of expected price variables as explanatory variables, and these proxy variables attach considerable weight to recent price outcomes. Common formulations include the frequently employed adaptive expectations model and other autoregressive moving average models. These models measure expected prices as a weighted average of current and past prices, with relatively more weight given to current prices than to past prices. These price expectation models have good explanatory powers. In the few cases where rational expectation models and the time series models of price expectations have been compared, the latter generally have performed as well as the rational expectations models (see, for example, Fisher and Tanner, 1978). Some early work on the terms of trade series by Blundell-Wignall and Gregory (1989) suggest that the terms of trade series may be represented as a random walk.

These types of empirical results on expectations indicate that current period prices have a large influence on industry expectations about future prices in making investment and production decisions. There is then a body of evidence supporting the key price expectations assumption of our commodity exchange rate model.

It is important to note that commodity price forecasts are subject to very large errors. Evaluation of Bureau of Agricultural Economics one year ahead price forecasts indicates mean absolute forecast errors of between 5 per cent and 10 per cent for most agricultural commodities and limited success in picking turning points (Freebairn, 1975). It is likely that similar qualitative results would be found for forecasts of mining commodity prices.

Econometric studies of private final consumption expenditure also support the hypothesis that short-term changes in real income levels influence short-term expenditure levels. Typical theoretical and empirical models of household behaviour based on the ideas of permanent or normal income and on life cycle determinants of consumption behaviour obtain estimates of the short-run marginal propensity to consume which exceed zero but are less than the long-run marginal propensity to consume. That is, part of a short-term increase (or fall) in real income associated with a world commodity boom (slump) would flow into increased (reduced) consumption outlays.

In the case of investment outlays, information on the link between changes in national income and investment is less clear cut. A number of studies provide a positive link between short-term swings in national expenditure and/or in profitability and investment outlays. Likely causal forces include the effects of commodity price changes on profitability, and the effects of changes in current profitability on both expectations of future profits and on the availability and cost of funds to finance investment.

There is considerable supporting evidence that a world commodity price boom or increase in Australia's terms of trade has a positive effect on expectations about future prices and about future real income and expenditure levels, and that a world commodity price slump has a negative effect, but that some weight also is given to longer-term trends in forming expectations and behavioural responses. That is, we have the assumptions for a modified commodity currency.

Overall then, the assumptions for a commodity currency approximately hold. First, Australia is heavily dependent on commodity exports. Second, world commodity export prices are highly correlated and volatile and, as a result, Australia's terms of trade also are volatile. Third, current commodity prices and the terms of trade have a large weight in expectations about future prices, terms of trade and real income. We turn now to consider evidence on the direct linkage between world commodity prices and the Australian real exchange rate.

2.3 Terms of Trade and the Real Exchange Rate

Evaluation of a reduced form relationship between the real exchange rate and the terms of trade encounters two sets of difficulties. First, there are a number of optional measures of the real exchange rate. Variations come from the choice of price indices (for example, between retail prices, wholesale prices, unit labour costs), the sectorial coverage, and the weighting system (for example, between import, export and trade shares). These options can give quite different pictures and there is no clear cut and unambiguous choice of the appropriate measure (Pitchford, 1986; McKenzie, 1986; and Shann, 1986). Second, a number of other factors as well as the terms of trade influence the real exchange rate. The problem is to ascertain the magnitude and relative importance of the terms of trade holding other causal forces constant. Subject to these very important caveats, data for the 1890–1984 period reported by McKenzie (1986) and for the June 1970 to June 1989 period reported by the Treasury (1989), and reproduced as Figures 9.4 and 9.5, lend support to the commodity currency model.

Figure 9.4 shows the long-term pattern of movements of the terms of trade and a measure of the real exchange rate over the period 1890–1984. The terms of trade is the ratio of export prices to import prices. The real exchange rate is a weighted average of the ratio of the domestic CPI to a weighted average of foreign country CPIs times the nominal exchange rate, with trade shares used as weights. The two series are broadly consistent with the commodity currency model. With two exceptions, large movements up and down in the terms of trade are associated with corresponding large movements up and down in the measured real exchange rate. The exceptions are the mid 1950s when the post-Korean war boom commodity collapse did not cause a real exchange rate fall – McKenzie suggests this could be due to a combination of a fixed nominal exchange rate and the boost to direct foreign investment in the import-competing manufacturing sector which was highly protected by import licensing – and the early 1980s when the collapse of the terms of trade was not accompanied by a fall in the real exchange rate – McKenzie suggests this could be due to the inflow of foreign capital to finance the anticipated commodity boom which in retrospect was not realised. Even in the 1890–1950 period where the large swings of the two series are highly correlated, there are important conflicts in movements in particular years.

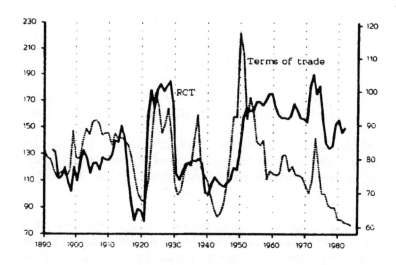

Source: For terms of trade: IMF International Financial Statistic (ratio of Laspeyres export price index for goods to Laspeyres import price index for goods).

Figure 9.4 Terms of trade index (left scale) and effective real exchange rate index, RCT (right scale) (1974 = 100)

By and large, Figure 9.4 shows a high correlation between movements in the terms of trade and movements in the real exchange rate over a period of nearly 100 years.

Data on the terms of trade and a measure of the real exchange rate for the more recent years are shown in Figure 9.5. Here the real exchange rate is measured as an index of relative labour costs; that is, the ratio of Australian labour costs per unit of output to a (import share) weighted average of unit labour costs in Australia's four main import source countries times the respective exchange rate. The figure shows a reasonably close relationship between world commodity prices and the real exchange rate. In particular, large changes to the real exchange rate closely follow the 1973–1974 world commodity price boom and the 1985–1986 slump in world commodity prices, and the subsequent recovery in world commodity prices. Such observations led the Treasury to conclude (1989, p. 2.17)

> Chart 9 [our Figure 9.5] illustrates the reasonably close relationship between the terms of trade and international competitiveness (the 'real exchange rate'). While other factors such as real interest rate differentials and investor

confidence can be influential especially over a short period of time, the terms of trade has been the dominant influence over a longer period.

Over the period 1902–1988 the correlation coefficient between the terms of trade and the real exchange rate (measured using consumer prices and trade weights) was 0.43. Thus, while there is a strong positive correlation between the two series, a number of other factors, including other exogenous factors influencing Australian investment activity and foreign capital inflows to finance part of that investment, are important determinants of the real exchange rate. A key implication of Figures 9.4 and 9.5 is that large swings in world commodity prices historically have led to accommodating adjustments in the real exchange rate.

Two related studies using econometric models provide strong support for the commodity currency model for Australia. Sjaastad (1990) reports two sets of equations estimated with quarterly data for the 1972–1988 period which indicate that the initial impact of world commodity price fluctuations on the Australian economy are partly offset by changes in the nominal Australian exchange rate and partly by changes in the Australian inflation rate. Estimates of equations explaining the nominal exchange rate indicate that between 60 per cent and 70 per cent of a terms of trade change is offset by changes in the nominal exchange rate in that quarter and in the long run about 90 per cent is offset. The nominal exchange rate is shown to be much more responsive to terms of trade changes in the post December 1983 floating exchange rate regime than in the earlier period of managed exchange rate policy. The terms of trade is estimated to have a significant positive effect on Australian consumer prices. That is, a world commodity price boom (slump) induces an appreciation (depreciation) of the Australian dollar and an increase (decrease) in the inflation rate, both of which cause the real exchange rate to appreciate (depreciate) as under a commodity currency.

Blundell-Wignall and Gregory (1989) report econometric work for quarterly data over the 1970–1988 period and monthly data for the 1984–1989 period which establish a highly significant positive causal relationship between the Australian terms of trade and the real exchange rate (using the real exchange rate measure based on the CPI and trade weights). The shift to a more freely floating exchange rate regime in 1983 is shown to speed up the adjustment speed between changes in the terms of trade and changes in the real exchange rate.

Overall, experience over the long term of the last 100 years and more detailed econometric work with data from the 1970s and 1980s supports the commodity currency model of determination of the Australian real exchange rate, but there also are other important causal forces. Further work which seeks to include the full set of different potential causal forces determining the real exchange rate in a comprehensive model, and work which investigates the stability or otherwise of key parameter values over the long sample period are desirable.

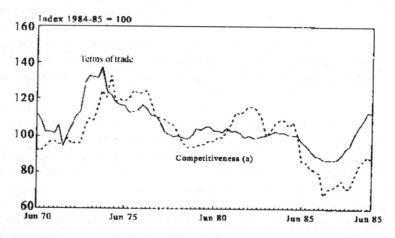

Notes:

Unit labour cost index of competitiveness. A rise (fall) in the index implies a deterioration (improvement) in Australian unit labour costs relative to those of our major trading partners after adjusting for exchange rate changes. The unit labour cost index is the ratio of unit labour costs in the non-farm sector of the Australian economy to the weighted average of the exchange rate adjusted unit labour cost indices for the business sector of Australian's four major import sources. The weights used are the average shares of Australian's imports from the USA, Japan, UK and Federal Republic of Germany from 1984–85 to 1987–88. Information on unit labour costs of these four countries is available to the March quarter 1989. Movements in the index in the June quarter 1989 are based on ODEC forecasts.

Source: The Treasury (1989, p. 2.18).

Figure 9.5 Australia's terms of trade and international competitiveness

3.0 SOME IMPLICATIONS OF A COMMODITY CURRENCY

Given that the Australian economy behaves along the lines of a modified commodity currency in response to fluctuations in world commodity prices, we consider some implications of such behaviour for different sectors of the

economy and for overall macroeconomic performance. The implications
provide information to assist more effective decision making by business
enterprises and by government.

In assessing the sectoral implications of a commodity currency we
consider the effects of fluctuations in world commodity prices on the
profitability of the export commodity sector, the import competing sector and
the non-traded sector. Profitability is influenced by changes in output prices
and input costs. Input costs include imported items, non-traded items and
nationally mobile factors such as labour. The effect of fluctuations in world
commodity prices on gross receipts to Australian exporters is cushioned in
their impact on Australian dollar commodity prices by partially offsetting
nominal exchange rate adjustments. The exchange rate adjustment at the
same time reduces Australian dollar prices of imports in the case of overseas
commodity price rises and increases them in the case of price falls. The real
income effect of commodity price changes and the associated expenditure
changes mean that prices of non-traded goods and services and also the prices
of mobile inputs rise (fall) with increases (decreases) in world commodity
prices. In these ways, fluctuations in world commodity prices directly and
indirectly affect the profitability of all sectors of the economy.

Figures 9.6, 9.7 and 9.8 provide a schematic summary of the implications
of world commodity price fluctuations for Australian sector profitability. In
the case of the export commodity (Figure 9.6), profitability moves in the
same direction as world export prices, and probably with more volatility,
however, there are some modifying influences. For world price rises, output
prices in Australian dollar terms rise but by a lesser amount than in foreign
currency terms because of the currency appreciation. Imported inputs are
cheaper in Australian dollar terms because of the currency appreciation.
There will be increases in costs of non-traded inputs and labour via the real
income benefits of the world commodity price boom. Given the typical
make-up of input costs, the profitability path in Australian currency terms
seems likely to be less variable than a first round assessment based on just
world commodity prices would suggest. By symmetrical arguments, the
indirect effects of a fall in world commodity prices leads to a much reduced
fall in profitability of the export sector than the direct world price slump
would suggest because of the offsetting nominal currency depreciation and
because of the lower inflation effects.

In the case of import competing activities, principally but not only
manufacturers, facing relatively stable world prices for manufactured goods,
world commodity price fluctuations tend to destabalise profitability of the
Australian industry in the opposite direction to the world commodity price

movements. This scenario is shown in Figure 9.7.

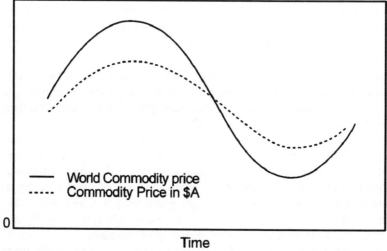

Figure 9.6 World commodity price fluctuations and Australian export commodity sector

When world commodity prices rise, the resulting real currency appreciation reduces Australian dollar prices of imports and increases the costs of non-traded inputs and mobile factors, and these effects will in all but exceptional cases exceed the benefits of lower imported input costs. By contrast, when world commodity prices fall, profitability of the import competing sector rises. This picture would apply also to exporters not directly affected by world commodity price fluctuations.

Figure 9.8 indicates that profitability of the non-traded sector most likely will fluctuate in the same direction as world commodity prices but with very much less amplitude.[5] Higher world commodity prices, via the increase in real income and expenditure, especially on non-traded goods and services, lead to increases in output prices of non-traded goods and services and also higher labour costs, a fall in costs of imported inputs and a rise in the cost of any export commodity inputs used by the non-traded sector. Lower world commodity prices have the opposite effect and reduce profitability of the non-traded sector.

Price, Profitability

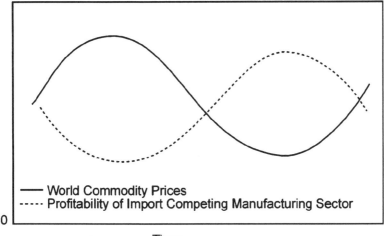

Figure 9.7 World commodity price fluctuations and Australian import
competing sector

Then, with a commodity currency, volatility of world commodity prices
generate changes in the profitability of all sectors of the economy, but with
much smaller amplitudes. Thus, enterprises in the non-traded and import
competing sectors, as well as the commodity export sector, need to keep an
eye on world commodity price movements and to take a medium and longer-
term perspective in making investment, production and marketing decisions.

Fluctuations in world commodity prices and associated changes in the
Australian real exchange rate include changes in relative prices and in the
overall inflation rate, and also these fluctuations likely will alter the
composition and aggregate levels of wages. The previous discussion and
Figures 9.6, 9.7 and 9.8 indicated significant changes in relative prices and
profitability of the export, import competing and non-traded sectors. Such
changes indicate the need for a flexible and dynamic economy that can adjust
to and take advantage of changes in relative prices, real prices and in wages,
both over time and across sectors of the economy. Further, to the extent that
knowledge of world commodity price fluctuations is shrouded in uncertainty
and imperfect foresight, flexibility needs to be complemented with
adaptability of individual, business and policy decisions to utilise new
information as it becomes available.

Price, Profitability

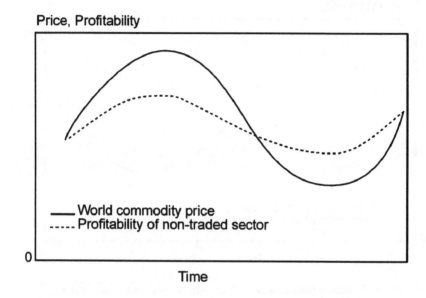

_____ World commodity price
- - - - Profitability of non-traded sector

0

Time

Figure 9.8 World commodity price fluctuations and non-traded sector

At the macroeconomic level, volatility of world commodity prices directly and indirectly generate fluctuations in national income and expenditure, employment, and inflation if the commodity currency model applies. An interesting question is whether these fluctuations are symmetric, in which case commodity price booms and slumps tend to even out over time, or whether there is a destabilising asymmetric response because of rigidities and inflexibility in the economy.

For policy makers, key issues are the choice of policy strategies to best live with the reality of fluctuations in world commodity prices. Options include the choice of a fixed or floating exchange rate, of active fiscal and monetary policy to counter real income fluctuations, of monetary policy to accommodate or sterilise international private capital flows, and of a host of microeconomic policies to influence flexibility and adaptability of the economy.

Some preliminary modeling of these issues by Blundell-Wignall and Gregory (1989) indicate how complex the policy choice task is; even with a highly simplified model of the economy, policy answers are shown to be sensitive to the choice of policy objectives, to the source and relative magnitude of economic shocks to the economy, to the economic characteristics of the economy in terms of supply and demand elasticities and their time profile, sectorial interdependencies, and so on, and to the quantity and quality of available information about world commodity prices, the state of the economy and how the economy operates. Plausible alternatives can have quite different policy implications.

A fairly robust finding is that floating exchange rates are preferred to fixed exchange rates. Blundell-Wignall and Gregory (1989) conclude that only a very unlikely and peculiar set of conditions would lead their models to point to the choice of a fixed exchange rate. In the context of the Australian economy, without very extreme restrictions on international capital flows, sticking to a fixed exchange rate, even if it is the mythical long-run equilibrium exchange rate, is unlikely to be a practical option. The information requirements necessary to establish a fixed exchange rate and to manipulate fiscal and monetary policies to support the chosen rate are enormous and unrealistic. Thus, as in the past, a large part of fluctuations in world commodity prices will be absorbed as changes in the nominal exchange rate.

An important factor bearing on the magnitude of nominal exchange rate changes in response to world commodity price fluctuations hinges on the way expectations of current and future commodity price movements are formed by key Australian and overseas market participants. The more myopic the assessment, the greater the exchange rate fluctuations and the greater the fluctuations in real economic activity and in inflation rates. Conversely, the more long-sighted the perspective the greater will be the importance of international capital inflows in offsetting the balance of trade fluctuations caused by world commodity price fluctuations. Government has a clear role in generating and disseminating information about the medium and longer-term patterns of world commodity prices.

An interesting set of policy issues for future assessment concern the desirability of, and the form of, macroeconomic and microeconomic policy responses to residual volatility of the nominal exchange and to disturbances to the inflation rate associated with fluctuations in the world prices of Australia's principal export commodities. To be realistic, such an assessment should be made in the context of imperfect knowledge about future commodity prices, imperfect knowledge of operation of the economy; the long lags in policy responses, and the lags in adjustment of the economy to changes in policy settings. These challenges seem worthy questions for further study.

4.0 CONCLUDING COMMENTS

Quite wide swings in world commodity prices for Australia's agricultural and mining exports are likely to be a continuing feature of the external environment to be faced by the Australian economy in the future. If the commodity currency story told in this study is valid, and continues to hold, our analysis points to important indirect effects of world commodity price fluctuations on the nominal exchange rate, inflation and wages, absolute profitability and relative profitability of different sectors of the economy, and on real economic activity. Understanding these processes and lines of causation is valuable information of itself for business and policy decision makers. Subsequent responses will in turn moderate the effect of the various lines of causation, and in general more informed responses will moderate the short-term destabilising effects of world commodity price fluctuations on the Australian economy.

ACKNOWLEDGEMENTS

The author is grateful to Hazel Ramsden for research assistance.

REFERENCES

Australian Bureau of Agricultural and Resource Economics, *Agriculture and Resources Quarterly*, various issues.

Blundell-Wignall, A. and R.G. Gregory (1989), 'Exchange Rate Policy in Advanced Commodity Exporting Countries: The Case of Australia and New Zealand', paper presented at International Monetary Fund Conference, *Exchange Rate Policy in Selected Industrial Industries*.

Cook, L.H. and M.G. Porter (1984), *The Mineral Sector and the Australian Economy*, Sydney: Allen and Unwin.

Fisher, B.S. and C. Tanner (1978), 'The formulation of price expectations: An empirical test of theoretical models', *American Journal of Agricultural Economics*, **60**, pp. 245–248.

Fitzgerald, V. and P. Urban (1989), 'Causes and consequences of changes in the terms of trade and balance of payments', in B. Chapman (ed.), *Australian Economic Growth*, Canberra: Macmillan.

Freebairn, J.W. (1975), 'Forecasting for Australian agriculture', *Australian Journal of Agricultural Economics*, **19**, pp. 154–174.

Maddock, R. and I.W. McLean (1987), *The Australian Economy in the Long Run*, Cambridge: Cambridge University Press.

Martin, W.J. (1989) 'Implications of changes in the composition of Australian exports for export sector stability', *Australian Economic Review*, 1st quarter, pp. 39–50.

McKenzie, I.M. (1986), 'Australia's real exchange rate during the twentieth century', *Economic Record*, Supplement, pp. 69–78.

Pitchford, J.D. (1986), 'The Australian economy: 1985 and prospects for 1986', *Economic Record*, **62**, pp. 1–21.

Review of Marketing and Agricultural Economics (1988), Forum: 'Exchange Rates and Interest Rates: Where to Now?', a collection of papers published in April issue.

Shann, E.W. (1986), 'Australia's real exchange rate during the twentieth century: comment', *Economic Record*, Supplement, pp. 79–81.

Sjaastad, L. (1990), 'Exchange rates and commodity prices: the Australian case', in K.W. Clements and J. Freebairn (eds), *Exchange Rates and Australian Commodity Exports*, Centre for Policy Studies, Monash University and The Economic Research Centre, The University of Western Australia.

The Treasury (1989), *Budget Statements 1989–90*, Canberra, AGPS.

Trewin, R. and P. O'Mara (1990), 'Commodity Exports and the Exchange Rate: ABARE Outlook and Research', in K.W. Clements and J. Freebairn (eds), *Exchange Rates and Australian Commodity Exports*, Centre for Policy Studies, Monash University and The Economic Research Centre, The University of Western Australia.

NOTES

1   Formally, the real exchange rate is measured as: $Er = En\ P/P^*$, where En is the nominal exchange rate (measured as units of foreign currency per unit of Australian currency), P is a measure of Australian prices or costs (such as CPI, WPI, unit labour costs) and P^* is a comparable measure of foreign country prices or costs. The real exchange rate often is referred to as an index of competitiveness. A fall in the real exchange rate, or a real depreciation, represents, ceteris paribus, an increase in international competitiveness.

2   A rising supply elasticity for the non-traded sector could be due to sector-specific inputs, including capital, skilled labour and management, or it could flow from a nearly fully employed economy in which case the sector would have to offer higher returns to bid nationally mobile labour and other resources away from the rest of the economy.

3   The following circumstances support the view that most surplus funds would be placed in overseas assets. With a perfectly elastic demand for and supply of international funds to Australia at a given world interest rate and no expectation of changes in the Australian exchange rate, and using covered interest parity, there would be no change in the domestic interest rate. Then, most of an increase in an Australian wealth portfolio would be allocated to foreign assets with its assumed highly elastic demand function at the world interest rate.

4   But note here that the commodity currency model has relative price movements as an endogenous variable driven by world commodity price movements. By contrast, the PPP model typically regards price movements as exogenous.

5   It is possible that the reverse could happen. For example, if the import competing sector has strong interlinkages with the non-traded sector, and the export sector/non-traded sector interlinkages are weak, it is conceivable that the non-traded sector will face a net demand fall. This type of outcome is unlikely in Australia.

Index